Blanding
Farmington
THE FOUR CORNERS
Tucson
THE FOUR CORNERS
See pp100–119
0 km
100
0 miles
100

EYEWITNESS TRAVEL

ARIZONA & THE GRAND CANYON

EYEWITNESS TRAVEL

ARIZONA & THE GRAND CANYON

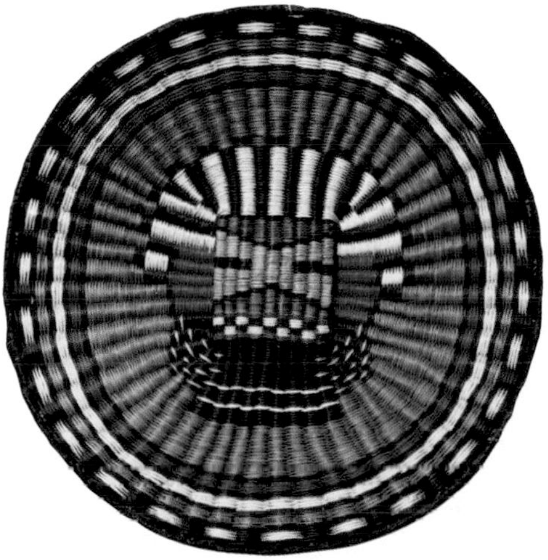

DK

LONDON, NEW YORK,
MELBOURNE, MUNICH AND DELHI
www.dk.com

MANAGING EDITOR Aruna Ghose
ART EDITOR Benu Joshi
SENIOR EDITOR Rimli Borooah
EDITOR Bhavna Seth Ranjan
DESIGNER Mathew Kurien
PICTURE RESEARCH Taiyaba Khatoon
DTP COORDINATOR Shailesh Sharma
DTP DESIGNER Vinod Harish

MAIN CONTRIBUTOR
Paul Franklin

PHOTOGRAPHERS
Demetrio Carrasco, Alan Keohane, Francesca Yorke

ILLUSTRATORS
P. Arun, Gary Cross, Eugene Fleurey, Claire Littlejohn, Chris Orr & Associates, Mel Pickering, Robbie Polley, John Woodcock

Reproduced by Colourscan (Singapore)
Printed and bound by L. Rex Printing Company Limited, China

First published in Great Britain in 2005
by Dorling Kindersley Limited
80 Strand, London WC2R 0RL

Reprinted with revisions 2006, 2008, 2010

A CIP CATALOGUE RECORD IS AVAILABLE FROM THE BRITISH LIBRARY.

ISBN 978-1-40535-393-9

FLOORS ARE REFERRED TO THROUGHOUT IN ACCORDANCE WITH AMERICAN USAGE; IE THE "FIRST FLOOR" IS AT GROUND LEVEL.

Front cover main image: Toroweap Point, Grand Canyon National Park

MIX
Paper from responsible sources
FSC www.fsc.org
FSC™ C018179

The information in this DK Eyewitness Travel Guide is checked regularly.

Every effort has been made to ensure that this book is as up-to-date as possible at the time of going to press. Some details, however, such as telephone numbers, opening hours, prices, gallery hanging arrangements and travel information are liable to change. The publishers cannot accept responsibility for any consequences arising from the use of this book, nor for any material on third party websites, and cannot guarantee that any website address in this book will be a suitable source of travel information. We value the views and suggestions of our readers very highly. Please write to: Publisher, DK Eyewitness Travel Guides, Dorling Kindersley, 80 Strand, London, WC2R 0RL, Great Britain.

◁ **Tall saguaro cacti in the Sonoran Desert, Southern Arizona**

Relaxing in the rose-colored sandstone of Antelope Canyon

CONTENTS

INTRODUCING ARIZONA

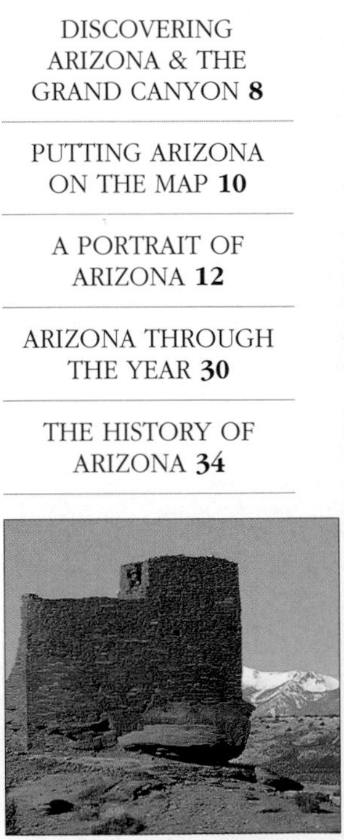

Wupatki National Monument with ruins of a 12th-century pueblo building

World famous Monument Valley in the Four Corners region

ARIZONA & THE FOUR CORNERS AREA BY AREA

Contemporary glass skyscrapers in downtown Phoenix

Hispanic pottery

TRAVELERS' NEEDS

SURVIVAL GUIDE

Visitors enjoying a trail ride at a dude ranch in Southern Arizona

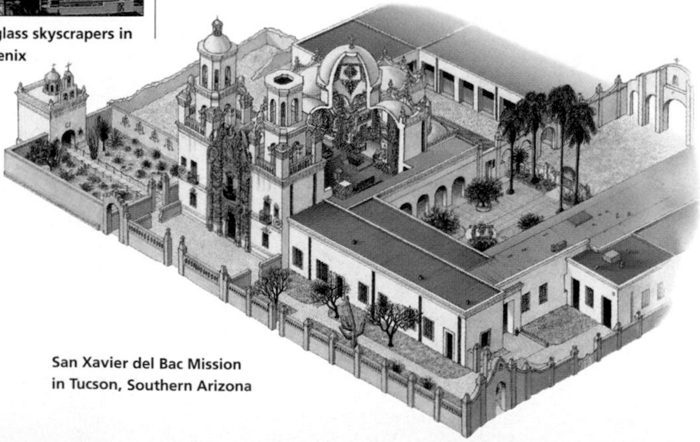

San Xavier del Bac Mission in Tucson, Southern Arizona

INTRODUCING ARIZONA

DISCOVERING ARIZONA & THE GRAND CANYON

Adventurers and explorers visit Arizona to enjoy the awesome site of the Grand Canyon and the haunting beauty of the Colorado Plateau. Across the state, the spirit of the Wild West lives on in ghost towns and historic re-creations like Oatman and Tombstone. Modern cities such as Phoenix and Tucson offer luxurious spas, excellent golf courses, and first-rate shops and museums. Beyond the towns, the desert awaits outdoor enthusiasts, while serrated mountains hide pine forests, alpine meadows, and tumbling streams. Below is an overview of each of these diverse regions.

Native petroglyph in Monument Valley

The luxuriant foliage surrounding Havasu Falls

GRAND CANYON AND NORTHERN ARIZONA

- **The unspoiled North Rim, the South Rim, and the Skywalk**
- **America's road: Route 66**
- **Romantic ghost towns**
- **Houseboats on Lake Powell**

There is no more familiar icon of the American West than the hauntingly beautiful desert and red-rock landscape of Northern Arizona and, in particular, the stunning spectacle of the **Grand Canyon** *(see pp48–61)*. The Grand Canyon has two distinct regions: the more remote and less visited **North Rim** *(see p55)* offers an unspoiled high-elevation realm of giant ponderosa pines, magnificent vistas, and seldom-traveled paths that wind through forests and along the canyon rim; the **South Rim** *(see pp54–5)* offers even more amazing views. Here, Grand Canyon Village has hotels, restaurants, shops, a campground, and other amenities. A paved rim-walk with dramatic views allows visitors to enjoy the canyon's beauty. Farther west, you can hike or take a horse-back ride into the **Havasu Canyon** *(see p48)* to see the stunning waterfalls. On the Hualapai Reservation, you can stroll 4,000 ft (1,200 m) above the canyon floor on the glass-paved **Skywalk** *(see p61)*, the area's newest attraction.

Northern Arizona is also home to **Route 66** *(see pp28–9)*, the road that took America westward in the mid-20th century. Miles of the original road still pass through charming towns such as Winslow and Holbrook, where you will find restored roadside hotels, excellent restaurants, and attractions that bring to life the era when America had a love affair with the automobile.

This area is famous for its ghost towns such as **Oatman** *(see p73)*. Gold was discovered here in 1915, leading to a sudden economic boom; when the gold ran out, the town was all but abandoned. Today, Oatman and other towns are making a comeback as romantic relics of the Wild West.

Anyone who loves the desert and the great outdoors should head to **Lake Powell** *(see pp62–3)*. Visitors can stay in shoreside resorts and rent boats or jet skis to take a spin on the lake. There are also luxurious houseboats for rent that allow leisurely multiday journeys into some of the most remote parts of this man-made lake. Surrounding the lake is the **Glen Canyon National Recreation Area** *(see pp62–3)*, a vast expanse of desert and red-rock canyon country that is very popular with wilderness hikers.

Driving through Northern Arizona on the legendary Route 66

◁ ***The Southwest,*** **oil on canvas by Walter Ufe (1876–1936)**

Glittering buildings dominating the Phoenix skyline

PHOENIX AND SOUTHERN ARIZONA

- **Sleek, modern Phoenix**
- **The Heard Museum**
- **Tucson and the San Xavier del Bac Mission**
- **Beautiful Sonora Desert**

Arizona's main urban oasis, **Phoenix** *(see pp76–83)* is also one of the largest cities in America. This busy city teems with cultural icons, including the renowned **Heard Museum** *(see p78–9)*, with its incredible collection of Native American art. Here, too, are the **Phoenix Art Museum** *(see p77)* and Frank Lloyd Wright's **Taliesin West** *(see pp80–81)*, now housing a school of architecture. The nearby village of **Scottsdale** *(see p80)* is a sophisticated hub of urban chic, with upscale art galleries, luxurious spas, and some of the world's best golf resorts.

Farther south, **Tucson** *(see pp88–94)* is a modern city that somehow manages to retain its aura of small-town western hospitality. The city's early Spanish history is on display at the magnificent **San Xavier del Bac Mission** *(see pp92–3)*, located just out of town. In fact, many of Tucson's best attractions are located outside the downtown area, including the **Old Tucson Studios** *(see p90)*; the excellent hiking, camping, and fishing around **Mount Lemmon** *(see p94)*; and the futuristic world of **Biosphere 2** *(see p94)*.

Tucson lies at the northern edge of the Sonora Desert, home to an incredible range of flora and fauna, including the towering saguaro cactus. Visitors can learn more about this area at Tucson's informative **Arizona-Sonora Desert Museum** *(see p90)*; or travel a short distance east to explore **Saguaro National Park** *(see p90)*. More adventurous travelers may want to make a longer trip to experience the remote grandeur of the **Organ Pipe Cactus National Monument** *(see p96)*.

THE FOUR CORNERS

- **The canyons of the Colorado Plateau**
- **Magnificent Monument Valley and Canyon de Chelly**
- **Mesa Verde National Park**
- **Captivating Chaco Canyon**

Named for the only point in America where four states meet, the Four Corners area has a fascinating history. Most of this region lies within the rocky splendor of the **Colorado Plateau** *(see pp116–17)*, a land whose ruggedness served as a hideout for many a Wild West desperado.

The towering buttes and mesas of **Monument Valley** *(see pp102–3)* are familiar to anyone who has ever watched American Western movies. Much of this land is home to several Native American tribes, such as the Hopi, the Ute, and the Navajo, whose vast reservation is larger than the state of West Virginia. The spiritual center of the Navajo world is the mazelike red-rock **Canyon de Chelly** *(see pp106–9)*. Visitors are welcome to enter the canyon on daylong tours that also visit the abandoned cliff dwellings of the Ancient Pueblo people, who lived here long before the Navajo.

No one knows why the Ancient Puebloans vanished from the region more than 700 years ago, but they left an extensive record of their culture in the massive cliff dwellings that fill the canyons of **Mesa Verde National Park** *(see pp118–19)*. Visitors can travel through the park to view the mesmerizing ruins of Cliff Palace and Spruce Tree House, and climb long ladders to stand inside a cliff dwelling at Balcony House.

Ancient Puebloan culture reached its zenith during the construction of a spectacular ceremonial city whose ruins today fill the **Chaco Culture National Historic Park** *(see pp112–13)*. This impressive cultural site is one of the largest and most complex pre-European cities in America. A tour road circles the canyon, taking visitors to Pueblo Bonito, Chetro Ketl, and other major ruins.

Pueblo Bonito, a well-preserved example of Ancient Puebloan culture

Putting Arizona on the Map

Arizona and the Four Corners area, which also takes in parts of Utah, Colorado, and New Mexico, lie in the southwest corner of the United States. Bordered by Mexico in the south, California in the west, and Texas in the east, the region covers around 113,000 sq miles (292,000 sq km). It is sparsely populated, with 60 percent of its population of around 5.3 million living in the cities. Arizona's most famous sight is the magnificent Grand Canyon.

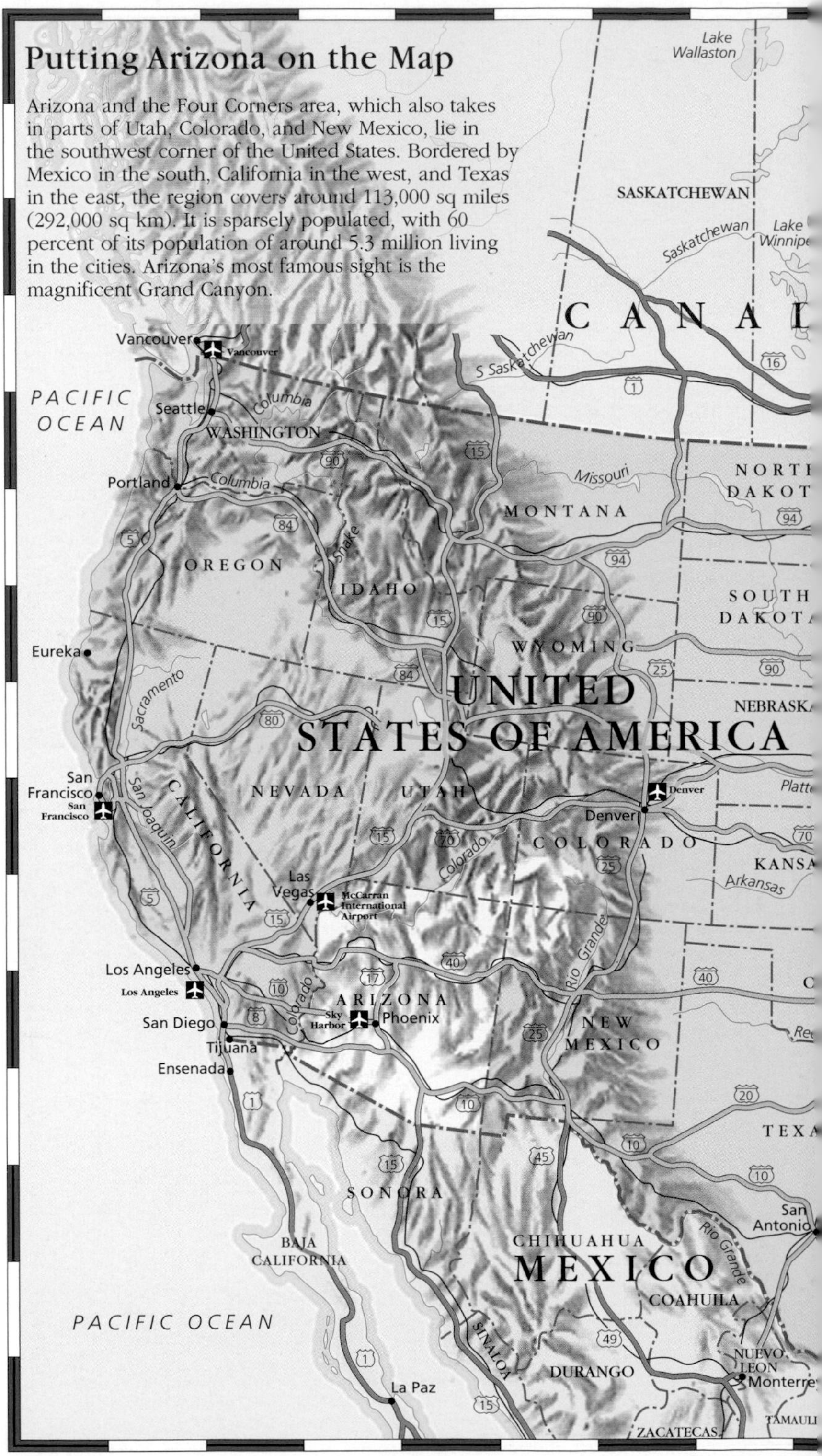

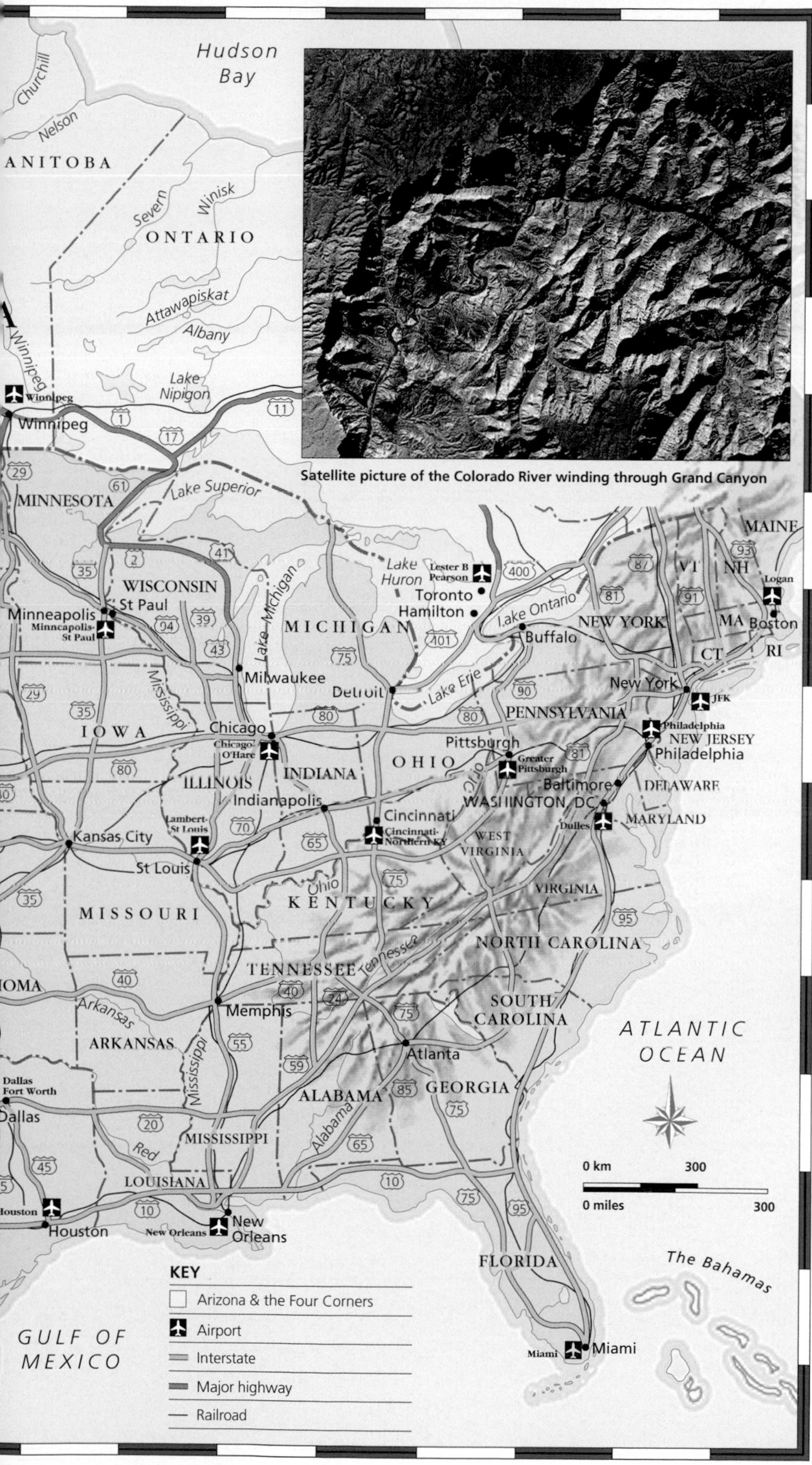

Satellite picture of the Colorado River winding through Grand Canyon

A PORTRAIT OF ARIZONA

At the heart of all things Arizonan lies its landscape – stark and stunning, vast and magnificent. There is little in Arizona that is "normal" – from towering red rock buttes and deserts that secretly hoard explosions of life, to deep canyons that are encyclopedias of the planet's history. Everywhere there is a sense of grandeur, drama, and contrast.

Skull of a buffalo

Native American tribes have lived in this region for thousands of years. They had flourishing civilizations that subsequently vanished, leaving mysterious and haunting ruins, which are today just a stone's throw from modern cities of glass and steel, towering above the ancient desert.

The Spanish, too, had a thriving culture here, a century before English colonists turned westward toward Arizona and the Southwest. When the Anglos finally reached the Southwest, their deeds and misdeeds gave rise to the legends of the Wild West.

CLIMATE & ENVIRONMENT

Elevation, to a great extent, controls the environment in Arizona. For every 1,000 ft (300 m) in altitude, temperatures fall 3–5°F (1–2°C), and different flora and fauna dominate. In Arizona's southwest corner, the Sonoran Desert is often little more than a 100 ft (30.5 m) above sea level. Here, days are searingly hot, nights are cold, and vegetation is sparse. Heading east, the land rises around 1,000 to 3,000 ft (300–1,000 m), and the desert often bursts into vibrant bloom after spring showers. The northern half of the state is dominated by the Colorado Plateau – a rock tableland covering a vast area of around 130,000 sq miles (336,700 sq km) and rising as high as 12,000 ft (3,660 m).

In southeastern Arizona, some mountains higher than 10,000 ft (3,048 m) are surrounded by desert, which has blocked the migration of plants and animals for millions of years, creating unique ecosystems called

Cacti and dried chilis adorn this flower shop in Tucson's historic El Presidio district

◁ Spring flowers, such as sand verbena and dune primrose, cover the desert landscape

"Sky Islands." Here are found animals such as the Mount Graham red squirrel that exist nowhere else.

In this land of contrasts, an hour's drive can lead from arid, barren lands of near-mystical silence, to mountains blanketed in lush and verdant forests fed by sparkling snow-melt streams.

Mount Graham red squirrel in the Sky Islands

Most parts of Arizona enjoy more than 300 days of sunshine a year, yet around 90 percent of the land receives as little as 2 in (5 cm) and no more than 20 in (50 cm) of annual rainfall. Sudden summer rainstorms on the Colorado Plateau cause flash floods. Summer temperatures in the desert often reach more than 100°F (38°C), but can drop by up to 50°F (10°C) after sunset.

A CULTURAL CROSSROADS

Modern Arizona has been forged by the same three great cultures that have helped shape much of America: Native American, Hispanic, and Anglo-American. Spanish is the second language in Arizona, and throughout the Southwest. Everyday English is peppered with a range of Spanish phrases, reflecting a regional heritage stretching back to the 16th century. While US history usually focuses on developments in the east coast British colonies, Spanish explorers were in the Southwest in 1539 *(see p38)*, 80 years before the Pilgrims landed at Plymouth Rock. Native Americans have a far older relationship with Arizona. The Hopis and Pueblos trace their ancestry to the ancient peoples *(see pp24–5)* who built the elaborate cliff dwellings at the sites of Mesa Verde, Canyon de Chelly, and Chaco Canyon. Today's Native populations have a hand in the government of their own lands and have employed a variety of ways to regenerate their economies – through casinos, tourism, coal production, and crafts such as pottery, basketry, and Hopi *kachina* dolls. Native American spiritual beliefs are complex, as each tribe has different practices, which are often tied to ancestors and the land. Most Native festivals and dances are open to visitors, although some are private affairs for spiritual reasons.

POLITICS & ECONOMY

Today, Arizona is the country's fifth-largest state. Despite the fact that its population is increasing, Arizona remains one of the least populated in the United States, with an average density of just 45 people per square mile. However, there is intense urbanization in certain areas – Phoenix, Tucson, and Flagstaff account for around 40 percent of the state's

Native Americans performing a traditional dance during the Navajo Nation Fair at Window Rock

Downtown Tucson – the city's historical and cultural heart – at night

population. This has put an immense pressure on the region's resources, particularly water, which has become one of the most pressing issues facing Arizona. In the 1930s, dam-building projects were initiated, starting with the Hoover Dam. The controversial Glen Canyon Dam, opened in 1963, flooded a vast area of natural beauty, as well as many sacred sites of the Native Americans. Today, many tribes have asserted ownership of the water on their lands. Water has also been channeled increasingly toward urban use as farmers in need of cash sell or lease their water rights.

Saxophone player, downtown Phoenix

Manufacturing, high technology, and the tourism industry have taken over from mining and ranching as the region's principal employers. However, mining and agriculture remain important elements of the economy.

ENTERTAINMENT & THE ARTS

Arizona's canyons, deserts, mountains, rivers, and man-made lakes offer a plethora of hiking, watersports, skiing, and golfing opportunities. One of the best ways to experience the landscape is on a trail ride, while armchair cowboys can attend that great Southwestern event – the rodeo. The state's federally-protected national parks, recreation areas, and monuments – such as Grand Canyon National Park, Glen Canyon National Recreation Area, and Saguaro National Park – are favorite haunts for hikers, rock climbers, and 4WD enthusiasts.

Beside outdoor sport and activities, Arizona's red rock landscapes and light have always inspired artists, many of whom have settled in Sedona, Flagstaff, and Prescott. For culture lovers, there are orchestras, theaters, operas, and dance companies, who perform regularly in Phoenix and Tucson. Both cities also have a vibrant nightclub scene, featuring country, jazz, and alternate sounds. A flourishing Hispanic music scene livens up nightclubs, while Native American musicians such as Carlos R. Nakai mix traditional sounds with classical music and jazz.

The attractions of the stunning landscape and a romantic sense of the past combine to conjure up the legends of the "Wild West." For many, the Southwest offers the chance to indulge that bit of cowboy in their souls.

Landscapes of Arizona

Arizona's colorful, beautiful, and varied landscape has been shaped by millions of years of volcanic eruption, uplift, and wind and water erosion. For much of the Paleozoic Era (between about 570 and 225 million years ago), the state was mostly covered by a vast inland sea that deposited over 10,000 ft (3,048 m) of sediment, which hardened into rock. Following the formation of the Rocky Mountains, some 80 million years ago, rivers and rainfall eroded the rock layers and formed the deep canyons and arches that distinguish Arizona's landscape.

The central geological feature of the region is the Colorado Plateau, which covers some 13,000 sq miles (34,000 sq km). It is cut through by many canyons, including the Grand Canyon *(see pp48–55)*.

Coral Pink Sand Dunes State Park's *shimmering pink sand dunes cover more than 50 percent of this 3,700-acre (1,500-ha) park.*

The butte formations of Monument Valley *(see pp102–103)* are the result of erosion, and their tops mark the level of an ancient plain.

Arizona's mountains *are part of the Rockies and were formed during volcanic activity and continental plate movement some 65 million years ago. Snow-covered peaks, forests of pine, juniper, spruce, and fir, and streams and small lakes fed by snowmelt, as well as alpine meadows are all found in this area.*

GEOGRAPHICAL REGIONS

Arizona's prominent features are the Colorado Plateau and the Sonoran Desert, which is divided into Colorado Desert and Arizona Upland. The High Country mountain ranges are surrounded by desert, creating the "Sky Islands" *(see p18)*.

KEY

- Colorado Desert
- Arizona Upland
- Colorado Plateau
- High Country
- Sky Islands

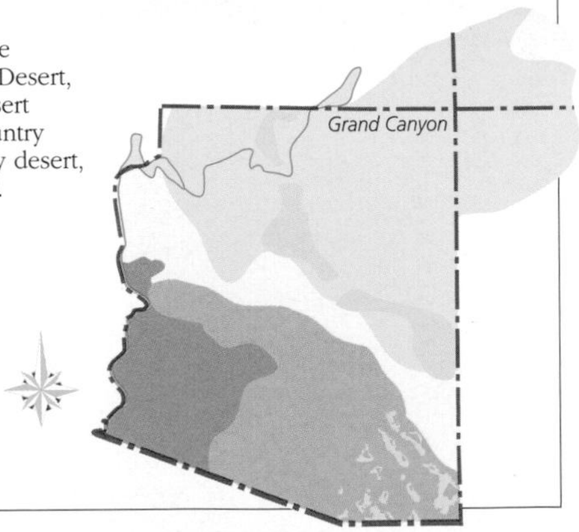

Lake Powell (see pp62–3) *was formed by the damming of Glen Canyon in 1963. The creation of the 185-mile (300-km) long lake was reviled by environmentalists, and celebrated by watersport enthusiasts and parched farmers and city dwellers.*

Antelope Canyon, *in the Glen Canyon area, is the most famous of Arizona's narrow "slot" canyons. The canyon's rose-colored sandstone chambers, sculpted into sensual curves by centuries of flash floodwaters and desert winds, are a favorite subject for photographers.*

The orange sand of Monument Valley's desert floor is dotted with plants such as sagebrush and cacti.

MESAS, BUTTES & SPIRES

Like canyons, mesas come in many sizes. Some large ones measure over 100 miles (160 km) across, and are often the result of land being forced up by geological forces. Other mesas, buttes, and spires are hard-rock remains left behind as a large plain cracked, and then eroded away.

The Colorado Plateau *is crossed by river-forged canyons. Elevations here range from 2,000 ft (600 m) above sea level to around 13,000 ft (3,900 m). Dramatic variations in the landscape include desert, verdant river valleys, thickly forested peaks, and eroded bizarre sandstone formations.*

Flora & Fauna

Despite the fact that over 70 percent of Arizona is occupied by desert, it is not an arid, lifeless wasteland. Here, elevation, more than any other factor, determines the flora and fauna of a location.

The Sonoran Desert in the south is divided into the low elevation, arid Colorado Desert, and the comparatively higher and more verdant Arizona Upland. Covering much of the state's northern third is the 13,000 sq mile (34,000 sq km) Colorado Plateau. Above 7,000 ft (2,134 m) is High Country, where green pine forests, alpine meadows, and sparkling rivers abound. In the extreme southeast of the state, where the Sonoran Desert gives way to a part of the Chihuahuan Desert, the green-topped mountains of the High Country are surrounded by arid desert, creating special eco-zones called Sky Islands, where unique species have developed over the millennia.

The mountain lion, *also known as cougar or puma, is found in remote desert and mountain areas in Arizona. The males may be up to 8 ft (2.4 m) long and weigh 150 lbs (68 kg).*

THE COLORADO DESERT

Dry for most of the year, this vast, arid portion of the Sonoran Desert gets a small amount of winter rain that results in a display of wildflowers in spring. Other flora and fauna found here include creosote bush, cacti, yucca, jackrabbits, desert tortoises, and bighorn sheep.

The blacktailed jackrabbit *is born with a full coat of muted fur to camouflage it from predators such as the coyote.*

The Joshua tree *was named by Mormons who pictured the upraised arms of Joshua in its branches.*

THE ARIZONA UPLAND

The summer "monsoon" and winter storms make the upland region – in the northeast of Arizona's Sonoran Desert – the greenest of the deserts. It is famous for its tall saguaro cactus *(see p90)*, some of which attain heights of 50 ft (15 m), and provide a home for animals such as the gila woodpecker and the elf owl.

Prickly pear cacti *flower in spring and are among the largest of the many types of cacti that flourish in the Sonoran Desert.*

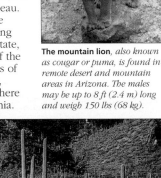

The desert tortoise *can live for more than 50 years. It is now a protected species and is increasingly difficult to spot.*

DANGERS IN THE DESERT

The danger of poisonous desert creatures has often been exaggerated. Although some desert creatures do, on rare occasions, bite or sting people, the bites are seldom fatal unless the victims are small children or have serious health problems. To avoid being hurt, never reach into dark spaces or overhead ledges where you can't see. Watch where you place your feet, and shake out clothes and shoes before putting them on. Never harass or handle a poisonous creature. If you are bitten, stay calm and seek medical help immediately.

The Arizona bark scorpion *is golden in color. America's most venomous scorpion, it has a sting that requires prompt medical help.*

The diamondback rattlesnake *is found in Arizona's deserts and mountains. Its bite is venomous, but seldom deadly if treated. It usually strikes only when surprised.*

THE COLORADO PLATEAU

Classically Western with canyons, cliffs, mesas, and buttes, the Colorado Plateau is dotted with cacti, sage, and mesquite in its lower reaches. At higher altitudes, the flora changes to piñon pines and junipers. Rattlesnakes, cougars, and coyotes are among the wildlife found on the plateau.

Piñon pines *are ball-shaped, less than 30 ft (9.1 m) tall, and are found between 4,000 and 6,000 ft (1,829 m).*

The coyote *is a small, highly intelligent member of the dog family. It hunts both solo and in packs, and can often be heard howling at night.*

THE HIGH COUNTRY

At higher elevations, Arizona's plants and animals are similar to those of Canada. Black bears, mule deer, and elk are some of the fauna. Ponderosa pines are found at 6,000–9,000 ft (1,829–2,743 m), aspen forests at 8,000–11,000 ft (2,438–3,353 m), and alpine meadows at 11,000–13,000 ft (3,353–3,962 m).

Black bears *inhabit Arizona's mountainous areas. Their diet consists of nuts, insects, and small mammals. They are shy, but may approach humans out of curiosity or if they smell food.*

Aspen trees *are common at elevations over 8,000 ft (2,438 m). Their leaves turn a rich golden color in fall.*

Art of Arizona

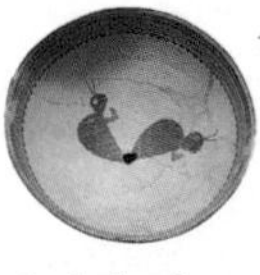

Ancient pottery bowl

Arizona's qualities of light, open spaces, and colorful landscapes have inspired art and craft for centuries – from intricate baskets and pottery of the Native Americans to the religious art of the early Spanish missions. In the 1800s, Frederic Remington and Charles Russell painted romantic images of the Wild West. Later, in the 20th century, Ansel Adams photographed the beauty and physical drama of the land. Today, Arizona is a dynamic center for the arts, with vibrant art museums, busy galleries, and a lively community of artists.

Basketwork *is associated with most Native tribes. Braided, twined or coiled from willow or yucca leaves, the baskets are decorated differently by each tribe.*

Anglo art *developed as European settlers moved westward. Works by Frederic Remington* (see p26), *such as* Cowboy on a Horse *seen above, and by Thomas Moran captured cowboy life and the stunning landscapes of the West. Today, this trend continues with artists portraying traditional and contemporary life in the West.*

TRADITIONAL NATIVE ART

Five hundred years before Columbus arrived in the New World, Native tribes in Arizona were producing baskets, pottery, and jewelry of stunning delicacy and beauty. Thousands of artifacts recovered from Ancient Puebloan, Hohokam, and Mogollon sites are on display at major institutions. The Heard Museum *(see pp78–9)* has one of the world's most comprehensive collections of both ancient and contemporary Native art, and the Arizona State Museum *(see p89)* has a significant display that covers 2,000 years of Native history. The Museum of Northern Arizona in Flagstaff *(see p66)* features superb examples of Sinagua pottery and artifacts from early Navajo, Hopi, and Zuni tribal life. Native tribes still produce traditional art and crafts, and trading posts are an excellent place to see and purchase them *(see pp146–7)*.

Pottery
One of the oldest of all Native art forms, exceptional pottery collections can be seen at the Edge of Cedars State Park (see p117).

CONTEMPORARY SCULPTURE

One of the most popular art forms in Arizona today, excellent examples of contemporary sculpture, such as the piece featured here – *Dineh* (1981) – can be seen in galleries throughout the state. *Dineh*, meaning "the people," is the word the Navajo use to describe themselves. This bronze displays clean lines and smooth surfaces that evoke the strength and dignity of the subjects.

MODERN NATIVE ARTISTS

Native artists often blend traditional themes with modern styles. The *Red-Tailed Hawk* (1986) by Daniel Namhinga reflects his Hopi-Tewa heritage in the stylized *kachina* and birdwing forms, boldly rendered in bright desert colors. It is part of the Native art collection at Heard Museum *(see p79)*.

Latin art *first appeared in Arizona during the Spanish Colonial period, usually representing religious themes. Today, it depicts the Hispanic cultures of the American Southwest and Mexico. Exhibits featuring the works of renowned contemporary Latin artists can be found at major art museums.*

Silver Jewelry
Made from silver and turquoise, jewelry is a relatively new art form developed by the Navajo and Zuni tribes in the late 1800s.

Rugs
Weaving began in the mid-1800s. Today, a fine Navajo rug can sell for thousands of dollars.

Carvings
Kachina *represent Hopi spirits. They can be traced to the tribe's early history, and ancient* kachinas *are valued collector's items.*

Architecture of Arizona

Arizona's distinctive architecture traces its influences to the Ancient Puebloan master-builders, whose stone and adobe cliff dwellings, such as Canyon de Chelly's Antelope House *(see p108)*, were suited to the region's harsh climate. Historic architecture can be seen in many old town districts, where adobes are arranged around a central plaza. But there are also other styles, from the Spanish Colonial of the 18th century to those of the 19th and early 20th century. Wooden storefronts, Victorian mansions, and miners' cottages all lend a rustic charm to the region's many mountain towns. Scottsdale *(see p80)* has an architecture school that was set up by Frank Lloyd Wright, one of the 20th century's most famous architects.

Immaculate Conception Church, Ajo

TRADITIONAL ADOBE

Adobe ovens such as these were once used for baking

The traditional building material of the Southwest is adobe, a mixture of mud or clay and sand, with straw or grass as a binder. This is formed into bricks, which harden in the sun, then built into walls, cemented with a similar material, and plastered over with more mud. Adobe deteriorates quickly and must be replastered every few years. Modern adobe-style buildings are often made of cement and covered with lime cement stucco painted to look like adobe. Original dwellings had dirt floors and wooden beams *(vigas)* as ceiling supports. These structures also had adobe ovens that were used for baking.

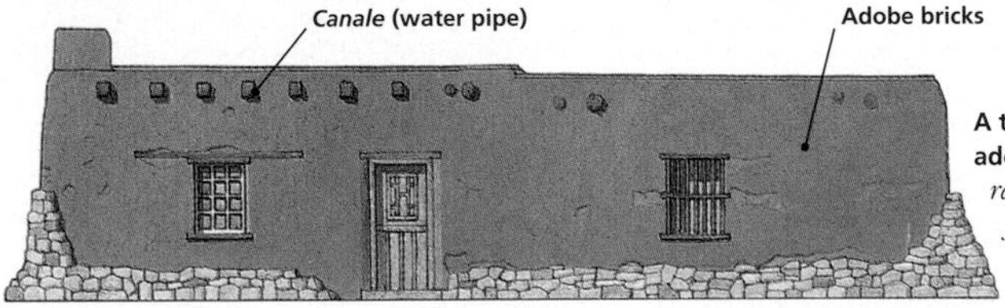

A traditional adobe rancho *or ranch house has a flat roof with pipes* (canales) *to drain away water.*

SPANISH COLONIAL

In the 17th and 18th centuries, Spanish Colonial missions combined the Baroque style of Mexican and European religious architecture with Native design, using local materials and craftsmen. This style underwent a resurgence as Spanish Colonial Revival, from 1915 to the 1930s, and was incorporated into private homes and public buildings. Red-tiled roofs, ornamental terracotta, and stone or iron grille work were combined with white stucco walls. A fine example is Tucson's Pima County Courthouse *(see p88)*, with its dome adorned with colored tiles.

Domes and towers of San Xavier del Bac Mission

San Xavier del Bac Mission (see pp92–3) *exemplifies the Baroque tradition of the Spanish Colonial churches.*

MISSION REVIVAL

Similar in spirit to Spanish Colonial trends, the early 20th-century Mission Revival style is characterized by stucco walls made of white lime cement, often with graceful arches, flat roofs, and courtyards, but with less ornamentation. A fine example of a Mission Revival-style bungalow is the J. Knox Corbett House in Tucson's Historic District *(see p88)*. Built of brick but plastered over in white to simulate adobe, it has a red-tile roof and a big screen porch at the back.

Façade of J. Knox Corbett House

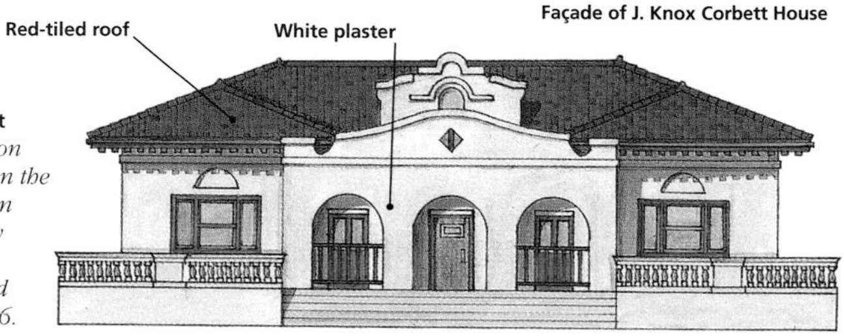

J. Knox Corbett House *in Tuscon was designed in the popular Mission Revival style by the Chicago architect David Holmes in 1906.*

CONTEMPORARY ARCHITECTURE

Arizona has inspired three of the 20th century's most prominent American architects. Frank Lloyd Wright (1867–1959) advocated "Organic Architecture" – the use of local materials and the importance of creating structures that blended with their settings. The architectural complex he built at Taliesin West in Scottsdale includes a school, offices, and his home. Constructed from desert stone and sand, the expansive proportions of the complex reflect the vastness of the Arizona Desert.

Interiors of the Frank Lloyd Wright-designed Taliesin West in Scottsdale, Phoenix

Mary Elizabeth Jane Colter (1870–1958) was one of the most influential architects in America at a time when women architects were virtually unknown. At the turn of the 20th century, the Santa Fe Railroad hired Colter to design several buildings in the Grand Canyon area. Colter was fascinated by Native American building styles and is credited with starting the architectural style called National Park Service Rustic. Her masterpiece is Hopi House *(see p54)*, completed in 1904.

In the 1940s, Italian Paolo Soleri (b. 1919) studied at Taliesin. In 1956, he established the Cosanti Foundation *(see p81)* devoted to what he termed "arcology." This synthesis of architecture and ecology minimizes energy waste, which is endemic in modern buildings and towns.

The visitor building at Arcosanti, designed by Paolo Soleri

Desert View's stone watchtower designed by Mary Colter, at Grand Canyon South Rim

Native Cultures of Arizona

Hopi wicker plaque

The Native peoples of Arizona have maintained many of their traditions, in spite of more than 400 years of armed conflict and brutal attempts at cultural assimilation since the arrival of the Spanish in 1539. Such hardships have forged their determination to retain cultural identities, though some have chosen to move between two worlds – living and working in the modern world while taking part in tribal life and traditional ceremonies. Since the mid-20th century, Native groups have led political campaigns for the restoration of homelands and compensation for past losses.

Today, there are 23 Native reservations in Arizona, the Navajo Reservation being the largest. Tourism and gambling have brought much-needed revenue, but battles over land rights and environmental issues continue.

Rodeo in session at the Apache reservation in Whiteriver, Arizona

THE APACHE

Despite their reputation as fierce warriors, reinforced by their legendary leaders Cochise and Geronimo *(see p38)*, traditionally the Apache were mainly hunter-gatherers. They are thought to have roamed south from their Athabascan-speaking homelands in northern Canada during the 15th century.

The largest Apache reservations are the adjoining San Carlos and Fort Apache-White Mountain reservations in the east-central part of Arizona. Over 12,000 Apaches live on them, with the primary industries being tourism, timber, hunting, and cattle ranching. Successful management of their natural resources has ensured a small degree of economic stability. Visitors are welcome at the Apache reservations to watch rituals such as the *nah'ih'es* or Sunrise Ceremony, which marks a girl's transition to womanhood. Dances, festivals, and rodeos are also held on the reservations *(see pp30–33)*.

THE NAVAJO

With a population of more than 200,000, the Navajo Nation is the largest reservation in southwestern USA, covering more than 25,000 sq miles (64,750 sq km) in Arizona, New Mexico, and southern Utah. The spiritual center of the Navajo Nation is Canyon de Chelly *(see pp106–9)*, where Navajo farmers still live, tend to their sheep, and make rugs using the sheep wool. The Navajo are generally welcoming to visitors, and act as guides in Monument Valley and other sites on their land *(see pp102–3)*. The Navajo economy is based on tourism and the sale of natural resources such as oil, coal, and uranium. However, in 2007, after years of debate, the Navajo decided to move forward with casino development to create much-needed jobs on the reservation.

While many Navajo now live off the reservation in cities and towns, the traditional dwelling, the *hogan*, remains an important focus of their cultural life. Today's *hogan* is an octagonal wood cabin, often fitted with electricity and other modern amenities, where family gatherings take place.

Navajo religious beliefs are still bound up with daily life, with farmers singing corn-growing songs and weavers incorporating a spirit thread into their rugs. Colorful and intricate sand paintings still play a part in healing ceremonies, which aim to restore *hozho*, or harmony, to ill or troubled individuals.

Navajo Indian woman shearing wool from a sheep

THE HOPI

The predominant Pueblo tribe in Arizona is the Hopi, whose reservation is located in the center of the Navajo Reservation. They are one of 20 Pueblo tribes in the Southwest. Pueblo tribes share many of the same religious and cultural beliefs, though there are linguistic differences from tribe to

HOPI SPIRITUALITY

Religion is a fundamental element of Hopi lifestyle. Their ceremonies focus on *kachina* (or *katsina*) – spirit figures that symbolize nature in all its forms. Familiar to visitors as the painted, carved wooden dolls available in many gift stores, the *kachina* lie at the heart of Hopi spirituality. During the growing season (December to July), these spirit figures are represented by *kachina* dancers who visit Hopi villages. During the rest of the year, the spirits are believed to reside in a shrine in the high San Francisco Peaks, north of Flagstaff. Hopi religious ceremonies are often held in the *kiva*, a round underground chamber, usually closed to visitors. Most celebrations are closed to non-Hopis, but some are open to the public. Photography of Pueblo villages and ceremonies is forbidden.

Young Hopi Rainbow dancer

tribe. Most Pueblo tribes trace their ancestry to the Ancestral Puebloan people *(see pp36–7)*, who spread across the area from around 300–200 BC. The town of Walpi on the Hopi Reservation has been continuously occupied since AD 1100.

The oldest Hopi villages are on three mesa-tops, called First, Second, and Third mesas. The groups on each mesa are distinct, exceling at different crafts – pottery on First Mesa, jewelry on Second Mesa, and basketry on Third Mesa. All the settlements produce colorful *kachinas*.

The land occupied by the Hopi is among the starkest and most barren in all America. However, using the ancient irrigation techniques of their ancestors, the Hopi grow corn, beans, and squash. Each village holds sacred dances and ceremonies throughout the year.

Young dancer at an Ute powwow, a gathering of Native Indians

THE TOHONO O'ODHAM

Along with their close relatives, the Pima people, the Tohono O'odham live in South Arizona's Sonoran Desert. Due to the harsh environment here, neither tribe has ever been moved off its ancestral lands. These tribes are among the most anglicized in the region. The Tohono O'odham are mainly Christian. However, they still practice traditional ceremonies, such as the Saguaro Wine Festival and the Tcirkwena Dance, and are known for their fine basketwork.

THE HAVASUPAI & HUALAPAI

These two tribes occupy two separate reservations that stretch along the southern rim of the Grand Canyon. They trace their ancestry to the ancient Hohokam people and share similar languages. The only town on the Havasupai reservation is Supai, 8 miles (13 km) from the nearest road. The reservation is the gateway to the beautiful Havasu Canyon and emerald green Havasu Falls *(see p48)*, a popular destination for hikers.

THE UTE

This tribe once reigned over a vast territory, covering 85 percent of Colorado until as late as the 1850s. Steady encroachment by settlers and mining interests eventually forced them to resettle. Today, the Ute welcome visitors to their two reservations along the southern Colorado border. The Ute Mountain Reservation is home to the little known but spectacular Ancestral Puebloan ruins of Ute Mountain Tribal Park *(see p110)*, and the southern Ute Reservation attracts thousands of visitors each year to the popular Sky Ute Casino, Lodge, and Museum. The southern Utes also hold a colorful Bear Dance on Memorial Day weekend, and a sun dance in mid-summer.

Ute woman sewing moccasins with Mount Ute in the background

The Wild West

Romanticized in a thousand cowboy movies, the "Wild West" conjures up images of tough men herding cattle across the country before living it up in a saloon. But frontier life was far from romantic. Settlers arriving in this wilderness were caught up in a first-come-first-serve battle for land and wealth, fighting Native Americans and each other for land.

The rugged life of the prospectors and ranch cowboys helped to create the idea of the American West. Visitors can still see mining ghost towns such as Chloride *(see p73)* or enjoy re-enacted gunfights on the streets of Tombstone. In the late 19th century, however, such survival skills as good shooting often co-existed with a kill-or-be-killed ethos.

Women in the *Wild West often had to step into the traditional roles of men. Calamity Jane, a woman scout, was known to be an excellent shot and horse rider.*

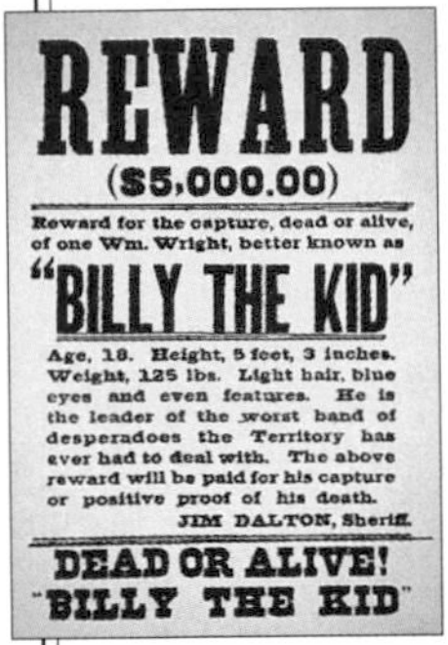

REWARD
($5,000.00)
Reward for the capture, dead or alive, of one Wm. Wright, better known as
"BILLY THE KID"
Age, 18. Height, 5 feet, 3 inches. Weight, 125 lbs. Light hair, blue eyes and even features. He is the leader of the worst band of desperadoes the Territory has ever had to deal with. The above reward will be paid for his capture or positive proof of his death.
JIM DALTON, Sheriff.
DEAD OR ALIVE!
"BILLY THE KID"

A reward poster *for William Bonney (better known as Billy the Kid), who was one of the Wild West's most notorious outlaws. He was eventually tracked and killed by Sheriff Pat Garrett at Fort Sumner, New Mexico, on July 14, 1881.*

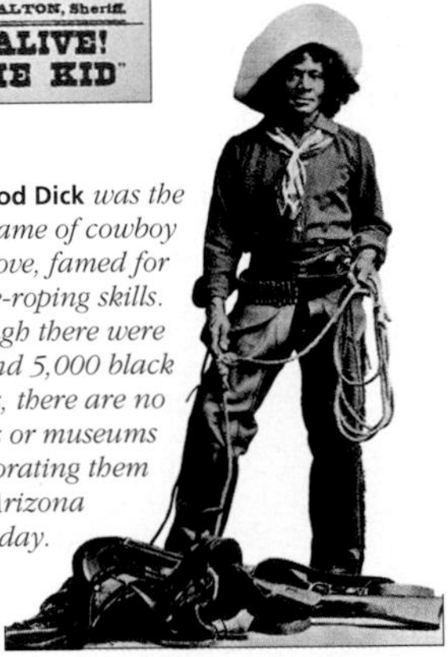

Deadwood Dick *was the nickname of cowboy Nat Love, famed for his cattle-roping skills. Although there were around 5,000 black cowboys, there are no sights or museums commemorating them in Arizona today.*

Cowboys were famous for their horsemanship and sense of camaraderie. The painting shows two friends attempting to save another.

The Conversation, or Dubious Company *(1902) by Frederic Remington highlights the tensions between Natives and the US army, which had played a central role in removing tribes from their ancestral lands.*

Cowboy fashion *began to appear in advertisements in around 1900. The ever popular Levi Strauss denim clothing can be bought across the region* (see p142).

Guided trail rides *are a great way to explore the Wild West and are part of the package of activities available at dude ranches* (see p152). *These ranches offer visitors the opportunity to experience the contemporary cowboy lifestyle.*

Horses were vividly depicted in Remington's dramatic action scenes. They were painted with astonishing realism, revealing a profound knowledge of their behavior and physique.

THE GUNFIGHT AT THE OK CORRAL

One of the most famous tales of the Wild West is the Gunfight at the OK Corral in Tombstone, Arizona *(see p98)*. This struggle pitted two clans against each other, the Clantons and the Earps. The usual, often disputed, version features the Clantons as no-good outlaws and the Earps as the forces of law and order. In 1881 Virgil Earp was the town marshal, and his brothers Morgan and Wyatt were temporary deputies. The showdown on October 26 had the Earps and their ally Doc Holliday on one side and Billy Clanton and the McLaury brothers, Tom and Frank, on the other. Of the seven combatants, only Wyatt Earp emerged untouched by a bullet. Billy, Tom, and Frank were all killed. Wyatt Earp moved to Los Angeles, where he died in 1929.

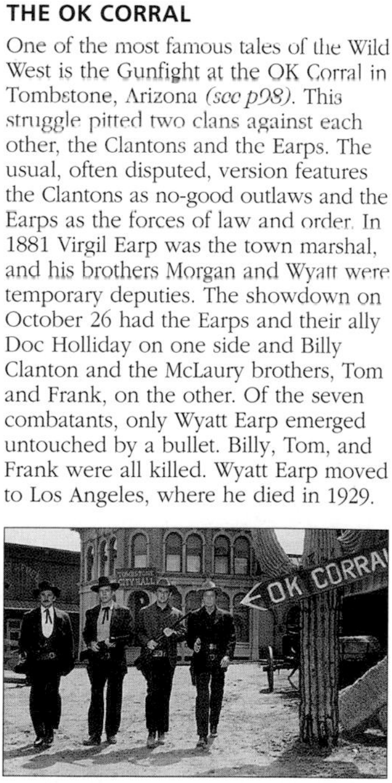

Scene from the 1957 film *Gunfight at the OK Corral*, with Burt Lancaster and Kirk Douglas

SOUTHWESTERN COWBOYS

New York-born artist Frederic Sackrider Remington (1861–1909) became well known for his epic portraits of cowboys, horses, soldiers, and Native Americans in the late 19th century. Featured above is *Aiding a Comrade* (1890), one of his works which celebrates the bravery and loyalty of the cowboy, at a time when they and small-scale ranchers were being superceded by powerful mining companies and ranching corporations. Remington lamented the passing of these heroes: "Cowboys! There are no cowboys anymore!"

Route 66 in Arizona

Route 66 Flagstaff sign

Route 66 is America's most famous road. Stretching for 2,448 miles (3,941 km) from Chicago to Los Angeles, it is part of the country's folklore, symbolizing the freedom of the open road and inextricably linked to the growth of automobile travel. Known also as "The Mother Road" and "America's Main Street," Route 66 was officially opened in 1926 after a 12-year construction process linked the main streets of hundreds of small towns that had been previously isolated. In the 1930s, a prolonged drought in Oklahoma deprived more than 200,000 farmers of their livelihoods and prompted their trek to California along Route 66. This was movingly depicted in John Steinbeck's novel *The Grapes of Wrath* (1939).

Seligman *features several Route 66 stores and diners. Set among Arizona's Upland mountains, the road here passes through scenery that evokes the days of the westward pioneers.*

Route 66 *in Arizona passes through long stretches of wilderness bearing none of the trappings of the modern world. The state has the longest remaining stretch of the original road.*

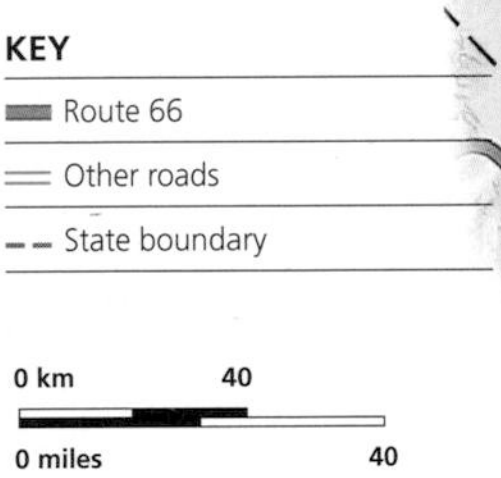

Oatman, *a former gold-mining boomtown* (see p73)*, has 19th-century buildings and boardwalks lining its historic main street. Mock gunfights are regularly staged here.*

The Grand Canyon Caverns, *discovered in 1927, are around 0.75 miles (1.2 km) below ground level. On a 45-minute guided tour visitors are led through football field-sized caverns adorned with stalagmites and seams of sparkling crystals.*

ROUTE 66 IN POPULAR CULTURE

In the 1940s and 1950s, as America's love affair with the car grew and more people moved west than ever before, hundreds of motels, restaurants, and tourist attractions appeared along Route 66, sporting a vibrant new style of architecture. The road's end as a major thoroughfare came in the 1970s with the building of a national network of multilane highways. Today, the road is a popular tourist destination in itself, and along the Arizona section, enthusiasts and conservationists have helped to ensure the preservation of many of its most evocative buildings and signs.

Bobby Troup, composer of the popular song *Route 66*, in a 1948 Buick convertible

LOCATOR MAP

— *Route 66*

☐ *Map area*

Holbrook *was founded in 1882 and is another Route 66 landmark. It is famous for Wigwam Village Motel* (see p125), *a restored 1950s motel, where visitors can stay in rooms that resemble Indian teepees.*

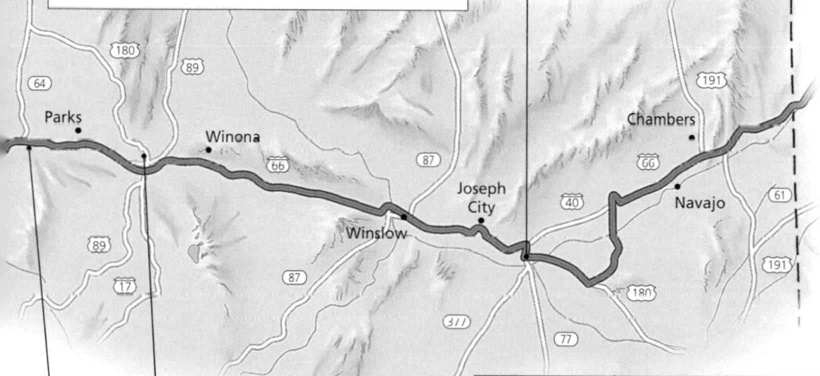

Flagstaff *is home to the famous Museum Club roadhouse* (see p149). *It became a nightclub nicknamed "The Zoo," which was favored by country musicians traveling the road, including such stars as Willie Nelson.*

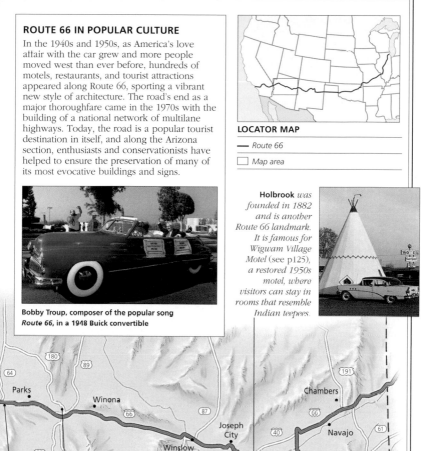

Williams *is known for its many nostalgic diners and motels. Twisters Soda Fountain* (see p136), *also known as The Route 66 Place, is crammed with road memorabilia, including the original 1950s soda fountain and bar stools.*

ARIZONA THROUGH THE YEAR

The weather in the state of Arizona is well known for its extremes, ranging from the heat of the desert to the ice and snow of the mountains. Temperatures vary according to altitude, and so the higher the elevation of the land, the cooler the area will be. Because the climate can be unbearably hot during the summer months, particularly in the southern parts of the state, many people prefer to travel to Arizona during spring and fall. This part of the world is particularly beautiful in fall, with an astounding array of golds, reds, and yellows in the forests and national parks. Besides Arizona's natural beauty, visitors can experience many different kinds of festivals and celebrations, which are unique to the state and reflect its diverse mix of the three main Southwestern cultures – Native American, Hispanic, and European.

Stringing *ristras* of hot chile peppers

SPRING

Everyone enjoys being outdoors in spring, and many festivals and celebrations are held at this time throughout Arizona.

MARCH

Cactus League Spring Training *(month long)* Phoenix and Tucson. Major league baseball teams play in pre-season practice and exhibition games.

Guild Indian Fair & Market *(first weekend)* Phoenix. Held at the Heard Museum, the fair features Indian dancing, arts, crafts, and Native American food.

Midnight at the Oasis Festival *(early Mar)* Yuma. Cars and nostalgia, with over 800 restored and unusual cars on display.

Native dancer at the Guild Indian Fair and Market, Phoenix

Rides at the Maricopa County fair held in Phoenix

Fourth Avenue Street Fair *(mid-Mar)* Tucson. Artists from all over the US, food vendors, live music performances, sidewalk performers, and kids' entertainment.

St. Patrick's Day Parade *(mid-Mar)* Sedona. Annual parade celebrates the green, preceded by a 3.1-mile (5-km) race.

National Festival of the West *(mid-Mar)* Scottsdale. Western music, cowboy poetry, cook-offs, and shooting championships.

APRIL

Phoenix Film Festival *(first or second week)* Phoenix. Week-long screenings of 130 carefully chosen films covering a wide range of subject matter.

Arizona Book Festival *(first Sat)* Phoenix. Event sees 200 local and national authors, and hundreds of exhibitors with new and used books.

Easter Pageant *(week preceding Easter)* Mesa. This extravagant annual outdoor theatrical production is held every night at the Mormon Mesa Arizona Temple with a cast of hundreds, in historical costumes.

Maricopa County Fair *(mid-Apr)* Phoenix. Carnival, entertainment, competitions, education, and fun times for all ages.

Tucson International Mariachi Conference *(mid–late Apr)* Tucson. Annual celebration of Mexican *mariachi* music and dancing.

Pima County Fair *(late Apr)* Tucson. Horses and cattle, gems and minerals, concerts, exhibits, rides, and food provide great family fun at this annual fair.

La Vuelta de Bisbee *(late Apr)* Bisbee. This professional 80-mile (129-km) bicycle race takes place in the Bisbee area.

SUMMER

Summer is warm and is the time for many open-air events, from carnivals and rodeos to cultural events. The weather in July and August, however, can be extreme, especially in Southern Arizona, which has very high temperatures and violent summer storms.

MAY

The Tucson Folk Festival *(early May)* Tucson. Three big-name headline acts, over 120 local and regional acts on four stages, and food, folk art, and craft stalls feature at this festival.

El Cinco de Mayo *(May 5)* Many Arizona towns. Festivities to mark the 1862 Mexican victory over the French include parades, dancing, and Mexican food.

Wyatt Earp Days *(Memorial Day weekend)* Tombstone. Mock gunfights, chili cook-off, "hangings," 1880s fashion show, street entertainment, and barbecue.

Phippen Western Art Show & Sale *(Memorial Day weekend)* Prescott. Western art and sculpture buyers, sellers, and admirers come for the juried fine arts show.

JUNE

Sharlot Hall Museum Folk Arts Fair *(first weekend)* Prescott. Demonstrations of the arts, skills, and entertainments of the territorial years.

Folk arts fair at Sharlot Hall Museum, Prescott

Sedona Taste *(Sunday before Father's Day)* Sedona. Chef's from top restaurants prepare food samples and serve fine wines.

Pine Country Pro Rodeo *(third weekend)* Flagstaff. Competitors take part in bronc and bull riding, roping, and barrel racing.

Hopi Festival of Arts and Culture *(late June–early July)* Flagstaff. A celebration of Hopi culture featuring film, music, art, and dance.

Shakespeare Sedona *(four weeks; late June–July)* Sedona. Theatrical productions of Shakespearean selections.

JULY

Fourth of July *(4 July)* Most Arizona towns. Celebrations include parades, fireworks, rodeos, sports, music festivals, and Indian dances.

Frontier Days *(first week)* Prescott. The oldest professional rodeo in the world, featuring calf roping and wild horse racing.

Arizona Highland Celtic Festival *(third Saturday)* Flagstaff. Entertainment and activities for all ages with bagpipers, dances, athletic demonstrations, and food.

White Mountain Native American Art Festival & Indian Market *(third weekend)* Pinetop-Lakeside. Features the region's finest Native artists, demonstrations, performances, and foods.

Arizona Cardinals Training Camp *(late July–mid-Aug)* Flagstaff. Most practice sessions of this NFL team are open to the public.

Cowpunchers Reunion Rodeo *(late July)* Williams. Watch cowboys in rodeo events, including bareback, team roping, calf roping, bull riding, and more.

AUGUST

Navajo Festival of Arts and Culture *(first weekend)* Flagstaff. Navajo artists and craftspeople display their work during a weekend of storytelling, dance, music, and art.

White Mountain Bluegrass Music Festival *(second weekend)* Pinetop-Lakeside. The region's finest bluegrass and gospel music, arts and crafts fair featuring children's crafts, music workshops, and food.

Payson Rodeo *(third weekend)* Payson. Sanctioned by the Professional Rodeo Cowboy Association (PRCA), the best of the best compete for sizeable prize money.

Arizona Cowboy Poets Gathering *(third weekend)* Prescott. Blend of traditional and contemporary poems, songs and stories about the lives of working cowboys on the Arizona range.

Hispanic musicians or *mariachis* play at a Cinco de Mayo celebration

FALL

The autumnal forests and mountains of Arizona are striking, ablaze with brilliant yellows, reds, and golds. Fall is one of the best seasons for touring and sightseeing because the temperature is cooler and more comfortable.

SEPTEMBER

Navajo Nation Fair & Rodeo *(early Sep)* Window Rock. Largest Native American fair in the US with a parade, a rodeo, traditional song and dance, and arts and crafts.
Rendezvous of the Gunfighters *(Labor Day weekend)* Tombstone. Includes a parade, stage-coach rides, chile cook-offs, and mock shootouts.
Coconino County Fair *(Labor Day weekend)* Flagstaff. Carnival rides, food, local arts and crafts exhibits, demolition derby and car shows, and live music.
Grand Canyon Music Festival *(mid-Sep)* Grand Canyon Village. Fine chamber music, from Baroque to classical, jazz, fusion, and cross over.
Andy Devine Days *(mid-Sep)* Kingman. PRCA rodeo, parade and activities honor the town of Kingman and actor Andy Devine.
Apache County Fair *(mid-Sep)* St. Johns. Horse racing, entertainment, and livestock shows and exhibits.
Jazz on the Rocks Festival *(third weekend)* Sedona. Great names in jazz perform for thousands of visitors.
Flagstaff Festival of Science *(late Sep)* Flagstaff. Ten days of events, including field trips, interactive exhibits, and open-houses at museums and observatories.

OCTOBER

Air Affaire *(first weekend)* Page. Air-show pilots entertain and thrill with aerobatics, showmanship, speed, and fun.
Route 66 Culture and Heritage Days *(second weekend)* Kingman. Music, food, and classic car show.
Fort Verde Days *(second weekend)* Camp Verde. Annual event with parade, horse events, barbecue, cavalry drills, and art show.
Helldorado Days *(third weekend)* Tombstone. Features re-enactments, parades, a carnival, and music and street entertainment.

Calf roping at a Southwest rodeo

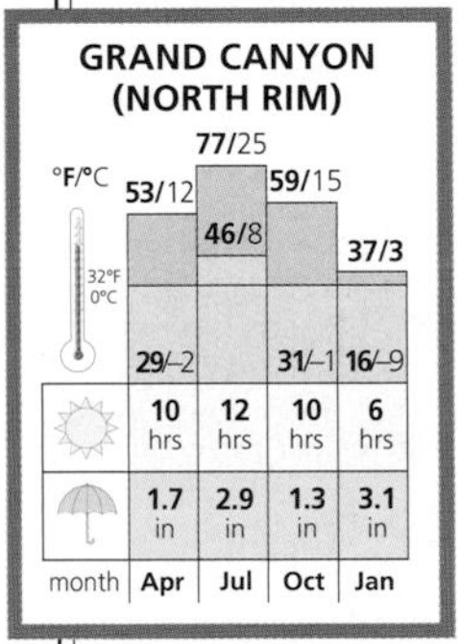

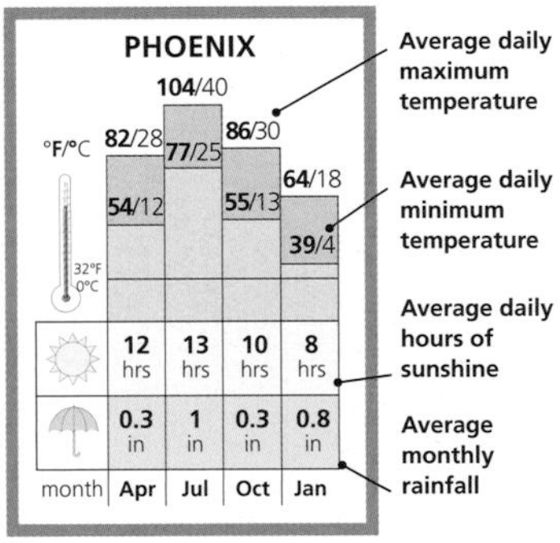

Climate

The climate varies across the state. Phoenix and the southern areas have hot and dry summers and mild, sunny winters, whereas towns, such as Flagstaff, in the northern areas have snowy winters. These areas are colder due to their higher elevation.

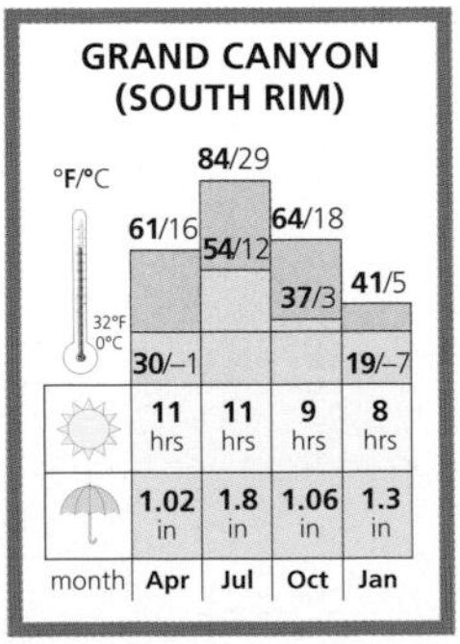

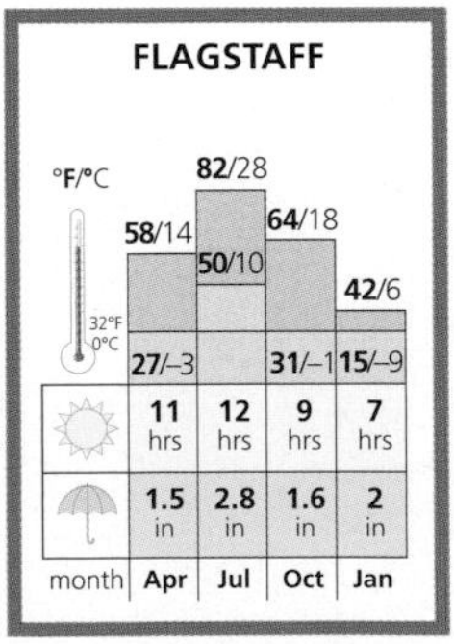

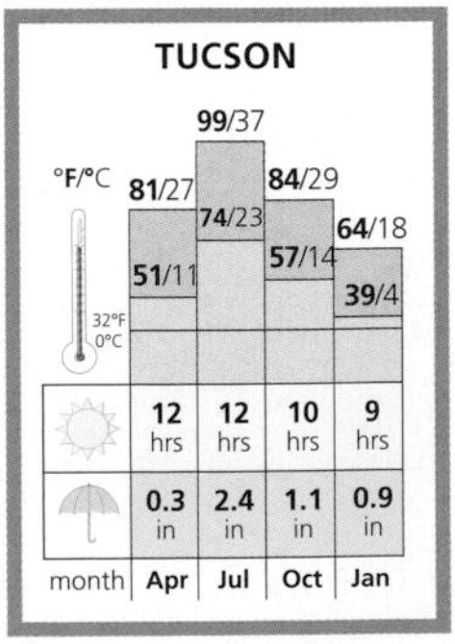

London Bridge Days *(late Oct)* Lake Havasu City. Annual celebration commemorates the dedication of the bridge with a parade, concerts, and a Renaissance Festival.

WINTER

Christmas in Arizona is celebrated in traditional American style, with lights decorating almost every building and tree. Much of the state – the low elevation areas – experiences mild, sunny winters. In areas above 7,000 ft (2,130 m), the ski season stretches from mid-December to early April.

NOVEMBER

El Tour de Tucson *(mid-Nov)* Tucson. Founded in 1983, this is America's largest perimeter cycling event for professional racers and amateurs.

Yuma Colorado River Crossing Balloon Festival *(late Nov)* Yuma. More than 50 hot air balloons fill the sky. Food, entertainment, and fireworks are part of the evening celebrations.

DECEMBER

La Fiesta de Tumacacori *(first weekend)* Tumacacori. Festival held on mission grounds to celebrate the Native American heritage of the upper Santa Cruz Valley.

Christmas City *(late Nov–Dec)* Prescott. Parades, bright lights, musical events, open houses, and shopping opportunities abound.

Fourth Avenue Street Fair *(early Dec)* Tucson. Artists, food vendors, live music, sidewalk performers, kids' entertainment, and fun activities for all.

Festival of Lights *(second Sat)* Sedona. Take part in the lighting of 6,000 luminarias in Tlaquepaque's courtyards, and enjoy carolers, musicians and dancers in this Spanish shopping center.

Saguaro cactus illuminated by Christmas lights

JANUARY

Fiesta Bowl Festival & Parade *(Dec 31 and New Year's Day)* Phoenix. Parade, street party, and college football at the Arizona State University Sun Devil Stadium.

Tucson Area Square Dance Festival *(mid-Jan)* Tucson. The festival attracts thousands of dancers.

FBR Open Golf Tournament *(late Jan or Feb)* Scottsdale. PGA's annual golf tournament.

Pow Wow – Gem & Mineral Show *(late Jan–early Feb)* Quartzsite. The largest of eight gem and mineral shows held during January and February.

Scottsdale Celebration of Fine Art *(mid-Jan–late Mar)* Scottsdale. Watch art being created as over 100 artists work in studios set up for the event.

FEBRUARY

Tubac Festival of the Arts *(early Feb)* Tubac. An important arts and crafts festival.

Silver Spur Rodeo *(first weekend)* Yuma. Features arts and crafts, rodeo, and Yuma's biggest parade.

Tucson Gem & Mineral Show *(mid-Feb)* Tucson. Open to visitors. One of the biggest gem and mineral shows in the US.

La Fiesta de los Vaqueros *(late Feb)* Tucson. Rodeo and other cowboy events, plus the world's largest non-motorized parade.

Flagstaff Winterfest *(month long)* Flagstaff. Competitive Nordic and Alpine skiing, dog sled races, stargazing and concerts, and family activities.

Sedona International Film Festival *(last weekend)* Sedona. Film fans gather to view films and attend workshops.

PUBLIC HOLIDAYS

New Year (Jan 1)
Martin Luther King Jr Day (third Mon in Jan)
Presidents' Day (third Mon in Feb)
Easter Sunday (variable)
El Cinco de Mayo (May 5)
Memorial Day (last Mon in May)
Independence Day (Jul 4)
Pioneer Day (Jul 24 – Utah)
Labor Day (first Mon in Sep)
Columbus Day (second Mon in Oct)
Veterans Day (Nov 11)
Thanksgiving (fourth Thu in Nov)
Christmas Day (Dec 25)

Skiers riding a chair lift outside Flagstaff

THE HISTORY OF ARIZONA

The story of Arizona's human history has been played out against a dramatic and hostile landscape. Despite the arid conditions, Native civilizations have lived here for thousands of years. Over the centuries, they have adjusted to the Hispanic colonizers of the 17th and 18th centuries, and the Anglo-Americans of the 19th and 20th. Each of these has molded the state's history.

Long before the appearance of the Spanish in the 1500s, the Southwest was inhabited by a variety of Native populations. Groups of hunters are believed to have walked to the region by crossing the Bering Straits over a land bridge that once joined Asia with North America around 25,000–35,000 years ago.

Kachina doll

The first Native American peoples of this region are known as Paleo-Indians. Skilled hunters of mammoths and other large Pleistocene animals, the Paleo-Indians roamed the area in small groups between 10,000 and 8,000 BC. As the large mammals died out, they turned to hunting small game and gathering roots and berries. These hunter-gatherers are called the Archaic Indians. Anthropologists believe settled farming societies appeared gradually as the population grew, and that new crops and farming techniques were introduced by migrants and traders from Mexico around 800 BC, when corn first began to be cultivated in the region. Among the early farmers were the Basketmakers, named for the finely wrought baskets they wove. Part of the early Ancestral Puebloan, or Anasazi, culture, these people are thought to have lived in extended family groups, in pithouse dwellings. By around AD 500, large villages, or pueblos, began to develop in the area. These usually centered around a big pithouse that was used for communal or religious purposes – the forerunner of the ceremonial *kiva* *(see pp36–7)*, which is still used today by the descendants of the Ancestral Puebloans to hold religious ceremonies.

By AD 700, there were three main cultures in the region: the Hohokam, Mogollon, and the Ancestral Puebloan. These were sophisticated agricultural societies that developed efficient and innovative techniques to utilize the desert's limited resources. The Mogollon were known for their pottery, and were one of the first groups to adjust to an agrarian lifestyle. The Hohokam farmed Central and Southern Arizona between 300 BC and AD 1350, and their irrigation systems enabled them to grow two crops a year.

TIMELINE

Stone spear point

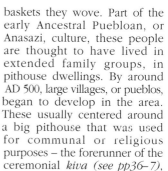

6,000 BC Appearance of Archaic Indians, skilled small-game hunters and tool makers

600 BC Corn arrives from Mexico. Start of agriculture, although the semi-nomadic quest for food predominates

200 BC Basketmakers in Four Corners region

10,000 BC | **5,000 BC** | **1,000 BC** | **AD 1**

10,000 BC Arrival of Paleo-Indians. A nomadic people, they hunted big game across the relatively temperate grasslands of Arizona

500 BC Beans and squash are grown, agriculture expands

300 BC Hohokam civilization in Central and Southern Arizona

◁ **Papago Indian woman from Pima County, Arizona, 1903**

The Ancestral Puebloans

The hauntingly beautiful and elaborate ruins left behind by the Ancestral Puebloan people are a key factor in the hold that this prehistoric culture has over the public imagination. Also known as "Anasazi," a name coined by the Navajo meaning "Ancient Enemy Ancestor," today they are more accurately known as the Ancestral Puebloans, and are seen as the ancestors of today's Pueblo peoples.

The first Ancestral Puebloans are thought to have settled at Mesa Verde *(see pp118–19)* in around AD 550, where they lived in pithouses. By around AD 800 they had developed masonry skills and began building housing complexes using sandstone. From AD 1100 to 1300, impressive levels of craftsmanship were reached in weaving, pottery, jewelry, and tool-making.

Ceramics, *such as this bowl, show the artistry of the Ancestral Puebloans. Pottery is just one of many ancient artifacts on show in museums in the region.*

Jackson Stairway *in Chaco Canyon is evidence of the engineering skills of the Ancestral Puebloans. They also built networks of roads between their communities and extensive irrigation systems.*

Kivas are round pit-like rooms dug into the ground and roofed with beams and earth.

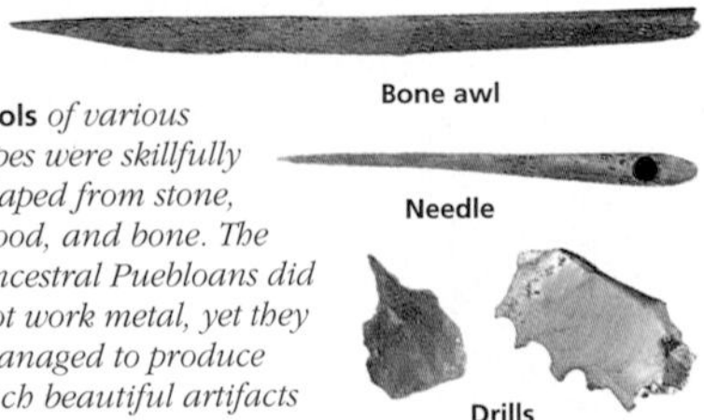

Tools *of various types were skillfully shaped from stone, wood, and bone. The Ancestral Puebloans did not work metal, yet they managed to produce such beautiful artifacts as baskets, pottery, and jewelry.*

The blue corn *growing on this Hopi Reservation today is a similar plant to that grown by Ancestral Puebloans. They were also skilled at utilizing the medicinal properties of plants, including cottonwood bark, which contains a painkiller.*

The kiva *was the religious and ceremonial center of Ancestral Puebloan life. Still used by modern Pueblo Indians, a* kiva *usually had no windows and the only access was through a hole in the roof. Small* kivas *were used by a single family unit, while large* kivas *were designed to accommodate the whole community.*

WHERE TO FIND ANCESTRAL PUEBLOAN RUINS

Navajo National Monument *(see p104)*; Canyon de Chelly National Monument *(see pp106–9)*; Hovenweep National Monument *(see p110)*; Chaco Culture National Historical Park *(see pp112–13)*; Mesa Verde National Park *(see pp118–19)*.

Petroglyphs *were often used by Ancestral Puebloans as astronomical markers for the different seasons. This one was found at the Petrified Forest National Park* (see p67).

Pueblo Bonito features many examples of the masonry skills used by the Puebloan peoples.

THE PUEBLO PEOPLE

By AD 1300 the Ancestral Puebloans had abandoned many of their cities and migrated to areas where new centers emerged. Theories on why this occurred include a 50-year drought; the strain that a larger population placed on the desert's limited resources; and a lengthy period of social upheaval, perhaps stimulated by increasing trade with tribes as far away as central Mexico. Most archeologists agree that the Ancestral Puebloans did not disappear but live on today in Puebloan descendants who trace their origins to Mesa Verde, Chaco, and other sacred ancestral sites.

Painstaking excavation at an Ancestral Puebloan *kiva* in Chaco Canyon

CHACO CANYON'S PUEBLO BONITO

At Chaco Canyon *(see pp112–13)* the largest "great house" ever built was Pueblo Bonito with more than 600 rooms and 40 *kivas*. One current theory is that these structures did not house populations but were, in fact, public buildings for commerce and ceremonial gatherings. The lives of the Ancestral Puebloans were short, barely 35 years, and as harsh as the environment in which they lived. Their diet was poor, and arthritis and dental problems were common. Women often showed signs of osteoporosis or brittle bones as early as their first childbirth.

ANCIENT CULTURES

By around AD 800, the Ancestral Puebloans began to build elaborate ceremonial centers, such as Chaco Canyon *(see pp112–13)*, and to move pueblos off open mesa tops to cliff recesses in canyons such as Mesa Verde *(see pp118–19)*. Their numbers started diminishing around 1250. Chaco Canyon was abandoned about 1275, and Mesa Verde by 1300. By 1350, there was virtually no trace of the Ancestral Puebloans on the Colorado Plateau. Soon after, the Hohokams and the Mogollons became extinct. Experts theorize that a combination of a long drought and social unrest caused them to break up into smaller groups that were easier to sustain. However, these groups may not have vanished entirely. It is believed that the Hopi are the descendants of the Ancestral Puebloans, and that the Pima and Tohono O'odham trace their ancestry to the Hohokam *(see pp24–5)*.

THE NAVAJO & THE APACHE

The Navajo and Apache originated in the Athabascan culture of Canada and Alaska. The Navajo moved south between 1200 and 1400, while the Apache are thought to have arrived in the late 15th century. The Navajo were hunters who took to herding sheep brought by the Spanish. The Apache groups – Jicarilla, Mescalero, Chiricahua, and Western Apache – continued their nomadic lifestyle. They were skillful warriors, especially the Chiricahua of Southern Arizona, whose leaders Cochise and Geronimo fought Hispanic and Anglo settlers to deter them from colonization in the late 19th century.

THE ARRIVAL OF THE SPANISH

In 1539, the Franciscan priest Fray Marcos de Niza led the first Spanish expedition into the Southwest. He was inspired by hopes of finding gold, and the desire to convert the Native inhabitants to Christianity. A year later, Francisco Vasquez de Coronado arrived with 330 soldiers, 1,000 Indian allies, and more than 1,000 heads of livestock. He conquered Zuni Pueblo, and spent two years traversing Arizona, New Mexico, Texas, and Kansas in search of the legendary city of gold, Cibola. His brutal treatment of the Pueblo people sowed the seeds for the Pueblo Revolt 140 years later.

Engraving by Norman Price of Coronado setting out to discover a legendary kingdom of gold in 1540

TIMELINE

600 Earliest date for settlement of Acoma and Hopi mesas

800 Large pueblos such as Chaco Canyon under construction

1020 Chaco Canyon is at its height as a trading and cultural center

1250 Ancient sites are mysteriously abandoned; new smaller pueblos are established along the Rio Grande

1300 Mesa Verde abandoned

1400 Navajo and Apache migrate from Canada to the Southwest

1539 Fray Marcos de Niza heads first expedition to the Southwest

1598 Juan de Oñate founds permanent colony in New Mexico

800 | 1000 | 1200 | 1400 | 1600

Illustration of the 1680 Pueblo Indian Revolt

THE COLONY OF NEW MEXICO

In 1598, Juan de Oñate arrived in the Southwest with 400 settlers, and set up a permanent colony called New Mexico. The colony included all of the present-day states of New Mexico and Arizona, as well as parts of Colorado, Utah, Nevada, and California.

Spanish attempts to conquer the Indian Pueblos led to hard and bloody battles but, despite the harsh conditions, more settlers, priests, and soldiers began to arrive in the area, determined to subdue the Natives, and to suppress their religious practices.

As the Spanish colonists spread out, they seized Pueblo farmlands and created huge ranches for themselves. A Pueblo uprising began on August 9, 1680, resulting in the deaths of 375 colonists and 21 priests, with the remaining 2,000 settlers driven south across the Rio Grande. In 1692, however, Don Diego de Vargas reclaimed Santa Fe, re-establishing Spanish control of the land. By the late 18th century, the Spanish were attempting to extend their power westward to California. Their first Arizona settlement was at Tubac, near Tucson, in 1752.

The beginning of the end of Spanish control came with the Louisiana Purchase of 1803. The French emperor, Napoleon, sold Louisiana, an enormous area of about 828,000 sq miles (2.2 million sq km) of land, to the recently formed United States. Land-hungry Americans began a rapid westward expansion toward the borders of Spanish-controlled Mexico. Compounding Spain's problems, Mexico's fight for independence began in 1810, but it was not until 1821 that independence was finally declared. The newly independent Mexicans were glad to do business with their Anglo-American neighbors, who brought much-needed trade.

THE MISSIONS

In the late 17th century, Jesuit missionary Father Eusebio Kino lived alongside and established a rapport with the Pima people of Southern Arizona. He initiated the Jesuit practice of bringing gifts of livestock and seeds for new crops, including wheat. Those Natives involved in the missionary program escaped forced labor. Kino inspired the Natives living south of Tucson, at a place called Bac, to begin work on the first mission there, which later became the Southwest's most beautiful mission church, San Xavier del Bac *(see pp92–3)*. When Kino died in 1711, there were around 20 missions across the region.

Father Eusebio Kino

Juan de Oñate

1680 Pueblo Revolt drives Spanish out of the Southwest

1711 Death of Father Kino; 20 missions in Southern Arizona

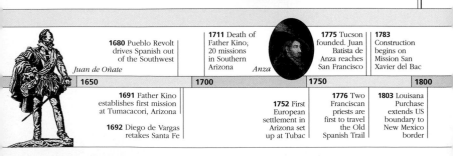

Anza

1775 Tucson founded. Juan Batista de Anza reaches San Francisco

1783 Construction begins on Mission San Xavier del Bac

1650 | **1700** | **1750** | **1800**

1691 Father Kino establishes first mission at Tumacacori, Arizona

1692 Diego de Vargas retakes Santa Fe

1752 First European settlement in Arizona set up at Tubac

1776 Two Franciscan priests are first to travel the Old Spanish Trail

1803 Louisana Purchase extends US boundary to New Mexico border

A group of cowboys roping a steer, painted by C. M. Russell (1897)

THE ARRIVAL OF ANGLO-AMERICANS

The first non-Spanish people of European descent, or Anglo-Americans, to arrive in the Southwest were "mountain men" and fur trappers in the early 1800s. They learned survival skills from Native tribes, married Native women, and usually spoke more than one Native language as well as Spanish.

While the Hispanic and the Natives were happy to trade with the Anglos, they were, at the same time, angered by the new settlers who built ranches and even towns on lands to which they had no legal right.

LAND DISPUTES & THE INDIAN WARS

After the Civil War (1861–65), reports of land and mineral wealth in the west filtered back east, and Anglo settlement in the west increased rapidly. By the 1840s, the US government had embarked on a vigorous expansion westward, with settlers accompanied by United States' soldiers. The primary problem they encountered were the constant raids by Natives, dubbed "the Indian problem." The US cavalry countered with raids and massacres of its own. In 1864, more than 8,000 Navajo were forced off their land, and made to march "The Long Walk" of 370 miles (595 km) east to a reservation at Bosque Redondo in New Mexico. Many died during harsh weather en route, and many more from disease at the reservation. In 1868, the Navajo were given 20,000 sq miles (51,800 sq km) across Arizona, New Mexico, and southern Utah.

In 1845, the US acquired Texas and, when Mexico resisted further moves, it set off the Mexican War. The Treaty of Guadalupe-Hidalgo ended the conflict in 1848, and gave the US the Mexican Cession (comprising California, Utah, Nevada, Northern Arizona, and parts of New Mexico, Wyoming, and Colorado) for $18.25 million. In 1854, the United States bought Southern Arizona through the Gadsden Purchase for $10 million. Finally, in 1863, the US government recognized Arizona as a separate territory, and drew the state line that exists between it and New Mexico today.

In the 1870s, vast areas of Arizona became huge cattle and sheep ranches, and by the 1880s, four major

TIMELINE

- **1821** Mexico declares independence from Spain
- **1824** Republic of Mexico established
- **1825**
- **1846–48** US expansionism leads to war with Mexico
- **1848** Mexican territory ceded to US under Treaty of Guadalupe-Hidalgo
- **1850**
- **1854** The US gets Southern Arizona with the Gadsden Purchase
- **1864** Colonel Kit Carson conducts a campaign against the Navajo at Canyon de Chelly. The survivors are forcibly marched to New Mexico on "The Long Walk"
- **1869** John Wesley Powell leads first US expedition through the Grand Canyon
- **1875**
- **1881** Gunfight at OK Corral
- **1886** Indian Wars end with the surrender of Geronimo
- **1900**
- **1901** Grand Canyon Railway brings tourists to the region
- **1912** Arizona admitted to Union, becomes the 48th state

Geronimo

APACHE WARRIORS

The nomadic Apache lived in small communities in southeastern Arizona, and southern and northwestern New Mexico. Seeing them as a threat to the settlement of these territories, the US military was determined to wipe them out. The hanging of one of Chief Cochise's relatives in 1861 instigated a war that lasted more than a decade until Apache reservations were established in 1872. In 1877, a new leader, Victorio, launched a three-year guerrilla war against the settlers that ended only with his death. The most famous Apache leader, Geronimo, led a campaign against the Mexicans and Anglos from 1851 until he surrendered in 1886. He was sent to a reservation in Florida.

Apache leader Geronimo, in a fierce pose in this picture from 1886

railroads crossed the region. These became a catalyst for new industries in the region. Arizona was granted statehood in 1912, and in the years leading up to and following World War I, the state experienced an economic boom because of its rich mineral resources.

THE DEMAND FOR WATER

As the region's population expanded, the supply of water became one of the most pressing issues, and a series of enormous dams were constructed. Dam- and road-building projects, in turn, benefited the region's economy and attracted even more settlers.

Mining boom prospector

The Hoover Dam was constructed between 1931 and 1936, but by the 1960s even that proved inadequate. Soon after, Glen Canyon Dam was completed in 1963, flooding an area of great beauty. The dam created the huge reservoir of Lake Powell, destroying a number of ancient Native ruins.

The issue of water continues to be a serious problem in the Southwest, and projects to harness water from available sources are under debate.

THE SOUTHWEST TODAY

Arizona's economy continues to prosper, and its population is still growing, augmented by thousands of winter residents from the north, or "snowbirds." An ever-increasing number of tourists visit the state's scenic and historic wonders, preserved in national parks, monuments, and recreational areas. Set up in the early 20th century, the parks highlight conservation issues and Native cultures, all of which will help guard Arizona's precious heritage for generations to come.

1931–36 Hoover Dam constructed

1974 Central Arizona Project initiated to harvest water from the Colorado River for thirsty Phoenix

2000–2003 Forest fires devastate large tracts of timber in Eastern and Northern Arizona

1925 | 1950 | 1975 | 2000 | 2025

Glen Canyon Dam

1963 Opening of the Glen Canyon Dam

1996 Bill Clinton signs Navajo-Hopi Land Dispute Settlement Act, ending violent conflicts between tribes

2007 The Grand Canyon Skywalk, a new tourist attraction, opens

ARIZONA & THE FOUR CORNERS AREA BY AREA

Introducing Arizona & the Four Corners

One of the Mittens in Monument Valley

This is a region of vast expanses and stunning natural beauty. In Arizona's southwest corner lies the hostile, but eerily beautiful, Sonoran Desert. Its boundaries are marked by the important cities of Tucson and Phoenix. To the north the landscape rises through the red rock canyonlands around Sedona to green mountain towns such as Flagstaff and Payson. Beyond lies the enormous Colorado Plateau, cut by the almost unimaginable depth and beauty of the Grand Canyon *(see pp48–55)*. In the east, the Four Corners area is the only place in the USA where four states – Utah, Colorado, Arizona, and New Mexico – meet at a single point. It is dominated by dramatic canyonlands such as Monument Valley and ancient ruins that stand as haunting epitaphs in a lonely but captivating landscape.

Lake Powell in Glen Canyon National Recreation Area

KEY

- Interstate
- Major highway
- Highway
- River
- State boundary

0 km 50

0 miles 50

◁ **Dramatic and magnificent expanse of the Grand Canyon**

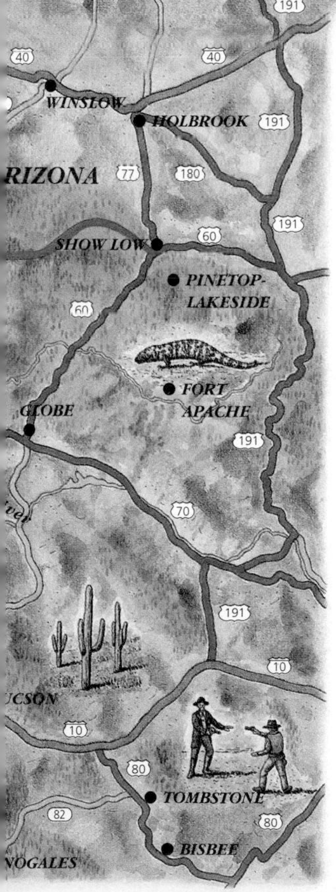

GETTING AROUND

Phoenix is a major hub for international and domestic flights, but many airlines fly directly to Tucson as well. The region is serviced by Amtrak train services and regular Greyhound buses. Driving, however, is the preferred option and the area has a network of well-maintained highways. Northern Arizona is bisected by I-40 and I-10 cuts across the south; I-17 is the main north–south artery. A private car is essential for getting around the Four Corners; a high-clearance 4WD vehicle is recommended for traveling many interesting, unpaved regional roads.

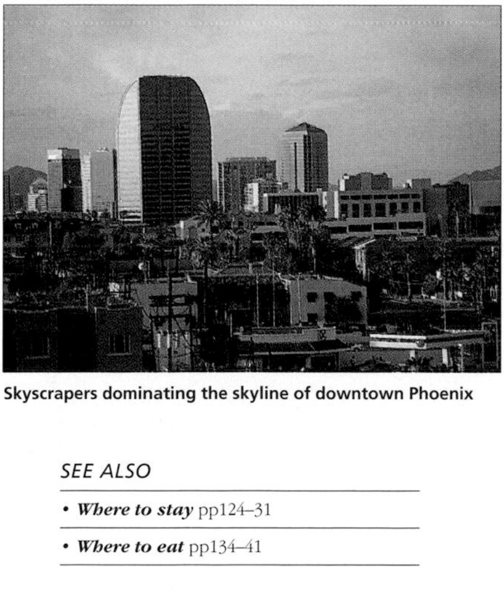

Skyscrapers dominating the skyline of downtown Phoenix

SEE ALSO

- ***Where to stay*** pp124–31
- ***Where to eat*** pp134–41

Phillips
66
Enjoy
Coca-Cola
5¢
DRINK
NuGrape
SODA

GRAND CANYON & NORTHERN ARIZONA

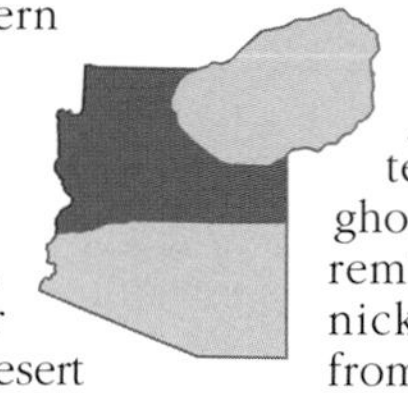

For most people, Northern Arizona is famous as the location of Grand Canyon, a gorge of breathtaking proportions carved out of rock by the Colorado River. Northern Arizona's other attractions include the high desert landscape of the Colorado Plateau, with its sagebrush and yucca, punctuated by the forested foothills of the San Francisco Peaks. The Kaibab, Prescott, and Coconino National Forests cover large areas, and provide the setting for the lively city of Flagstaff as well as for the charming towns of Sedona and Jerome. The region is dotted with fascinating mining ghost towns such as Oatman, a reminder that Arizona won its nickname, the Copper State, from the mineral mining boom of the first half of the 20th century.

More than 25 percent of Arizona is Native American reservation land. The state is also home to several centuries-old Puebloan ruins, most notably the hilltop village of Tuzigoot and the hillside remains of Montezuma Castle.

SIGHTS AT A GLANCE

Historic Towns & Sights
Camp Verde 16
Flagstaff 3
Hoover Dam 18
Jerome 13
Kingman 20
Lake Havasu City 22
Oatman 21
Prescott 17
Quartzsite 23
Sedona 9
Williams 11

National Parks & Monuments
Grand Canyon 1
Meteor Crater 7
Montezuma Castle National Monument 15
Petrified Forest National Park 8
Sunset Crater Volcano National Monument 5
Tuzigoot National Monument 12
Walnut Canyon National Monument 6
Wupatki National Monument 4

Areas of Natural Beauty
Heart of Arizona Tour 14
Lake Mead National Recreation Area 19
Lake Powell & Glen Canyon National Recreation Area 2
Oak Creek Canyon 10

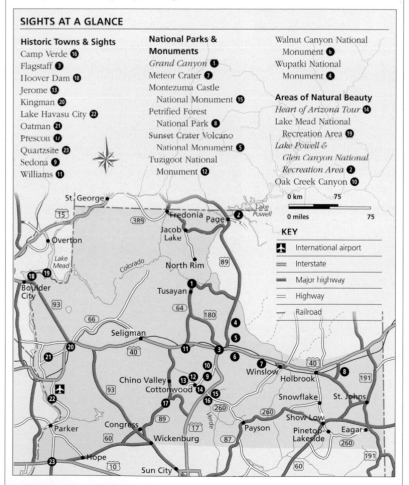

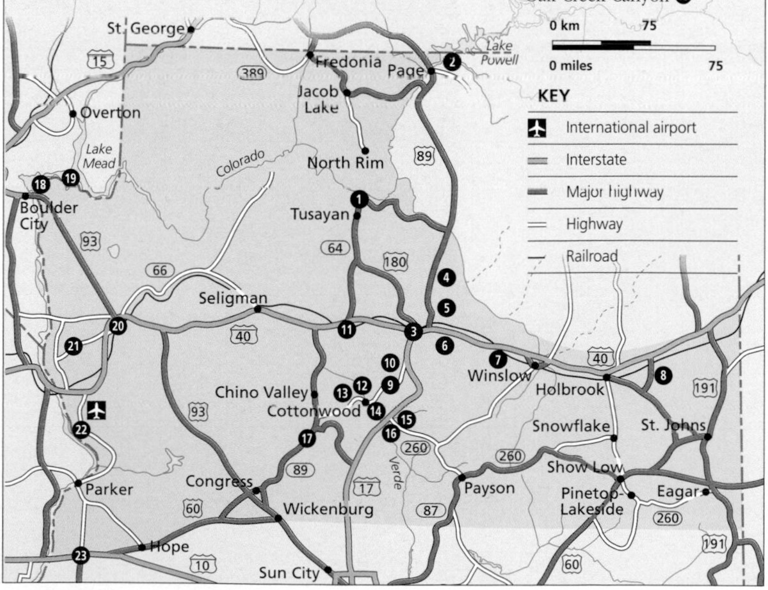

◁ **Route 66 memorabilia decorating a shop on the Arizona section of the famous road**

Grand Canyon ❶

Grand Canyon is one of the world's great natural wonders and an instantly recognizable symbol of the Southwest. The canyon runs through Grand Canyon National Park *(see pp50–51)*, and is 277 miles (446 km) long, an average of 10 miles (16 km) wide, and around 5,000 ft (1,500 m) deep. It was formed over a period of six million years by the Colorado River, whose fast-flowing waters sliced their way through the Colorado Plateau *(see p17)*, which includes the gorge and most of Northern Arizona and the Four Corners region. The plateau's geological vagaries have defined the river's twisted course, and exposed vast cliffs and pinnacles that are ringed by rocks of different colors, variegated hues of limestone, sandstone, and shale *(see pp52–3)*. The canyon is spectacular by any standard, but its beauty is in the ever-shifting light patterns, and the colors that the rocks take on – bleached white at midday, but red and ocher at sunset.

Mule Trip Convoy
A mule ride is a popular method of exploring the Grand Canyon.

Havasu Canyon
The 10-mile (16-km) trail to the beautiful Havasu Falls is a popular hike. The land is owned by the Havasupai tribe, who offer horseback rides and guided tours into the canyon.

Grandview Point
At 7,400 ft (2,250 m), Grandview Point is one of the highest places on the South Rim, the canyon's southern edge. It is one of the stops along Desert View Drive (see p51). *The point is thought to be the spot from where the Spanish had their first glimpse of the canyon in 1540.*

North Rim
The North Rim receives roughly one-tenth the number of visitors of the South Rim. While less accessible, it is a more peaceful destination offering a sense of unexplored wilderness. It has a range of hikes, such as the North Kaibab Trail, a steep descent down to Phantom Ranch on the canyon floor.

VISITORS' CHECKLIST

Road map B2. *Grand Canyon Airport, Tusayan.* *Grand Canyon Railway from Williams.* *From Flagstaff.* *Visitor Center, Canyon View Information Plaza, south of Mather Point, AZ, (928) 638-7888.* **www**.nps.gov/grca *South Rim: year round. North Rim: summer only.* *North Rim: mid-Oct–mid-May: closed by snow.* *partial.*

Grand Canyon Skywalk
This horseshoe-shaped glass walkway is suspended 4,000 ft (1,200 m) above the Colorado River. Some 450 tons of steel were used in the construction of this spectacular structure (see p61).

YAVAPAI POINT AT THE SOUTH RIM

Situated 5 miles (8 km) north of the canyon's South Entrance, along a stretch of the Rim Trail, is Yavapai Point. Its observation station offers spectacular views of the canyon, and a viewing panel identifies several of the central canyon's landmarks.

Bright Angel Trail
Used by both Native Americans and early settlers, the Bright Angel Trail follows a natural route along one of the canyon's enormous fault lines. It is an appealing option for day hikers because, unlike some other trails in the area, it offers some shade and several seasonal water sources.

Grand Canyon National Park

A World Heritage Site, Grand Canyon National Park is located entirely within the state of Arizona. The park covers 1,904 sq miles (4,930 sq km), and is made up of the canyon itself, which starts where the Paria River empties into the Colorado, and stretches from Lees Ferry to Lake Mead *(see p72)* and adjoining lands. The area won protective status as a National Monument in 1908 after Theodore Roosevelt visited in 1903, observing that it should be kept intact for future generations as "… the one great sight which every American … should see." The National Park was created in 1919.

The park has two main entrances, on the North and South Rims of the canyon. However, the southern section of the park receives the most visitors and can become very congested during the summer season *(see pp54–5)*.

North Kaibab Trail follows Roaring Springs Canyon, past Roaring Springs, and descends to Phantom Ranch.

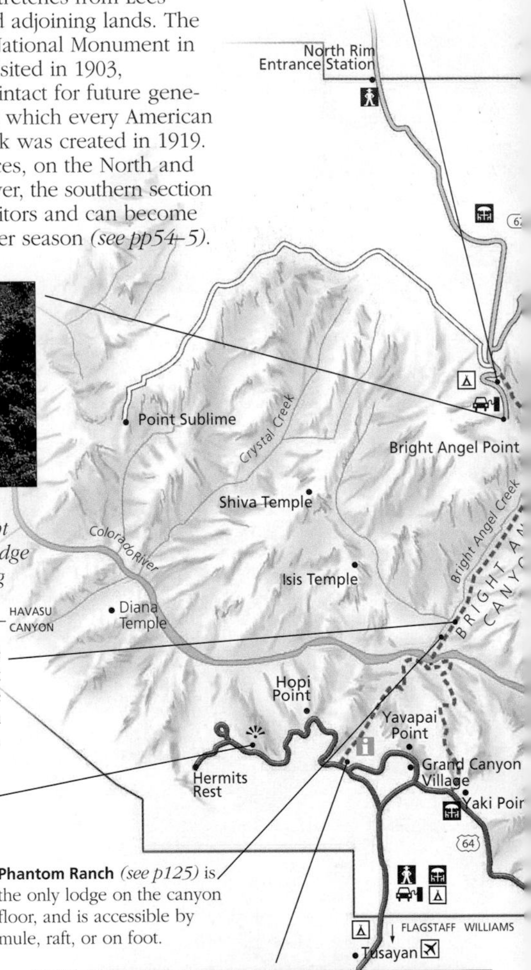

Grand Canyon Lodge
Perched above the canyon at Bright Angel Point, the Grand Canyon Lodge has rooms and a number of dining options (see pp55, 125 & 135).

Bright Angel Trail starts from the South Rim. It is well maintained but demanding. It descends into the canyon and connects with the North Kaibab Trail up on the North Rim.

Phantom Ranch *(see p125)* is the only lodge on the canyon floor, and is accessible by mule, raft, or on foot.

Hermit Road
A free shuttle bus runs along this route to the Hermits Rest viewpoint during the summer. It is closed to private vehicles March to November.

Kolb Studio
Built in 1904 by brothers Emery and Ellsworth Kolb, who photographed the canyon extensively, the Kolb Studio is now a National Historic Site and book store.

Point Imperial is the highest point on the North Rim at 8,803 ft (2,683 m), and offers views of Mt. Hayden and the Painted Desert *(see p55)*.

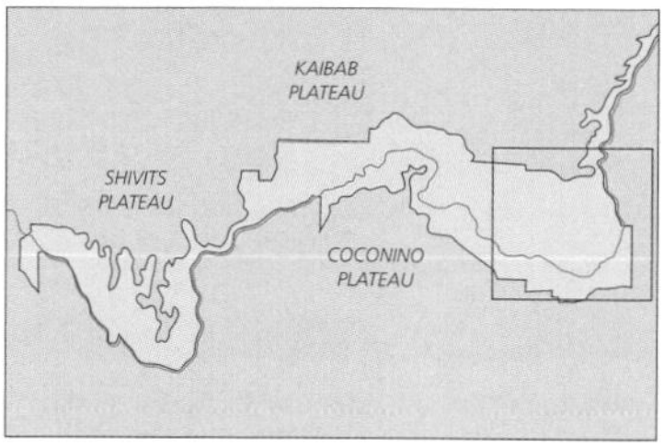

LOCATOR MAP

Grand Canyon National Park area

Colorado River

Aided by wind and rain, the Colorado River has shaped the Grand Canyon. The river winds for 277 miles (446 km) through the canyon.

KEY

- Major highway
- Park boundary
- Rivers
- Highway
- Trail route
- Gas station
- Ranger station
- Campground/RV
- Picnic area
- Visitor information
- Viewpoint

0 km 5

0 miles 5

The Tusayan Ruin was a pueblo abandoned by the Ancestral Puebloans around 1150. The Tusayan Museum now sits next to the site.

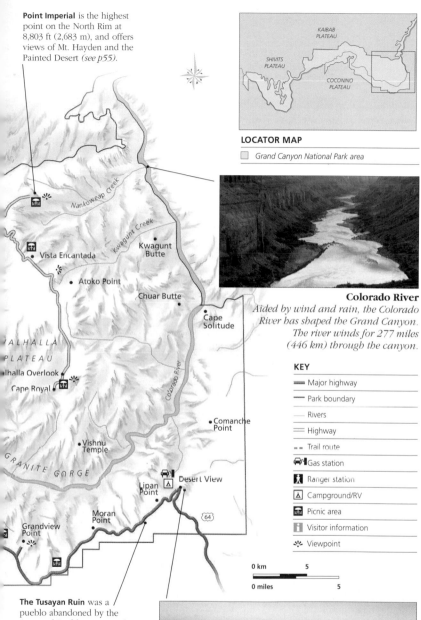

Desert View Drive

This route connects Grand Canyon Village with Desert View, and offers breathtaking views of both the central and eastern canyon.

The Geology of the Grand Canyon

Grand Canyon's multicolored layers of rock provide the best record of the Earth's formation anywhere in the world. Each stratum of rock reveals a different period in the Earth's geological history beginning with the earliest, the Precambrian Era, which covers geological time up to 570 million years ago. Almost two billion years of history have been recorded in the canyon, although the most dramatic changes took place relatively recently, five to six million years ago, when the Colorado River began to carve its path through the canyon walls. The sloping nature of the Kaibab Plateau has led to increased erosion in some parts of the canyon.

A view of Grand Canyon's plateau and South Rim

The canyon's size *is awe-inspiring, attracting millions of visitors every year. Pictured here is the North Rim.*

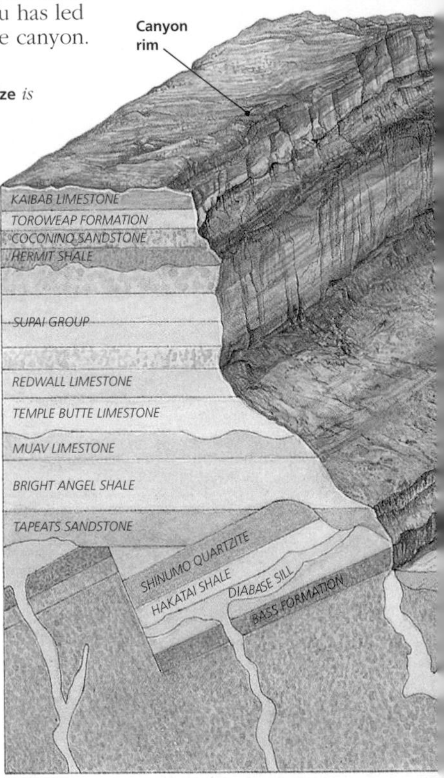

RECORD OF LIFE

The fossils found in each layer tell the story of the development of life on Earth. The oldest layer, the Vishnu Schist, was formed in the Proterozoic era, when the first bacteria and algae were just emerging. Later layers were created by billions of small marine creatures whose hard shells eventually built up into thick layers of limestone.

An asymmetrical canyon, *the Grand Canyon's North Rim is more eroded than the South Rim. The entire Kaibab Plateau slopes to the south, so rain falling at the North Rim flows toward the canyon and over the rim, creating deep side canyons and a wide space between the rim and the river.*

The Surprise Canyon formation, *a new strata classified by geologists in 1985, can be seen only in remote parts of the canyon. It was formed 335 million years ago.*

The Colorado River *changed its course about 5 million years ago. It is thought that it was encompassed by another, smaller river that flowed through the Kaibab Plateau. The force of the combined waters carved out the deep Grand Canyon.*

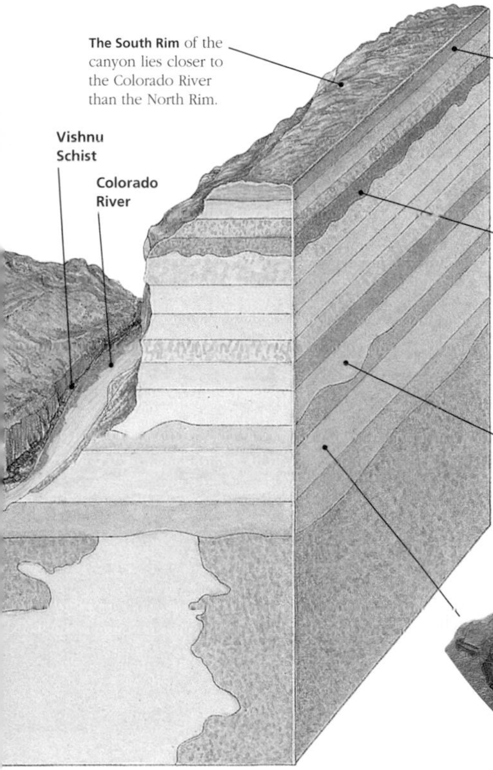

The South Rim of the canyon lies closer to the Colorado River than the North Rim.

Fish plate *fossils are found in the Kaibab limestone.*

Seedfern leaf *fossils are found in the Hermit Shale layer.*

Temple Butte limestone *contains fossils of marine creatures.*

Trilobite fossils *occur in the canyon's Bright Angel Shale layer.*

HOW THE CANYON WAS FORMED

While the Colorado River accounts for the canyon's depth, its width and formations are the work of even greater forces. Wind rushing through the canyon erodes the limestone and sandstone a few grains at a time. Rain pouring over the canyon rim cuts deep side canyons through the softer rock. Perhaps the greatest canyon-building force is ice. Water from rain and snowmelt works into cracks in the rock. When frozen, it expands, forcing the rock away from the canyon walls. The layers vary in hardness. Soft layers erode quickly into sloped faces. Harder rock resists erosion, leaving sheer vertical faces.

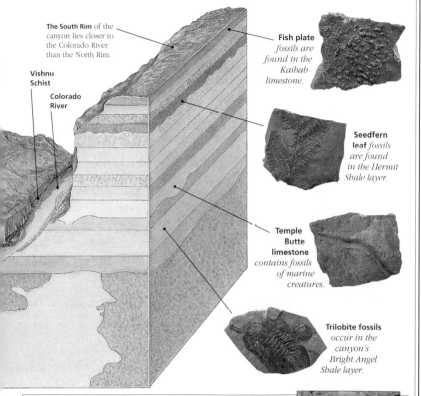

Crack formed by ice and water erosion

Exploring Grand Canyon National Park

Bell near Hermits Rest

Grand Canyon offers awe-inspiring beauty on a vast scale. The magnificent rock formations with towers, cliffs, steep walls, and buttes recede as far as the eye can see, their bands of colored rock varying in shade as light changes through the day. The park's main roads, Hermit Road and Desert View Drive, both accessible from the South Entrance, overlook the canyon. Grand Canyon Village is located on the South Rim and offers a range of facilities. Visitors can also enter the park from the north, although this route (Hwy 67) is closed during winter. Walking trails along the North and South Rims offer staggering views but, to experience the canyon at its most fascinating, the trails that go down toward the canyon floor should be explored.

The Bright Angel Trail on the South Rim, and the North Kaibab Trail on the North Rim, descend to the canyon floor, and are tough hikes involving an overnight stop.

Adobe pueblo-style architecture of Hopi House, Grand Canyon Village

Grand Canyon Village

Grand Canyon National Park.
Tel *(928) 638-7888.* *partial.*

Grand Canyon Village has its roots in the late 19th century. The extensive building of visitor accommodations started after the Santa Fe Railroad opened a branch line here from Williams in 1901, though some hotels had been built in the late 1890s. The Fred Harvey Company constructed a clutch of well-designed, attractive buildings. The most prominent is **El Tovar Hotel** *(see p125)*. Opened in 1905, it is named for a Spanish explorer who reached the gorge in 1540. The **Hopi House** also opened in 1905 – a rendition of a traditional Hopi dwelling, where locals could sell their craftwork as souvenirs. It was built by Hopi craftsmen and designed by Mary E. J. Colter. An ex-schoolteacher and trained architect, Colter drew on Southwestern influences, mixing both Native American and Hispanic styles *(see p23)*. She is responsible for many of the historic structures that now grace the South Rim, including the 1914 **Lookout Studio** and **Hermits Rest**, and the rustic 1922 **Phantom Ranch** on the canyon floor.

Today, Grand Canyon Village has a wide range of hotels, restaurants, and stores. It is surprisingly easy to get lost here since the buildings are spread out and discreetly placed among wooded areas. The village is not only the starting point for most of the mule trips through the canyon, but also the terminus for the Grand Canyon Railway.

South Rim

Most of the Grand Canyon's 4.5 million annual visitors come to the South Rim, since, unlike the North Rim, it is open year-round and is easily accessible along Highway 180/64 from Flagstaff *(see p64)* or Williams. **Hermit Road** and **Desert View Drive** (Hwy 64) start at Grand Canyon Village and encompass a selection of the choicest views of the gorge. Hermit Road is closed to private vehicles from March to November each year but there are free shuttle buses. Desert View Drive is open all year.

From the village, Hermit Road meanders along the South Rim, extending for 8 miles (13 km). Its first viewpoint is **Trailview Overlook**, which provides an overview of the canyon and the winding course of the Bright Angel Trail. Moving on, **Maricopa Point** offers especially panoramic views of the canyon but not of the Colorado River, which is more apparent from nearby **Hopi Point**. At the end of Hermit Road lies Hermits Rest, where a gift shop, decorated in rustic style, is located in yet another Mary Colter-designed building. The longer Desert View Drive runs in the opposite direction, and covers 26 miles (42 km). It winds for 12 miles (20 km) before reaching **Grandview Point**, where the Spaniards may have had their first glimpse of the canyon in

The interior of the Hermits Rest gift store with crafts for sale lining the walls

Desert View's stone watchtower, on Desert View Drive

CALIFORNIA CONDORS

America's largest bird, the California condor, has a wingspan of over 9 ft (2.7 m). Nearly extinct in the 1980s, the last 22 condors were captured for breeding in captivity. In 1996, the first captive-bred birds were released in Northern Arizona. Today, more than 60 condors fly the skies over Northern Arizona. They are frequent visitors to the South Rim, though visitors should not approach or attempt to feed them.

A pair of California condors

1540. About 10 miles (16 km) farther on lie the pueblo remains of **Tusayan Ruin**, where there is a small museum with exhibits on Ancestral Puebloan life. The road continues on to the stunning overlook of **Desert View**. The watchtower here was Colter's most fanciful creation, its upper floor decorated with early 20th-century Hopi murals.

Just east of Grand Canyon Village is **Yavapai Point** from where it is possible to see Phantom Ranch *(see p125)*. This is the only roofed accommodation available on the canyon floor, across the Colorado River.

North Rim

Standing at about 8,000 ft (2,400 m), the North Rim is higher, cooler, and greener than the South Rim, with dense forests of ponderosa pine, aspen, and Douglas fir. Visitors are most likely to spot wildlife such as the mule deer, Kaibab squirrel, and wild turkey on the North Rim.

The Rim can be reached via Highway 67, off Highway 89A, ending at **Grand Canyon Lodge** *(see p125 & p135)*, where there are visitor services, a campground, a gas station, restaurant, and a general store. Nearby, there is a National Park information center, which offers maps of the area. The North Rim and all its facilities are closed mid-October to mid-May, when it is often snowed in.

The North Rim is twice as far from the river as the South Rim, and the canyon really stretches out from the overlooks giving a sense of its 10-mile (16-km) width. There are about 30 miles (45 km) of scenic roads along the North Rim, as well as hiking trails to high viewpoints or down to the canyon floor, particularly the **North Kaibab Trail** that links to the South Rim's Bright Angel Trail. The picturesque **Cape Royal Drive** starts north of Grand Canyon Lodge and travels 23 miles (37 km) to Cape Royal on the Walhalla Plateau. From here, several famous buttes and peaks can be seen, including Wotans Throne and Vishnu Temple. There are also several short walking trails around Cape Royal. A 3-mile (5-km) detour leads to **Point Imperial**, the highest point on the canyon rim, while along the way the **Vista Encantada** has delightful views and picnic tables overlooking the gorge.

Mule deer on the canyon's North Rim

Bright Angel Trail

This is the most popular of all Grand Canyon hiking trails. The Bright Angel trailhead is at Grand Canyon Village on the South Rim. The trail begins near the **Kolb Studio** at the western end of the village. It then switches dramatically down the side of the canyon for 9 miles (14 km). The trail crosses the river over a suspension bridge, ending a little further on at Phantom Ranch. There are two resthouses and a fully equipped campground along the way. It is not advisable to attempt the whole trip in one day. Many walk from the South Rim to one of the rest stops and then return up to the Rim. Temperatures at the bottom of the canyon can reach 110°F (43°C) or higher during the summer. Day hikers should, therefore, carry a quart (just over a liter) of water per person per hour for summer hiking. Carrying a first-aid kit is also recommended.

Hikers taking a break on the South Rim's Bright Angel Trail

Breathtaking view of Grand Canyon at dusk ▷

Grand Canyon Adventures

The Grand Canyon's beauty and grandeur, the diversity of activities it offers, and the availability of top-notch tours and outfitters have made it one of the most popular outdoor adventure sites in the world. Many of the classic Grand Canyon experiences, such as mule and helicopters tours, Rim-to-Rim hikes and whitewater raft trips, rate as once-in-a-lifetime adventures for many people. But not all Grand Canyon adventures involve white-knuckle thrills. There are activities geared for every interest and physical ability, from birdwatching to ranger-led interpretive walks along the North and South Rims, to a host of educational programs lasting an hour or a week. If there is anything to stymie the would-be adventurer, it is only the sheer number of experiences to choose from.

Hikers studying a map of the Grand Canyon

HIKING

The most popular day hikes in the park involve a descent into the canyon and a fairly strenuous climb back up, on well-maintained trails, such as Bright Angel and Hermits Rest *(see pp48–55)*. Once below the Rim, these trails offer ever changing views of the canyon on the way down, sometimes passing by steep overlooks and a few shaded rest areas. Visitors are strongly advised to carry water on these hikes.

For those wanting an easier stroll, there are relatively level trails that follow the edge of the canyon. At the South Rim, the 13-mile (21-km) long Rim Trail can be crowded where it passes through the Grand Canyon Village, but provides wonderful solitude and stunning vistas just a mile away. At the North Rim, the Transept Trail is an easy 1-mile (1.6-km) hike that winds through thick woods to come out at various points along the canyon's edge. Try to head out early to avoid the crowds

Many hikers consider a Rim-to-Rim hike (descending from one Rim and hiking up to the other Rim) to be the ultimate canyon hiking experience, but it is also extremely demanding, with more than 10,000 ft (3,048 m) of a vertical descent and ascent over 22 miles (35 km). Bright Angel to North Kaibab, or the reverse, is the most popular Rim-to-Rim route, as it offers the only accessible river crossing. Most Rim-to-Rim hikers spend one or two nights at the Bright Angel campground (advance reservations required).

CANYON HIKING TIPS

Over 400 people require medical evacuations from the canyon each year. Most are healthy people under 40 who are dehydrated or exhausted.

- *Drink plenty of water and/or electrolyte liquids as you hike, even if you don't feel thirsty.*
- *Eat often, even while you are hiking. High-carb and salty foods are good.*
- *Hats, sun-protective clothing, and sunscreen are essential.*
- *Do not attempt to hike to the bottom of the canyon and back in a single day.*

BACKCOUNTRY CAMPING

In the Grand Canyon Park, backcountry camping exists primarily to facilitate multi-day hikes into the canyon. In fact, demand far outpaces supply, so visitors should try and reserve camp spaces early if they are contemplating spending a few nights in the canyon. Reservations can be made up to four months in advance. If no camp spaces are available for the time of your visit, it is possible to sign up for a guided hike with companies that pre-book campsites. **Grand Canyon Hikes** and **Discovery Treks** are two of the many tour companies in the Grand Canyon that offer three- to seven-day hikes, both for beginners and for experienced hikers.

Camping out in Grand Canyon National Park

Mountain bikers in Toroweap Valley, Grand Canyon National Park

MOUNTAIN BIKING

Although mountain bikes are not allowed on hiking trails within the National Park, there are several scenic roads on which they are permitted. At the North Rim, just outside the park, the Kaibab National Forest offers mountain bikers the 18-mile (29-km) long Rainbow Rim Trail and the Arizona Trail, both of which follow the Rim and offer superb views of the canyon. Both trails have varied sections ranked easy to difficult. **Escape Adventures** offers five-day mountain bike adventures on the North Rim.

At the South Rim, a paved, multi-purpose trail follows the rim itself from Monument Creek Vista to Hermits Rest and offers panoramic views.

BIRDWATCHING

Birdwatching is a popular pastime at the Grand Canyon for both serious and casual birders. Hawks and bald eagles can be seen gliding silently above the canyon. Other species, such as canyon wrens, pygmy nuthatch, mountain chickadee, and red crossbill, are quite tame, and can be seen along the tourist trails. Also, many people visit the South Rim for a glimpse of the rare California condors. For those who want a more in-depth experience, birdwatching is a major component of many of the outdoor programs offered by the **Grand Canyon Field Institute**.

EDUCATIONAL TOURS

The Grand Canyon is a natural classroom for the study of desert and canyon ecology, history, archeology, geology, and natural history. One of the most accessible sources of short educational courses are ranger-led day-programs offered by the National Park. More in-depth, single and multi-day programs are offered by the renowned Grand Canyon Field Institute. Begun in 1993, the institute's programs include wilderness studies, ecology, and photography. The **Museum of Northern Arizona** also offers a variety of educational tours, as do numerous commercial hiking tour operators such as **Discovery Treks**.

MULE TRIPS

Since their inception in 1904, mule rides have been one of the most popular of all Grand Canyon adventures. Although thousands of people undertake these trips each year, they should not be taken lightly – this is a demanding adventure. Run by **Xanterra Parks & Resorts**, the trips fill early and may be booked up to two years in advance. The trip takes two days, descending Bright Angel Trail, with an overnight stay and hearty steak dinner at Phantom Ranch *(see p125 & p134)*. The ride offers ever-changing panoramas of the canyon in both directions. Guides stop frequently to ensure everyone is drinking water, as dehydration is a common and sometimes serious problem. Riders must be at least 4.7 ft (1.38 m) tall, weigh less than 200 lbs (91 kg), understand fluent English, and be unafraid of heights. One-day trips that go only half-way into the canyon before returning are also available.

Those wanting a tamer adventure can opt for short trail rides on horseback, which are offered by **Apache Stables** at the South Rim, just outside the park's boundary. For a longer horseback adventure, contact the **Havasupai Tourist Enterprise**, which offers one-day and multi-day adventures into the beautiful Havasu Canyon *(see p48)*.

Mule rides into Grand Canyon National Park – a popular adventure

A helicopter conducts an aerial tour of the Grand Canyon, offering breathtaking views

AIR TOURS

An airplane trip over the Grand Canyon offers a unique opportunity to view the vastness of the canyon, and is a particularly good option for those with limited mobility. Some flights land close to the Skywalk. Tours leave hourly on demand from the Grand Canyon Airport. **Air Grand Canyon** offers tours in small, high-wing aircraft that seat five and provide everyone a window seat. **Grand Canyon Airlines** offer tours in larger twin-engine aircraft that seat 19. Helicopters, which fly at just 500 ft (150 m), compared to 900 ft (275 m) for airplanes, offer an even more intimate look at the canyon. Several operators, such as **Maverick Helicopters**, offer 25- to 50-minute tours over the canyon.

The aircraft are not allowed to enter the canyon within the National Park, but full-day trips into the Havasu Canyon (fly in, explore, and fly out) with an optional horseback ride to the Havasu Falls are offered by **Papillon Grand Canyon Helicopters**.

RIVER TRIPS

Perhaps no adventure puts visitors in touch with the essence and natural beauty of the canyon as much as a paddling trip down the Colorado River. The classic river trip, offered by outfits such as **Canyon Explorations**, **OARS**, and **Arizona Raft Adventures** is undertaken in moderate-sized rubber rafts that seat four to seven people, and are powered by a highly trained guide at the oars. Several rafts usually make the run together, with one or two reserved for provisions. A full-river trip starts at Lees Ferry and covers 280 miles (451 km) over 14–16 days, taking out at Diamond Creek. Stretches of quiet water are interspersed with 49 of America's most impressive whitewater runs. The rafts stop every night to pitch camp and most tour operators pride themselves on providing excellent meals. They also offer hikes into the canyons on the sides, so tourists can view the flora and fauna, and waterfalls in the area. Also available are half-river trips lasting five to nine days that begin or end at Phantom Ranch and require hiking in or out of the canyon. Some tour companies, such as **Hatch River Expeditions**, offer trips in larger, motorized rafts that seat 15, and can run the canyon in just seven days.

DORY TRIPS AND KAYAK SUPPORT TRIPS

Dories were the first type of boat used to run the Colorado river. Although similar in many ways to rubber rafts, dories are smaller, and many paddlers feel they offer a simpler and more intimate river experience. Several tour operators, including **Grand Canyon Dories** and **Grand Canyon Expeditions**, offer 7- to 14-day dory trips through the canyon.

Dory running on the Specter Rapids, Colorado River

Many skilled watersports enthusiasts may long for the opportunity to challenge the river under their own power, in a whitewater kayak. However, they should be aware that waiting lists for solo permits are extremely long. A suitable alternative might be to sign up for a kayak support trip; operators provide groups of paddlers with supplies, camping gear, and food, which follows along in a support raft. Full and half-river trips are available through several outfitters, including **Canyon Explorations**.

GRAND CANYON SKYWALK

This horseshoe-shaped bridge allows thrill-seekers to walk 70 ft (21 m) beyond the canyon rim on a glass-floored walkway. At the apex of the walk, visitors stand suspended 4,000 ft (1,200 m) above the canyon floor. You must wear special footwear that protects the glass floor, and cameras are not allowed on the walkway. Shuttles to the Skywalk are available from the nearby town of Dolan; most tours leave from Las Vegas.

Spectacular views on the Grand Canyon Skywalk

DIRECTORY

BACKCOUNTRY CAMPING

Discovery Treks
28248 N Tatum Blvd,
Suite B1-#414,
Cave Creek, AZ 85331.
Tel *(888) 256-8731.*
www.discoverytreks.com

Grand Canyon Hikes
7010 Bader Road,
Flagstaff, AZ 86001.
Tel *(877) 506-6233,*
(928) 779-1614.
www.grandcanyonhikes.com

MOUNTAIN BIKING

Escape Adventures
8221 W Chareston, #101,
Las Vegas, NV 89117.
Tel *(800) 596-2953,*
(702) 596-2953.
www.escapeadventures.com

BIRDWATCHING

Grand Canyon Field Institute
PO Box 399,
Grand Canyon, AZ 86023.
Tel *(866) 471-4435.*
www.grandcanyon.org/fieldinstitute

EDUCATIONAL TOURS

Discovery Treks
28248 N Tatum Blvd,
Suite B1-#414,
Cave Creek, AZ 85331.
Tel *(888) 256-8731.*
www.discoverytreks.com

Museum of Northern Arizona
3101 N Fort Valley Rd,
Flagstaff, AZ 86001.
Tel *(928) 774-5213.*
www.musnaz.org

MULE TRIPS

Apache Stables
PO Box 158,
Grand Canyon, AZ 86023.
Tel *(928) 638-2891.*
www.apachestables.com

Havasupai Tourist Enterprise
Supai, AZ 86435.
Tel *(928) 448-2121.*

Xanterra Parks & Resorts
POBox 699, 10 Albright,
Grand Canyon, AZ 86023.
Tel *(888) 297-2757.*
www.grandcanyonlodges.com

AIR TOURS

Air Grand Canyon
PO Box 3028,
Grand Canyon,
AZ 86023.
Tel *(800) 247-4726,*
(928) 638-2686.
www.airgrandcanyon.com

Grand Canyon Airlines
Grand Canyon National Airport, Highway 64,
Grand Canyon, AZ 86023.
Tel *(928) 638-2359.*
www.grandcanyonairlines.com

Maverick Helicopters
Grand Canyon National Airport, Highway 64,
Grand Canyon, AZ 86023.
Tel *(888) 261-4414,*
(928) 638-2622.
www.maverickhelicopter.com

Papillon Grand Canyon Helicopters
PO Box 455,
Grand Canyon,
AZ 86023.
Tel *(800) 528-2418,*
(928) 638-2419.
www.papillon.com

RIVER TRIPS

Arizona Raft Adventures
4050 E Huntington Dr,
Flagstaff, AZ 86004.
Tel *(800) 786-7238,*
(928) 526-8200.
www.azraft.com

Canyon Explorations
PO Box 310,
Flagstaff, AZ 86002.
Tel *(800) 654-0723,*
(928) 774-4559.
www.canyonx.com

Hatch River Expeditions
HC 67 Box 35,
Marble Canyon,
AZ 86036.
Tel *(800) 856-8966.*
www.hatchriverexpeditions.com

OARS
PO Box 67,
Angels Camp,
CA 95222
Tel *(800) 346-6277.*
www.oars.com

DORY TRIPS AND KAYAK SUPPORT TRIPS

Canyon Explorations
PO Box 310,
Flagstaff, AZ 86002.
Tel *(800) 654-0723,*
(928) 774-4559.
www.canyonx.com

Grand Canyon Dories
PO Box 216,
Altaville, CA 95221.
Tel *(800) 877-3679.*
www.oars.com

Grand Canyon Expeditions
PO Box 0 Kanab,
UT 84741.
Tel *(800) 544-2691.*
www.gcex.com

GRAND CANYON SKYWALK

Destination Grand Canyon
6206 West Desert Inn,
Suite B, Las Vegas,
NV 89146.
Tel *(877) 716-9378,*
(702) 878-9378.
www.destinationgrandcanyon.com

Lake Powell & Glen Canyon National Recreation Area ❷

The building of Glen Canyon Dam in 1963 created the 185-mile- (298-km-) long Lake Powell. Originally intended as a reservoir for drinking and irrigation water, in 1972 the Glen Canyon National Recreation Area (NRA) was opened to allow public access. Covering more than one million acres of desert and canyon country, mostly along the Utah side of Lake Powell, the area is a popular hiking and 4WD destination. Initially built for dam workers, the town of Page is now the starting point for exploring Lake Powell and the NRA. Along the lake shore, the Wahweap and Bullfrog marinas hum with activity, and water-sports are popular. In recent years, prolonged drought has lowered lake levels by approximately 40 percent.

Rainbow Bridge National Monument
Rising 290 ft (88 m) above Lake Powell, this natural bridge is accessible by boat from Wahweap or Bullfrog marinas, then a mile- (1.6-km-) long walk.

View of Lake Powell
The blue waters of the man-made Lake Powell are encircled by colorful sandstone coves – once Glen Canyon's side canyons – and dramatic buttes and mesas.

Glen Canyon Dam was completed in 1963 and rises 710 ft (213 m) above the bedrock of the Colorado River.

Antelope Canyon
Bands of sandstone curve sinuously together, sometimes just a few feet apart, in this famously deep "slot" canyon.

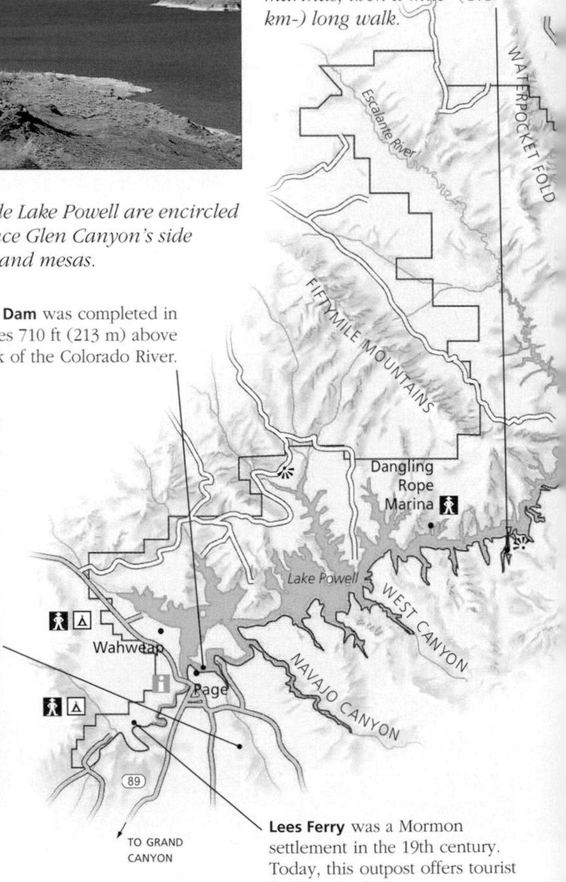

Lees Ferry was a Mormon settlement in the 19th century. Today, this outpost offers tourist facilities, including a ranger station and campground.

For hotels and restaurants in this region see pp124–7 and pp134–7

Wahweap Marina
One of the best ways of touring the area is by boat; Wahweap Marina offers tours and boats for hire.

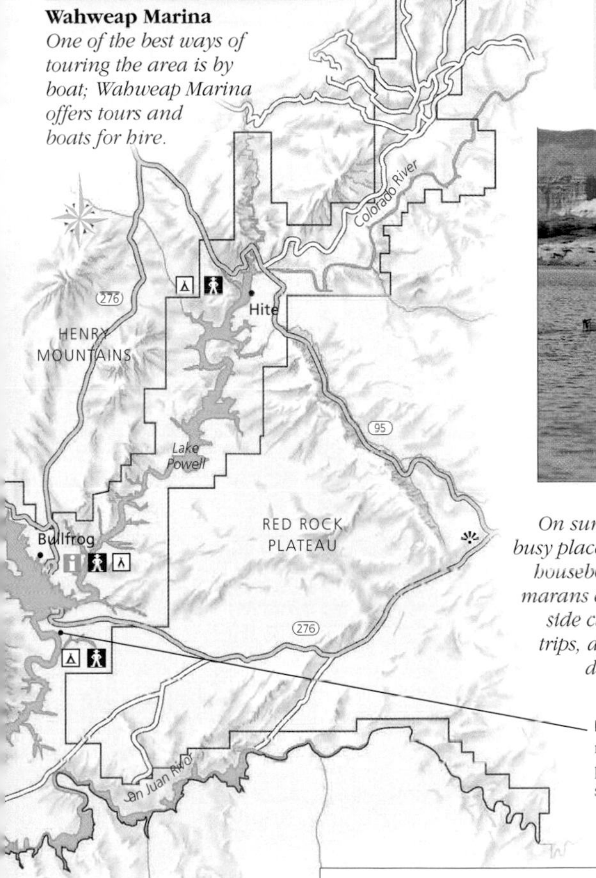

Halls Crossing has a marina and is the starting point for the regular ferry service to Bullfrog Bay.

0 km 20

0 miles 20

KEY

- Highway
- Unpaved road
- Ranger station
- Campground/RV
- Visitor information
- Viewpoint

VISITORS' CHECKLIST

Road map C1. 2m (3 km) N of Page on Hwy 89, off Hwy 160. *to Page, Bullfrog Marina.* *Carl Hayden Visitor Center, Page, (928) 608-6404.* *8am–5pm (summer: to 6pm; winter: to 4pm).* **www**.nps.gov/glca **www**.lakepowell.com *visitor center only.* *Page & Wahweap only.*

Boating on Lake Powell
On summer weekends, the lake is a busy place as powerboats, waterskiers, houseboat parties, jetskis, and catamarans explore its myriad sandstone side canyons. Colorado River float trips, available below Glen Canyon dam, are a special attraction.

CANYON CONTROVERSY

The completion of Glen Canyon Dam flooded the area described by explorer John Wesley Powell as "a curious ensemble of wonderful features". Controversial from the start, the project spurred the environmentalist Sierra Club to campaign against the original plans. Today, they continue to argue for the restoration of Glen Canyon, believing that ancient ecosystems are being ruined. Pro-dam advocates point out the value of the dam's ability to store water, generate power, and provide recreation.

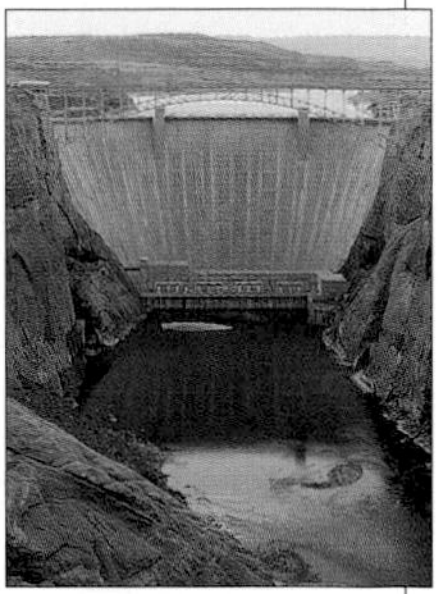

Lake Powell behind the vast Glen Canyon Dam

Flagstaff ❸

Colorful Lowell Observatory sign

Nestling among the pine forests of Northern Arizona's San Francisco Peaks, Flagstaff is one of the region's most attractive towns. It is a lively, easy-going place with a good selection of bars and restaurants among the maze of old red-brick buildings that make up its compact downtown. Flagstaff's first Anglo settlers were sheep ranchers who arrived in 1876. The railroad came in 1882, and the town developed as a lumber center.

Flagstaff is the home of Northern Arizona University, which has two appealing art galleries, and is a good base for visiting Grand Canyon's South Rim, just under two hours' drive away. The surrounding mountains attract hikers in summer and skiers in winter.

The town of Flagstaff with the San Francisco Peaks as a backdrop

Exploring Flagstaff

Flagstaff's center is narrow and slender, channeling north toward the Museum of Northern Arizona and south to the university. At its heart is a pocket-sized historic district, an attractive ensemble of red-brick buildings, which houses the best restaurants and bars. Lowell Observatory is located on Mars Hill, a short distance from downtown, and the popular Arizona Snowbowl ski resort is an enjoyable ten-minute drive to the north of the town.

Lowell Observatory

1400 W Mars Hill Rd. ***Tel*** *(928) 774-3358.* *Mar–Oct: 9am–5pm; Nov–Feb: noon–5pm. Evening hours all year; call for details.* *public hols.* **www**.lowell.edu

Tucked away on a hill about a mile northwest of the town center, the Lowell Observatory was founded in 1894 and named for its benefactor, Percival Lowell, a member of one of Boston's wealthiest families. He financed the observatory to look for life on Mars and chose the town because of its high altitude and clear mountain air. The observatory went on to establish an international reputation with its documented evidence of an expanding universe, data that was disclosed to the public in 1912. One of the observatory's famous astronomers, Clyde Tombaugh, discovered the planet Pluto on February 18, 1930 (Pluto has now been reclassified as a dwarf planet).

The 1930 Pluto dome, Flagstaff Lowell Observatory

Visitors have access to the main rotunda, exhibit halls, and the new John Vickers McAllister Space Theater, which shows presentations on the night sky and current research at Lowell. Campus tours are available daily, and telescope viewings nightly.

Historic Downtown District

Just ten minutes' walk from end to end, Flagstaff's historic downtown dates mainly from the 1890s. Many buildings sport decorative stone and stucco friezes, and are now occupied by cafés, bars, and stores. Architecturally, several buildings stand out, particularly the restored Babbitt Building and the 1926 train station that today houses the visitor center. Perhaps the most attractive building is the Weatherford Hotel, which was opened on January 1, 1900. It was named for its owner, Texan entrepreneur John W. Weatherford, and was much admired for its grand two-story wraparound veranda and its sunroom.

Northern Arizona University

624 S Knoles Dr. ***Tel*** *(928) 523-9011.* *times vary; call in advance.* **www**.nau.edu

Flagstaff's lively café society owes much to the 16,000 students of Northern Arizona University. The main entrance point to the campus is located on Knoles Drive. Green lawns, stately trees, and several historic buildings make this a pleasant place to visit. Of particular note are two campus art galleries: the Beasley Gallery in the Fine Art Building, which features temporary exhibitions and student work, and the Old Main Art Museum and Gallery housed in Old Main Building – the university's oldest. This features the permanent Weiss Collection, which includes works by the famous Mexican artist Diego Rivera.

For hotels and restaurants in this region see pp124–7 and pp134–7

Arts and Crafts swinging settee at Riordan Mansion

Riordan Mansion State Historic Park

409 W Riordan Rd. ***Tel*** *(928) 779-4395.* *May–Oct: 8:30am–5pm; Nov–Apr: 10:30am–5pm.* *Dec 25.* **www**.azstateparks.com

In the mid-1880s, Michael and Timothy Riordan established a lumber company that quickly made them a fortune. The brothers then built a house of grandiose proportions, a 40-room log mansion with two wings, one for each of them. Completed in 1904 and now preserved as a State Historic Park, the house has a rustic, timber-clad exterior, and Arts and Crafts furniture inside.

Pioneer Museum

2340 Fort Valley Rd. ***Tel*** *(928) 774-6272.* *9am–5pm Mon–Sat.* *public hols.* **www**.arizonahistoricalsociety.org

This museum occupies an elegant stone building that was originally erected as a hospital in 1908. It opened in 1960 and incorporates the Ben Doney homestead cabin. On display in the grounds are a steam locomotive of 1929 and a Santa Fe Railroad caboose. Inside, a particular highlight is a selection of Grand Canyon photographs taken in the early 1900s by Ellsworth and Emery Kolb.

Arizona Snowbowl

Snowbowl Rd, off Hwy 180. ***Tel*** *(928) 779-1951.* *Flagstaff Snow Report: (928) 779-4577.* *Dec–mid-Apr.* **www**.arizonasnowbowl.com

Downhill skiing can be enjoyed at Arizona Snowbowl just 7 miles (11 km) north of town. The mountains here are the San Francisco Peaks, which receive an average of 260 in (660 cm) of snow annually, enough to supply the various ski runs that pattern the lower slopes of the 12,356-ft (3,707-m) high Agassiz Peak. Facilities include four chairlifts, and a ski school for beginners. In summer, there is a hiking trail up to the peak, while for those less inclined to walk, the Arizona Scenic Skyride is a cable car trip that offers spectacular views of the scenery.

Museum of Northern Arizona

(see p66).

VISITORS' CHECKLIST

Road map C3. *58,000.*
Pulliam Airport, 4 miles (6 km) south of town.
Amtrak Flagstaff Station, 1 E Rte 66. *Flagstaff bus station, 399 S Malpais Lane.*
Flagstaff Visitor Center, at Amtrak depot, 1 E Rte 66, Flagstaff, (928) 774-9541.
8am–5pm Mon–Sat, 9am–4pm Sun.
Thanksgiving, Dec 25.
www.flagstaffarizona.org

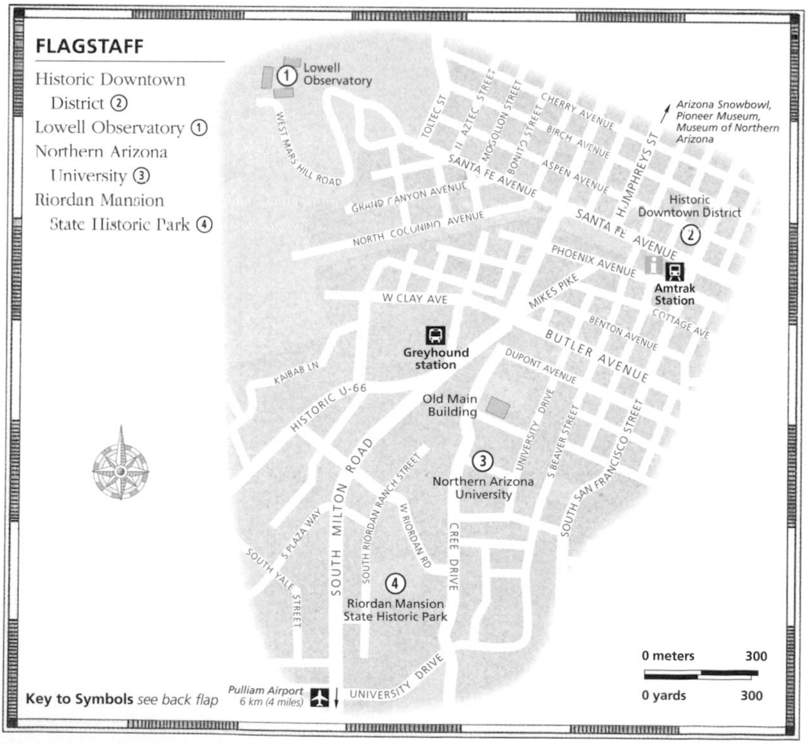

Flagstaff: Museum of Northern Arizona

The Museum of Northern Arizona holds one of the Southwest's most comprehensive collections of archeological artifacts, as well as fine art and natural science exhibits. The collections are arranged in galleries around a central courtyard. The Archaeology Gallery gives an introduction to the historic cultures. The Ethnology Gallery documents 12,000 years of tribal cultures on the Colorado Plateau, while the Babbitt Gallery showcases traditional and modern pottery of the Hopi people. The museum shop sells contemporary native fine arts and the bookstore specializes in native arts and crafts.

VISITORS' CHECKLIST

3101 N Fort Valley Rd. ***Tel*** *(928) 774-5213.* *9am–5pm.* *public hols.*
www.musnaz.org

★ Ethnology Gallery
This gallery highlights the living cultures of the Hopi, Navajo, Pai, and Zuni people.

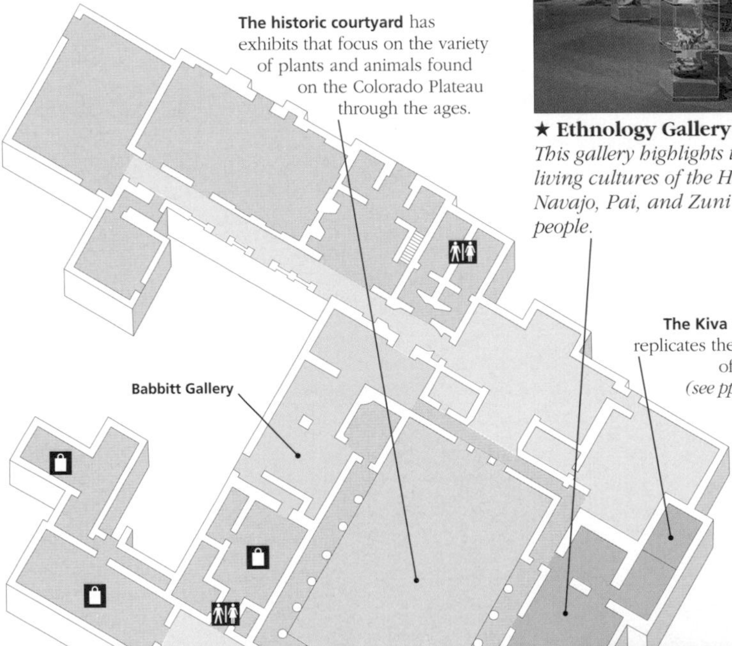
The historic courtyard has exhibits that focus on the variety of plants and animals found on the Colorado Plateau through the ages.
The Kiva Gallery replicates the inside of a *kiva* (see pp36–7).
Babbitt Gallery
Entrance
Archaeology Gallery

Geology Gallery
A lifesize skeletal model of a Dilophosaurus is ringed by dioramas of ancient Arizona desert scenes.

KEY

- Archaeology Gallery
- Ethnology Gallery
- Babbitt Gallery
- Geology Gallery
- Historic courtyard
- Changing Exhibition Gallery
- Non-exhibition space

STAR SIGHT

★ Ethnology Gallery

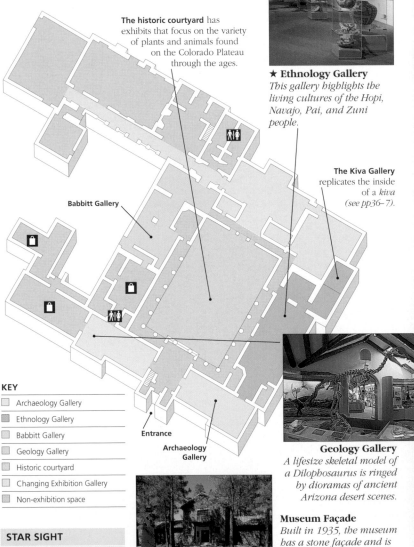

Museum Façade
Built in 1935, the museum has a stone façade and is listed on the National Register of Historic Places.

Wupatki National Monument ❹

Road map C3. Forest Service Rd 545, Sunset Crater/Wupatki Loop Rd. ***Tel*** *(928) 679-2365.* *Flagstaff.* *Flagstaff.* *9am–5pm daily.* *Dec 25.* *partial.* **www**.nps.gov/wupa

Covering more than 35,000 acres (14,000 ha) of sun-scorched wilderness to the north of Flagstaff, the Wupatki National Monument incorporates about 2,700 historic sites once inhabited by the ancestors of the Hopi people. The area was first settled after the eruption of Sunset Crater in 1064. The Sinagua people and their Ancestral Puebloan cousins *(see pp36–7)* realized that the volcanic ash had made the soil more fertile and consequently favourable for farming. The power of the volcanic eruption may also have have appealed to their spirituality. They left the region in the early 13th century, but no one really knows why.

The largest site here is the Wupatki Pueblo, built in the 12th century and once a four story pueblo complex of 100 rooms, housing more than 100 Sinagua. The structures rise from their rocky outcrop overlooking the desert. A trail from the visitor center explores the remains of the complex, whose most unusual feature is its ballcourt. Here the Sinagua may have played at dropping a ball through a stone ring without using their hands or feet.

Ruins of a 12th-century pueblo building at Wupatki National Monument

Sunset Crater Volcano National Monument ❺

Road map C3. Hwy 545 off Hwy 89, Sunset Crater/Wupatki Loop Rd. ***Tel*** *(928) 526-0502.* *Flagstaff.* *Flagstaff.* *Nov–Apr: 9am–5pm; May–Oct: 8am–5pm.* *Dec 25.* **www**.nps.gov/sucr

A mighty volcanic eruption in 1064 formed the 400-ft (120-m) deep Sunset Crater, leaving a cinder cone that is 1,000-ft (300-m) high. The cone is black at the base and tinged with reds and oranges farther up. The one-mile (1.6-km) Lava Trail offers an easy stroll around the ashy landscape with its lava tubes, bubbles, and vents.

Petroglyph from Walnut Canyon

Walnut Canyon National Monument ❻

Road map C3. Hwy 40 exit 204. ***Tel*** *(928) 526-3367.* *Flagstaff.* *Flagstaff.* *Nov–Apr: 9am–5pm; May–Oct: 8am–5pm.* *Dec 25.* *partial.* **www**.nps.gov/waca

Located about ten miles (16 km) east of Flagstaff, off Interstate Highway 40, the Walnut Canyon National Monument houses a collection of single-story cliff dwellings. These were inhabited by the Sinagua people in the 12th and 13th centuries.

Today, visitors to Walnut Canyon can tour the 25 cliff dwellings huddled underneath the natural overhangs of its eroded sandstone and limestone walls. Sinagua artifacts are on display in the Walnut Canyon Visitor Center, which also houses a small museum.

Meteor Crater ❼

Road map C3. South 6 miles off Hwy 40 exit 233. ***Tel*** *(928) 289-2362.* *Flagstaff.* *Flagstaff.* *Jun–Aug: 7am–7pm; Sep–May: 8am–5pm.* *Dec 25.* *partial.* **www**.meteorcrater.com

This meteorite impact crater so closely resembles a moon crater that NASA astronauts trained here in the 1960s. It was formed nearly 50,000 years ago and is 550 ft (168 m) deep and 2.4 miles (3.8 km) in circumference. The informative visitor center has exhibits and a film.

Petrified Forest National Park ❽

Road map D3. Off Hwy I-40. ***Tel*** *(928) 524-6228.* *7am–6pm (summer: 7am–7pm; winter: 8am–5pm).* *Dec 25.* *partial.* **www**.nps.gov/pefo

Millions of years ago rivers swept trees downstream into a vast swamp. Groundwater transported silica dioxide, eventually turning the timber into the quartz stone logs seen today, with colored crystals preserving the trees' shape and structure. Running the length of the forest is the famous Painted Desert, an area of colored bands of sand and rock that change from blues to reds as the shifting light catches the different mineral deposits.

From here, a 28-mile (45-km) scenic road has nine overlooks. Near the south end of the road is the **Rainbow Forest Museum.**

Rainbow Forest Museum
Off Hwy 180 (S entrance). ***Tel*** *(928) 524-6822.* *as Petrified Forest National Park (above).* *Dec 25.*

Sedona ❾

Sign of Sedona city

Founded by Theodore Schnelby in 1902, and named for his wife, Sedona was a quiet town until 1981. That year, author and renowned psychic Page Bryant claimed to have located seven "vortexes" emanating powerful spiritual energy in and around this beautiful town, and declared it the "heart-chakra of the planet." Since then, New Agers have developed Sedona as a spiritual, artistic, and outdoor-oriented resort town. Today, artists of all kinds sell their works in a growing number of galleries, such as those in Tlaquepaque, a superbly rendered village of artists, craftspeople, and imaginative shops.

VISITORS' CHECKLIST

Road map B3. *16,000.* *Pulliam Airport, Flagstaff (no commercial flights into Sedona Airport).* *331 Forest Road, (800) 288-7336.* *8:30am–5pm Mon–Sat; 9am–3pm Sun.* *Red Rocks Music Festival (late Sep).* **www**.visitsedona.com
Spas *Mii Amo at Enchantment Resort, (888) 749-2137; Los Abrigados Resort & Spa, (800) 418-6499.* **Art Shopping** *Tlaquepaque Art Village, (928) 282-4838.*

CATHEDRAL ROCK
One of Sedona's seven "energy vortexes," Cathedral Rock is revered in Native American mythology as the birthplace of the "First Man" and "First Woman." It is a popular place for sunrise and sunset hikes, and the view of Cathedral Rock overlooking Oak Creek is one of the most photographed scenes in Arizona.

Crystal Therapy
Sedona's New Age centers offer a dazzling array of alternative therapies.

Havasupai Storyteller
Native American themes and traditions are often components of many of the programs offered in and around Sedona.

Tlaquepaque Art Village
Sedona has attracted many artists and crafts-people, whose creations are on display in fine shops and galleries.

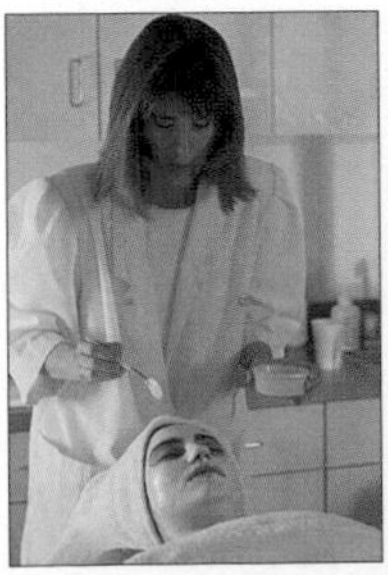

Spa Resorts
Sedona's natural desert beauty and reputed healing energies have made it a premier center for spas and resorts.

For hotels and restaurants in this region see pp124–7 and pp134–7

Oak Creek Canyon ⑩

Road map B3. *(800) 228-7336.*

Just south of Flagstaff, Highway 89A weaves a charming route through Oak Creek Canyon on its way to Sedona. In the canyon, dense woods shadow the road, and the steep cliffs are colored in bands of red and yellow sandstone, pale limestone, and black basalt. The canyon is a popular summer vacation area with many day-hiking trails, such as the East Pocket Trail, a steep, wooded climb to the canyon rim. One of the prettiest and easiest hikes in Oak Creek is along the 3-mile (5-km) West Fork Trail, which follows a stream past abandoned apple orchards and into a narrow red rock canyon. At nearby Slide Rock State Park, swimmers enjoy sliding over the rocks that form a natural water chute.

Picturesque Oak Creek Canyon – a popular summer destination

Williams ⑪

Road map B3. *2,700.* *200 W Railroad Ave, (928) 635-4061.* **www**.williamschamber.com

This distinctive little town was named in 1851 for Bill Williams (1787–1849), a legendary mountain man and trapper who lived for a time with the Osage Indians in Missouri. The town grew around the railroad that came in the 1880s, and when this was followed by a spur track to Grand Canyon's South Rim in 1901, Williams became established as a tourist center. By the late 1920s, it was also a popular rest stop on Route 66 *(see pp28–9)*.

The town has retained its frontier atmosphere, complete with Stetson-wearing locals. Most hotels and diners are located on a loop that follows Route 66 on one side, and Interstate Highway 40 on the other. Diners evoke the 1950s, and are filled with Route 66 memorabilia, including original soda fountains and posters.

Tuzigoot National Monument ⑫

Road map B3. *Follow signs from Hwy 89A.* ***Tel*** *(928) 634-5564.* *end May–early Sep: 8am–6pm; early Sep–end May: 8am–5pm.* *Dec 25.* **www**.nps.gov/tuzi

Perched on a solitary limestone ridge, the ruins of Tuzigoot National Monument offer fine views of the Verde River Valley. The pueblo was built by the Sinagua people between the 12th and 15th centuries and, at its peak, had a population of around 300. It was abandoned in the early 15th century, when the Sinagua are believed to have migrated north.

Tuzigoot was partly rebuilt by a local and federally funded program during the Depression in the 1930s. This emphasized one of the most unusual features of pueblo building, the lack of doorways. The normal pueblo room was entered by ladder through a hatchway in the roof. Sinaguan artifacts and art are on display at the visitor center here.

Jerome ⑬

Road map B3. *500.* *Box K, Jerome.* **www**.azjerome.com

Approached from the east along Highway 89A, Jerome is easy to spot, with its old brick buildings high above the valley. Silver mining began here in the 1870s, but the town's big break came in 1912 when prospectors struck substantial copper. World War I sent the price of copper sky-high, and Jerome boomed. In the Wall Street Crash of 1929, however, copper prices tumbled, and the boom times were over. Jerome was a ghost town by the early 1960s, but its fortunes have now been revived by an influx of artists and artisans.

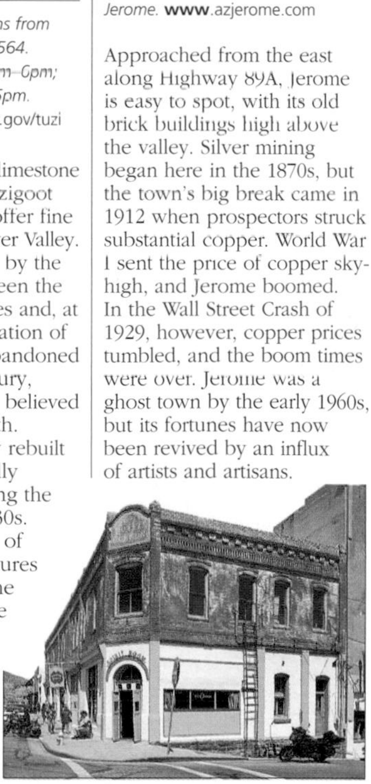

Façade of an early 20th-century store on Jerome's historic Main Street

Heart of Arizona Tour ⓮

The Verde River passes through the wooded hills and fertile meadows of Central Arizona, before opening into a wide, green valley between Flagstaff and Phoenix. The heart of Arizona is full of charming towns such as Sedona, hidden away among stunning scenery, and the former mining town of Jerome. Over the hills lies Prescott, once state capital and now a busy, likable little town with a center full of dignified Victorian buildings. The area's ancient history can be seen in its two beautiful pueblo ruins, Montezuma Castle and Tuzigoot.

TIPS FOR DRIVERS

Recommended route: *From Sedona, take Hwy 89A to Tuzigoot, Jerome, and Prescott. Hwy 69 runs east from Prescott to Interstate Hwy 17, which connects to Camp Verde, Fort Verde, and Montezuma Castle.*
Tour length: *85 miles (137 km).*
When to go: *Spring and fall are delightful; summer is very hot.*

Sedona ①
Set among dramatic red rock hills, Sedona *(see p68)* is a popular resort, known for its New Age stores and galleries, as well as for its friendly ambience.

KEY

Tour route

Other roads

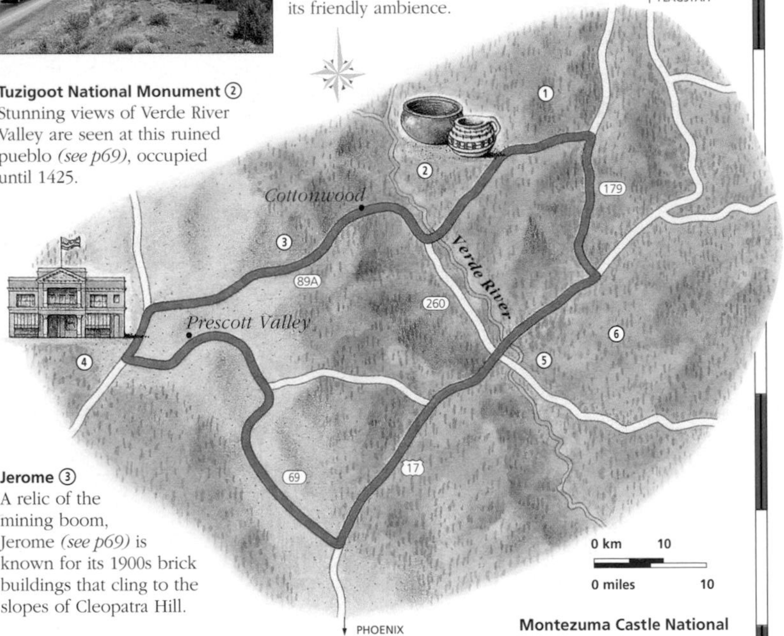

Tuzigoot National Monument ②
Stunning views of Verde River Valley are seen at this ruined pueblo *(see p69)*, occupied until 1425.

Jerome ③
A relic of the mining boom, Jerome *(see p69)* is known for its 1900s brick buildings that cling to the slopes of Cleopatra Hill.

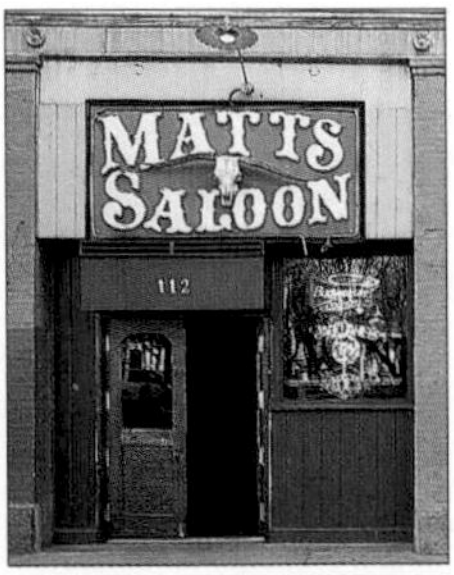

Prescott ④
This cool hilltop town is set among the rugged peaks and lush woods of Prescott National Forest, making it a popular center for many outdoor activities.

Montezuma Castle National Monument ⑥
The Ancestral Puebloan ruins here date from the 1100s and occupy one of the loveliest sites in the Southwest.

Camp Verde ⑤
A highlight of this little town is Fort Verde. Built by the US Army in 1865, the fort is manned by costumed guides.

Montezuma Castle National Monument ⓯

Road map B3. Hwy I-17 exit 289. ***Tel*** *(928) 567-3322.* *early Sep–end May: 8am–5pm; end May–early Sep: 8am–6pm.* **www**.nps.gov/moca

Dating from the 1100s, the pueblo remains that make up Montezuma Castle occupy an idyllic location, built into the limestone cliffs high above Beaver Creek, a couple of miles to the east of Interstate Highway 17. Once home to the Sinagua people, this cliff dwelling originally contained 20 rooms on five floors. Montezuma Castle was declared a National Monument in 1906 to preserve its excellent condition. The visitor center has a display on Sinaguan life, and is found at the start of an easy trail along Beaver Creek. The National Monument also incorporates Montezuma Well, situated about 11 miles (18 km) to the northeast. This natural sinkhole, 50 ft (15 m) deep and 470 ft (140 m) in diameter, had religious significance for Native Americans, who believed it was the site of the Creation. Over 1,000 gallons (3,790 liters) of water flow through the sinkhole every minute, an inexhaustible supply that has long been used for irrigation. A narrow trail leads around the rim before twisting its way down to the water's edge.

Pueblo remains of Montezuma Castle, built into limestone cliffs

Camp Verde ⓰

Road map B3. *6,000.* *385 S Main St, (928) 567-9294.* **www**.visitcampverde.com

Farmers founded the small settlement of Camp Verde in the heart of the Verde River Valley in the 1860s. It was a risky enterprise as the Apache lived nearby, but the US Army quickly moved in to protect the settlers, building **Fort Verde** in 1865. Today, Camp Verde remains at the center of a large and prosperous farming and ranching community. It was from Fort Verde that the army orchestrated a series of brutal campaigns against the Apache, which ended with the Battle of the Big Dry Wash in 1882. Once the Apache had been sent to reservations, Fort Verde was no longer needed and it was decommissioned in 1891. Four of its original buildings have survived. The former army administration building contains a collection of exhibits on army life. The interiors of the other three houses, on Officers' Row, have been restored. At times, volunteers dressed in period costume act as guides and re-enact scenes from the fort's daily life. Call ahead for a schedule of such events.

Costumed guides at Fort Verde State Historic Park

Fort Verde at Camp Verde State Historic Park
Off Hwy I-17. ***Tel*** *(928) 567-3275.* *9am–5pm Thu–Mon.*

Prescott ⓱

Road map B3. *34,000.* *117 W Goodwin St, (928) 445-2000.* **www**.prescott.org

Surrounded by high-country and lakes, this attractive Victorian town gives little evidence of its early days as a hard-drinking frontier area. Perhaps the three years spent as the early capital of the Arizona Territories gave it some respectability. Palace Saloon is the only structure left from "Whiskey Row," where over 20 saloons once stood. The Governor's Mansion – really just a large log cabin – is part of the **Sharlot Hall Museum**. This exceptional museum is named for Sharlot Hall, a pioneer, writer, and early activist who served as Arizona's first salaried historian. Her paintings and photographs form the core of a collection that fills nine buildings.

Fans of Native history should visit **Smoki Museum**. Located in a replica of a Hopi pueblo, the museum contains over 2,000 Native artifacts from prehistoric to modern. The museum's basket collection is said to be one of the best in the United States. Also of note is the **Phippen Art Museum**, which has an impressive collection of historic and contemporary Western art.

Sharlot Hall Museum
415 W Gurly St. ***Tel*** *(928) 445-3122.* *May–Oct: 10am–5pm Mon–Sat, noon–4pm Sun; Nov–Apr: 10am–4pm Mon–Sat, noon–4pm Sun.* **www**.sharlot.org

Smoki Museum
147 N Arizona St. ***Tel*** *(928) 445-1230.* *10am–4pm Tue–Sat; 1–4pm Sun.* **www**.smokimuseum.org

Phippen Art Museum
4701 Hwy 89 N. ***Tel*** *(928) 778-1385.* *10am–4pm Tue–Sat, 1–4pm Sun.* *early Jan, Thanksgiving, Dec 25.* **www**.phippenartmuseum.org

Hoover Dam ⓲

Road map A2. *Hoover Dam Visitor Center, Hoover Dam, Boulder City, (702) 494-2517.* *9am–4:45pm.* *Thanksgiving, Dec 25.* **www**.usbr.gov/lc/hooverdam

Named for Herbert Hoover, the 31st president, the historic Hoover Dam is situated at Arizona's border with Nevada. Built between 1931 and 1935 across the Colorado River's Black Canyon, the dam is 30 miles (48 km) east of the city of Las Vegas. Hailed as an engineering victory, the dam gave this desert region a reliable water supply and provided inexpensive electricity. Today, it supplies water and electricity to the three states of Nevada, Arizona, and California, and has created Lake Mead – a popular tourist center. Visitors to the dam can take the Powerplant Tour, which includes a trip to the observation deck and elevator ride deep inside the dam to the generator viewing area.

Located eight miles (13 km) west of Hoover Dam is **Boulder City**, which was built as a model community to house dam construction workers. With its neat yards and suburban streets, it is one of Nevada's most attractive and well-ordered towns. Its Christian founders banned casinos, and there are none here today. Several of its original 1930s buildings remain, including the restored 1933 Boulder Dam Hotel, which houses the **Hoover Dam Museum**.

The museum tells the history and development of Boulder City, Hoover Dam, Lake Mead, and the Lower Colorado River region through 3-D interactive displays and exhibits. Several artifacts and photographs, which highlight the lives of the workers who built the dam, provide a sense of the complexity and the immense scale of the Hoover Dam project.

Hoover Dam Museum
1305 Arizona St, Boulder City. ***Tel*** *(702) 294-1988.* *10am–5pm Mon–Sat; noon–5pm Sun.* *public hols.* **www**.bcmha.org

THE CONSTRUCTION OF THE HOOVER DAM

Hoover Dam sign

More than 1,400 miles (2,250 km) in length, the Colorado River flows through seven states from the Rocky Mountains to the Gulf of California. A treacherous, unpredictable river, it used to be a raging torrent in spring and a trickle in the heat of summer. As a source of water it was therefore unreliable and, in 1928, the seven states it served signed the Boulder Canyon Project Act to define how much water each state could siphon off. The agreement paved the way for the Hoover Dam, and its construction began in 1931. It was a mammoth task, and more than 5,000 men toiled day and night to build what was, at 726 ft (218 m), the world's tallest dam. The dam contains 17 hydroelectric generating units.

View of the Hoover Dam

Lake Mead, a popular tourist destination for watersports

Lake Mead National Recreation Area ⓳

Road map A2. *Las Vegas. Alan Bible Visitor Center* ***Tel*** *(702) 293-8990.* *8:30am–4:30pm.* *Jan 1, Thanksgiving, Dec 25.* *limited.* **www**.nps.gov/lame

After the completion of the Hoover Dam, the waters of the Colorado River filled the deep canyons that once towered above the river to create a huge reservoir – the largest artifical lake in America. This lake, with its 700 miles (1,130 km) of shoreline, is the centerpiece of Lake Mead National Recreation Area, a 1.5-million-acre (600,000-ha) tract of land. The focus is on watersports, especially sailing, waterskiing, and fishing. Striped bass and rainbow trout are popular catches. There are also several campgrounds and marinas.

Kingman ⓴

Road map A3. *35,000.* *120 W Route 66, (928) 753-6106.* **www**.kingmantourism.org

Located in the middle of the desert, Kingman was founded by the Santa Fe Railroad as a construction camp in 1882. In the 1920s, the town became an important stop on Route 66 *(see pp28–9)*, and during the 1930s depression it was crowded with migrants fleeing the Midwest. Today, Kingman's claim to fame is being situated on the longest remaining stretch of Route 66.

For hotels and restaurants in this region see pp124–7 and pp134–7

Renewed interest in the road has resulted in the renovation of many of Kingman's Route 66 diners, motels, and tourist stops. The visitor center, housed in the "Powerhouse," which was built in 1907, features a replica Route 66 diner and the Route 66 Museum, which traces the road's journey from its origins.

Chloride, a former mining town, is an enjoyable day trip from Kingman. A boomtown during the late 19th century, it still has many of its original structures, including a raised wooden sidewalk, and some shops and galleries.

Oatman – a boomtown of the early 20th century

Oatman ㉑

Road map A3. 100. PO Box 123, Oatman, (928) 768-6222. **www**.oatmangoldroad.org

Prospectors struck gold in 1904 in the Black Mountains, and Oatman became their main supply center. Today, it is popular with visitors wanting a taste of its boomtown past, such as the 1920s Oatman Hotel, where Carole Lombard and Clark Gable honeymooned in 1939.

Lake Havasu City ㉒

Road map A3. 45,000. 314 London Bridge Rd, (928) 453-3444. **www**.golakehavasu.com

California businessman Robert McCulloch founded Lake Havasu City in 1964. The resort city he built on the Colorado River was popular with the landlocked citizens of Arizona. His real brainwave, however, came four years later when he bought the historic London Bridge and transported it all the way from England to Lake Havasu.

Some people mocked McCulloch, suggesting that he had thought he was buying London's Gothic Tower Bridge, not this much more ordinary one. There was more hilarity when it appeared that there was nothing in Havasu City for the bridge to span. Undaunted, McCulloch simply created the waterway he needed by dredging a mile-long channel through the area. Today, Lake Havasu City is one of the most visited outdoor recreation areas in Arizona, attracting families and sports enthusiasts alike. The town is always busy with visitors enjoying the shops and restaurants. There are also watersports of every kind, from powerboating and houseboating to jetskiing and kayaking. Golf, hiking, and 4WD adventures are also very popular.

Quartzsite ㉓

Road map A4. 3,300. Quartzsite Chamber of Commerce, 100 E Main, (928) 927-9321. **www**.quartzsitebusinesschamber.com

This quiet village, located in the low desert, 10 miles (16 km) east of the Colorado River, has long been a favorite collecting site for rockhounds. In the 1970s, the winter population began to swell as escapees from the northern cold arrived in droves to park their RVs for a modest sum on government land. Many were rockhounds, and they started Quartzsite's first gem and mineral show.

Today, over a million people visit the town every winter, and eight major gem and mineral shows take place in January and February. Everything from antiques and collectibles to solar panels to eyeglasses can be purchased in what must be the most curious and diverse flea market in America.

London Bridge spanning a man-made waterway in Lake Havasu City

PHOENIX & SOUTHERN ARIZONA

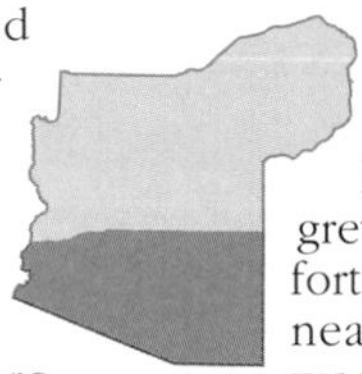

Mountain ranges and sun-bleached plateaus ripple the wide landscapes of Southern Arizona, a spectacular region dominated by pristine tracts of desert, parts of which are protected within the Saguaro National Park and the Organ Pipe Cactus National Monument. This land was first farmed around 400 BC by the Hohokam people *(see p35)*, who carefully used the meager water supplies to irrigate their crops. When the Spanish arrived in the 16th century they built forts and established settlements across the region. This Hispanic heritage is recalled by the beautiful mission churches of San Xavier del Bac and Tumacacori, and in the popular historic city of Tucson that grew up around the 1776 Spanish fort. When silver was discovered nearby in the 1870s, the scene was set for a decade of rowdy frontier life. Today, towns such as Tombstone, famous for the "Gunfight at the OK Corral," re-create this Wild West era. The influx of miners also spurred the growth of Phoenix, a farming town established on the banks of the Salt River in the 1860s. Phoenix is now the largest city in the Southwest, known for its warm winter climate and recreational facilities.

SIGHTS AT A GLANCE

Historic Towns & Cities

Bisbee 11
Globe 4
Nogales 10
Phoenix 1
Tombstone 12
Tubac 9
Tucson 6
Yuma 7

Parks, Museums & National Monuments

Amerind Foundation 14
Casa Grande Ruins National Monument 5
Chiricahua National Monument 15
Kartchner Caverns State Park 13
Organ Pipe Cactus National Monument 8

Areas of Natural Beauty

Apache Trail Tour 2
Salt River Canyon 3

KEY

International airport
Interstate
Major highway
Highway
Railroad

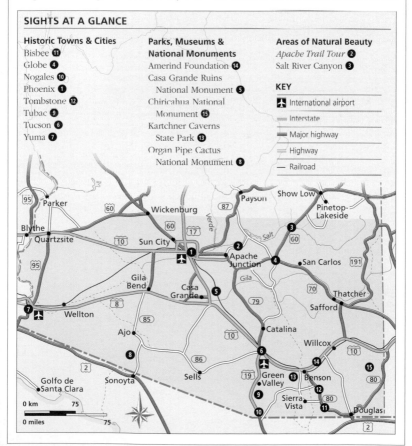

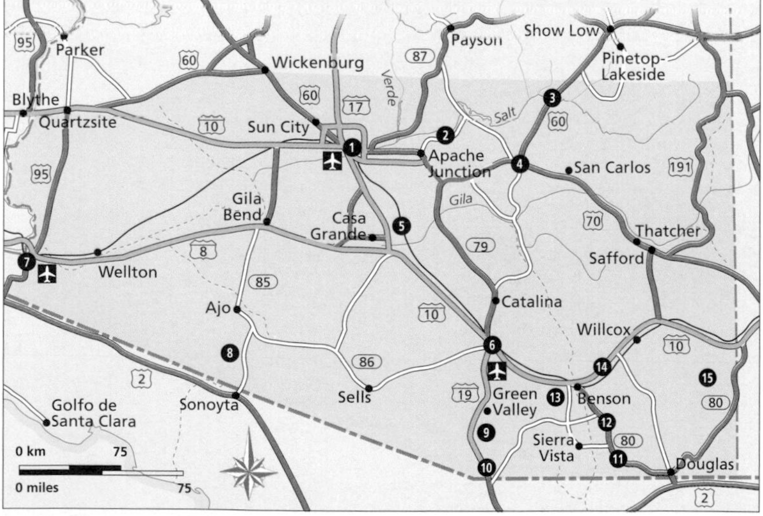

◁ **Visitors riding the range at the Lazy K Bar Guest Ranch near Tucson**

Phoenix ❶

Cash register at the Museum of History

Phoenix is a huge metropolis, stretching across the Salt River Valley. Farmers and ranchers settled here in the 1860s. By 1912, the city had developed into the political and economic focus of Arizona and was the state capital. As it grew, it absorbed surrounding towns, although each district still maintains its identity. Downtown Phoenix is now being reinvigorated and is home to many historic attractions. These include restored Victorian houses in Heritage Square, the Phoenix Art Museum, and the Heard Museum *(see pp78–9)* with its excellent collection of Native American artifacts.

The 1900 façade of the Arizona State Capitol Building

Exploring Downtown Phoenix

Downtown Phoenix, where the city began in the 19th century, is centered on Washington and Jefferson Streets, which run east to west between 7th Street and 19th Avenue. Central Avenue is the main north-south axis: to its east, parallel roads are labeled as "Streets," while roads to the west are "Avenues." City sights are mostly too far apart to see on foot, and driving is the best option. A DASH bus runs from downtown to the State Capitol regularly on weekdays.

Arizona State Capitol Museum

1700 W Washington St.
Tel *(602) 926-3620.*
9am–4pm Mon–Fri.
pub hols.
www.lib.az.us/museum

Completed in 1900, the Arizona State Capitol housed the state legislature until they moved into new premises in 1960. The handsome building is topped by a copper dome. The interior is now a museum; guided tours include both original legislative chambers, which have been carefully restored, and a series of sepia photographs that document the history of Phoenix.

Arizona Mining & Mineral Museum

1502 W Washington St. ***Tel*** *(602) 771-1611.* *8am–5pm Mon–Fri; 11am–4pm Sat.* *public hols.*
www.admmr.state.az.us

Azurite and malachite rock

The search for precious stones and metals brought waves of prospectors to the Southwest in the years following the Civil War (1861–65). The riches they unearthed in Arizona's sun-seared hills were fabulous. A mountain of silver was discovered in the Dragoon Mountains near Tucson, while quantities of gold, silver, copper, and turquoise were found farther north in the Cerbat Mountains outside Kingman *(see p72)*. As word of the fortunes to be made in the area spread, thousands of prospectors converged on the Superstition Mountains *(see p84)* to the east of Phoenix. However, many ended up destitute, never discovering the large deposits of gold rumored to be hidden in the hills.

This museum traces the history of Arizona mining through photographs and displays of historic tools. There are also glittering examples of the various rocks the miners quarried, the most striking of which are the copper-bearing ores such as malachite and azurite, in vivid greens and blues. All together there are over 3000 pieces on show.

Heritage Square

115 N 6th St. *partial.*
Rosson House ***Tel*** *(602) 262-5070.*
www.rossonhousemuseum.org

Phoenix is a thoroughly modern city, which grew rapidly after World War II. Many of its older buildings did not survive this intensive expansion. However, a few late 19th- and early 20th-century buildings remain, and the most interesting of these are found on Heritage Square. **Rosson House**, on Monroe Street, was built for Dr and Mrs Roland Lee Rosson in 1895. A handsome wooden mansion, it has a

Key to Symbols *see back flap*

wraparound veranda and distinctive hexagonal turret. Visitors may tour the house, which is furnished in period style. Next door is the Burgess Carriage House, constructed in an expansive colonial style rare in the Southwest. The 1900 Silva House features exhibits detailing Arizona's history. The tree-lined square with its cafés is pleasant for a stroll.

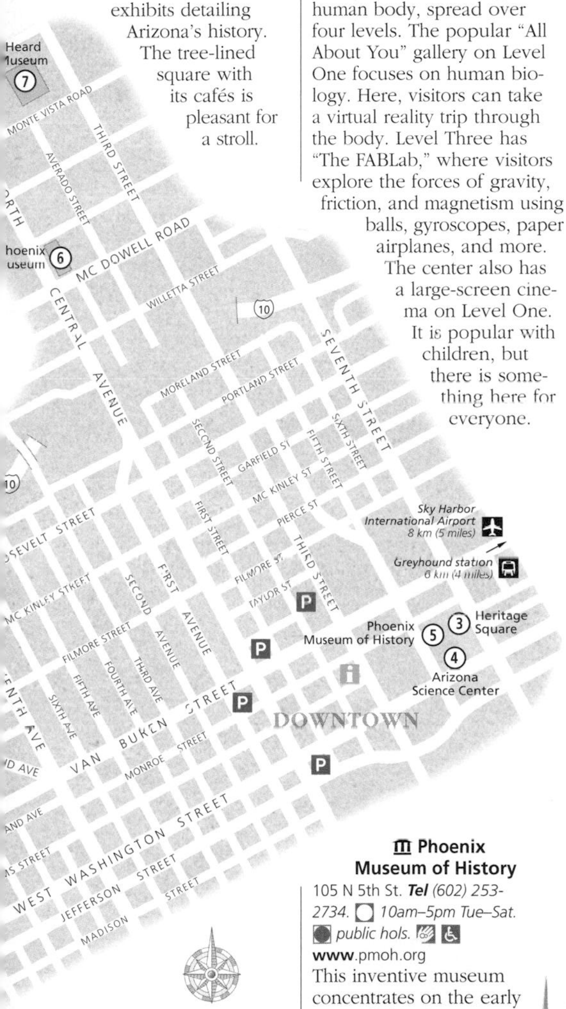

SIGHTS AT A GLANCE

Arizona Mining & Mineral Museum ②
Arizona State Capitol Museum ①
Arizona Science Center ④
Heard Museum ⑦
Heritage Square ③
Phoenix Art Museum ⑥
Phoenix Museum of History ⑤

Arizona Science Center

600 E Washington St. ***Tel*** *(602) 716-2000.* *10am–5pm.* *Thanksgiving, Dec 25.* **www**.azscience.org

This ultra-modern facility has over 300 interactive science exhibits, covering everything from physics and energy to the human body, spread over four levels. The popular "All About You" gallery on Level One focuses on human biology. Here, visitors can take a virtual reality trip through the body. Level Three has "The FABLab," where visitors explore the forces of gravity, friction, and magnetism using balls, gyroscopes, paper airplanes, and more. The center also has a large-screen cinema on Level One. It is popular with children, but there is something here for everyone.

Phoenix Museum of History

105 N 5th St. ***Tel*** *(602) 253-2734.* *10am–5pm Tue–Sat.* *public hols.* **www**.pmoh.org

This inventive museum concentrates on the early years of the city's history. There is a fascinating range of unusual artifacts, including 19th-century land surveying equipment, a steam-powered bicycle, Phoenix's first printing press, and reconstructions of a general store and the first jail.

VISITORS' CHECKLIST

Road map B4. *1,320,000 (city only).* *Sky Harbor International Airport, 3 miles (1.5 km) E of downtown.* *Greyhound Bus, 2115 E. Buckeye Rd.* *Greater Phoenix Convention & Visitors Bureau, 50 North 2nd St, (602) 254-6500.* *The PGA's FBR Golf Open, Jan, Feb.* **www**.visitphoenix.com

Phoenix Art Museum

1625 N Central Ave. ***Tel*** *(602) 257 1222.* *10am–9pm Tue; 10am–5pm Wed–Sun.* *public hols.* **www** phxart.org

Housed in a dramatic modern building, this acclaimed museum has an enviable reputation for the quality of its temporary exhibitions. The stunning Katz Wing houses a permanent collection of contemporary fashion design and photographic works. The museum is also renowned for its collection of US and European art; many of the 18th- and 19th-century American artists featured are associated with the Southwest. The exhibits include first-rate work from the Taos art colony of the 1900s, including paintings by Georgia O'Keeffe (1887–1986), the most distinguished member of the group. Among other featured artists are Gilbert Stewart (1755–1828), whose celebrated *Portrait of George Washington* (1796) is seen on every dollar bill.

Outside view of the Phoenix Museum of History

Phoenix: Heard Museum

The Heard Museum was founded in 1929 by Dwight Heard, a wealthy rancher and businessman who, with his wife, Maie, assembled an extraordinary collection of Southwest Native American art in the 1920s. Several benefactors later added to the collection; they included Senator Barry Goldwater of Arizona and the Fred Harvey Company, who donated their *kachina* dolls. The museum exhibits more than 40,000 works, but its star attraction is their display of more than 500 dolls. Additionally, the museum showcases baskets, pottery, textiles, and fine art, as well as sumptuous silverwork by the Navajo, Zuni, and Hopi peoples.

Heard Museum's Spanish Colonial Revival style, retained in the 1999 expansion

Flagsong *(1983)*
This sculpture by Native American artist Doug Hyde is located in one of the Heard's tranquil courtyards.

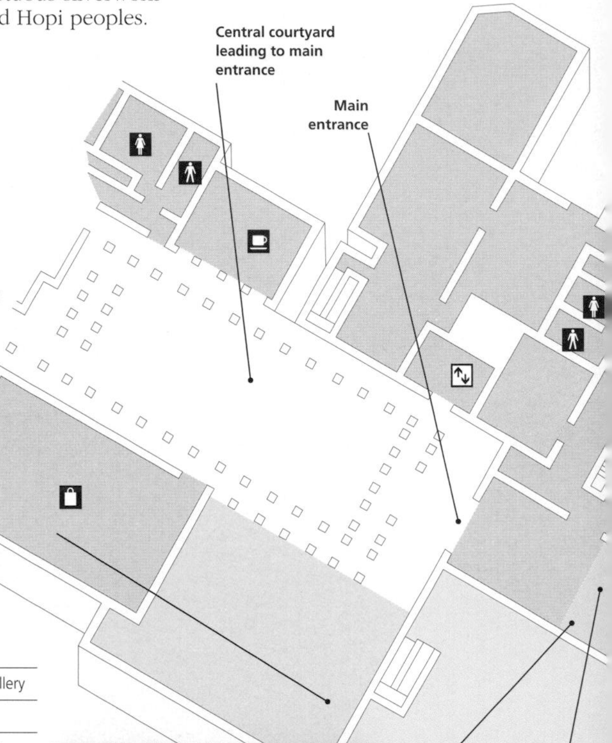

KEY

- Samuel and Betty Kitchell Gallery
- Crossroads Gallery
- Sandra Day O'Connor Gallery
- Ullman Learning Center
- Freeman Gallery
- Home: Native People in the Southwest Gallery
- Lincoln Hall
- Pritzlaff Courtyard
- Edward Jacobson Gallery of Indian Art
- Maureen and Dean Nichols Garden
- Temporary exhibition space
- Non-exhibition space

Red-Tailed Hawk *(1986)*
Dan Namingha's impressionistic view of a Hopi kachina *in hawk form is displayed as part of the Heard's fine art collection.*

The Samuel and Betty Kitchell Gallery explores the traditions of Native art.

For hotels and restaurants in this region see pp127–30 and pp137–9

VISITORS' CHECKLIST

2301 N Central Ave, Phoenix, AZ 85004. *Phoenix Greyhound Station.* **Tel** *(602) 252-8840.* *(602) 252-8848.* *9:30am–5pm Mon–Sat, 11am–5pm Sun.* *public hols.* **www**.heard.org

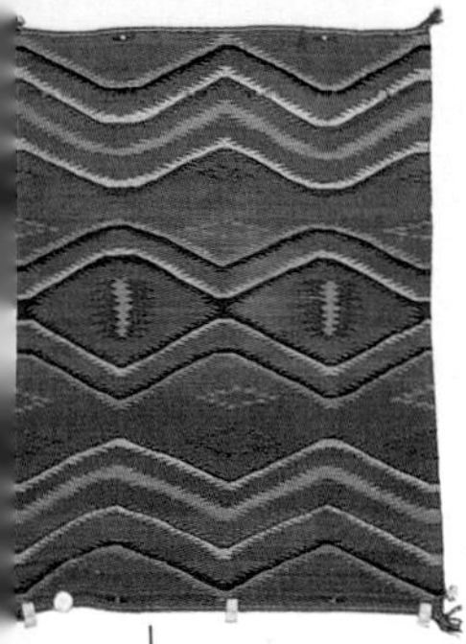

Navajo Child's Blanket
Woven in the 1870s, this richly colored, traditional blanket is one of the highlights of the Sandra Day O'Connor Gallery. The museum's history is documented at the gallery, which also showcases the Heard family's early collection of Native American artifacts.

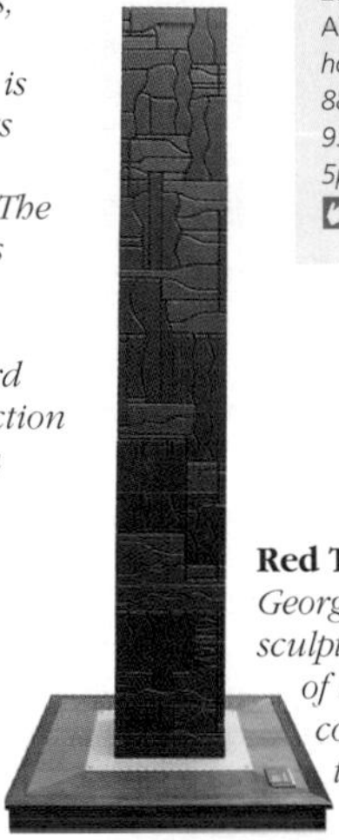

Red Totem *(1980)*
George Morrison's sculpture reflects the fusion of traditional and contemporary styles in the Native American Fine Art Movement.

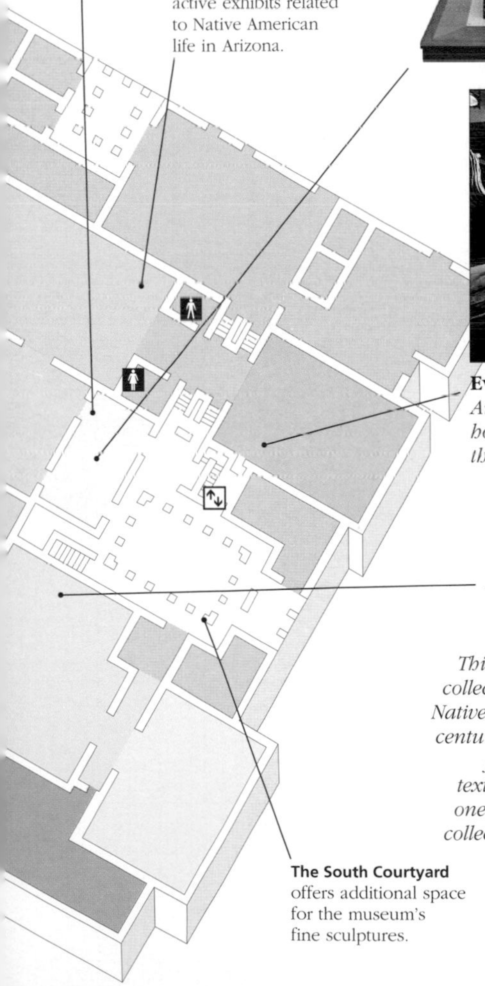

Ullman Learning Center features interactive exhibits related to Native American life in Arizona.

Every Picture Tells a Story
An interactive hands-on display shows how artists interpret their environments through art.

★ Home: Native People in the Southwest
This award-winning collection of over 2,000 Native artifacts spans 14 centuries, and includes jewelry, basketry, textiles, pottery, and one of the West's best collections of kachinas.

The South Courtyard offers additional space for the museum's fine sculptures.

STAR COLLECTION

★ Home: Native People in the Southwest

Exploring Metropolitan Phoenix

Phoenix is one of North America's largest cities. In addition to its city population of well over one million, Phoenix has a burgeoning number of residents in its metropolitan area, totaling more than three million. The city fills the Salt River Valley, occupying more than 2,000 sq miles (5,200 sq km) of the Sonoran Desert. It is famous for winter temperatures of 60–70°F (16–21°C) and around 300 days of sunshine a year. This makes Phoenix a popular destination with both tourists and "snowbirds," visitors who spend their winters here.

Metropolitan Phoenix includes the former town of Scottsdale, 12 miles (19 km) northeast of downtown. With air-conditioned malls, designer stores, hotels, and restaurants, it is a good base for visiting Taliesin West and Papago Park, and is famous for its world-class golf courses *(see pp154–5)*. Tempe, 6 miles (10 km) east of downtown, is home to Arizona State University and the Pueblo Grande Museum, while Mesa has the Arizona Temple, a large Mormon church built in 1927.

SIGHTS AT A GLANCE

Camelback Mountain ④
Challenger Space Center ⑧
Cosanti Foundation ③
Mystery Castle ⑦
Papago Park ⑥
Pioneer Living History Village ⑨
Pueblo Grande Museum & Archeological Park ⑤
Scottsdale ①
Taliesin West ②

KEY

- Downtown Phoenix
- Metropolitan Phoenix
- International airport
- Interstate
- Major highway
- Highway
- Railroad

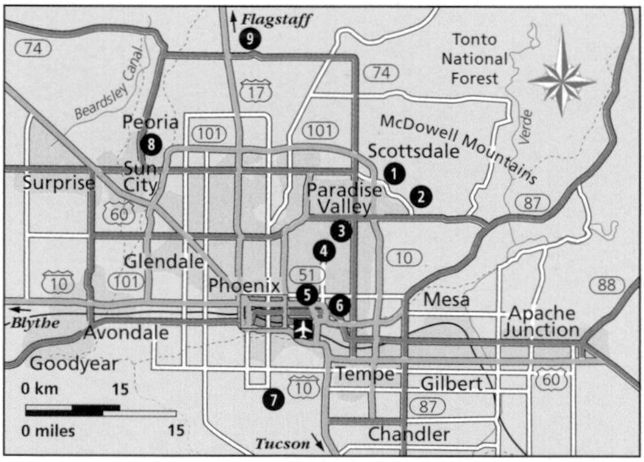

Scottsdale

Founded in the late 19th century, Scottsdale was named after its developer, army chaplain Winfield Scott (1837–1910), whose religious scruples helped keep the early settlement free from saloons and gambling. Scottsdale's quiet, tree-lined streets and desert setting attracted the architect Frank Lloyd Wright *(see p23)*, who established Taliesin West here in 1937. The area still attracts artists and designers, but it is best known for its many golf courses – there are 175 in and around Scottsdale. At the center of the district, to either side of Scottsdale Road between 2nd Street and Indian School Road, the streets are lined with low, brightly painted adobe buildings, which house many of the city's most fashionable restaurants as well as bars, antiques stores, and art galleries. In addition to the Renaissance-style Borgata shopping mall, there is the El Pedregal Festival Marketplace, and Scottsdale Downtown with its arts shopping district around Main Street, Marshall Way, Old Town, and Fifth Avenue. Scottsdale is also the location for Phoenix's most popular shopping mall, **Fashion Square**, which has an array of designer stores and excellent restaurants *(see p144)*.

Scottsdale's elegant shopping mall, Fashion Square

Taliesin West

Cactus Rd at Frank Lloyd Wright Blvd, Scottsdale. ***Tel*** *(480) 860-8810.* *9am–4pm.* *Jan 1, Thanksgiving, Dec 25.*
www.franklloydwright.org

Generally regarded as the greatest American architect of all time, Frank Lloyd Wright (1869–1959) established the 600-acre (240-ha) Taliesin West complex as a winter school for his students in 1937. Wright had come to prominence in Chicago during the 1890s with a series of strikingly original houses that featured an elegant open-plan style. Although noted for his use of local materials such as desert rocks and earth, he also pioneered the use of pre-cast concrete. Today, Taliesin West is home to the

Innovative design of the Cosanti Foundation gift shop

Frank Lloyd Wright School of Architecture, where students live and work for up to five years. The students also work as guides to the complex. There are a variety of tours, from one to three hours. Ninety-minute tours begin every hour from 10am to 4pm.

Taleisin West is approached along a winding desert road. The muted tones of the low-lying buildings reflect Wright's enthusiasm for the desert setting. He was careful to enhance, rather than dominate, the landscape.

Cosanti Foundation

6433 Doubletree Ranch Rd, Paradise Valley. ***Tel*** *(480) 948-6145.* *9am–5pm Mon–Sat; 11am–5pm Sun.* *public hols.* *donation requested.* **www.**arcosanti.org

In 1947, Italian architect Paolo Soleri (b. 1919) came to study at Taliesin West. He set up the Cosanti Foundation in Scottsdale nine years later to further his investigations into what he termed "arcology": a combination of architecture and ecology to create new urban habitats *(see p23)*.

Today, the Cosanti site consists of simple, low structures housing studios, a gallery, and workshops. This is where Soleri and his workers make and sell their trademark windbells. Guided visits can be arranged with advance notice.

Visitors can also take an interesting tour of Soleri's main project, Arcosanti, which lies 60 miles (100 km) north of Phoenix on Interstate Highway 17. The educational project began in 1970 as a way to test the "arcology concept", with its aim of reducing human impact on the environment while improving quality of life. Structures combine work and leisure space and accommodations and tours are available.

Camelback Mountain

Named for its humped shape, this mountain rises high above its suburban surroundings just 7 miles (11 km) northeast of downtown Phoenix. One of the city's most distinctive landmarks, the mountain is a granite and sandstone outcrop formed by prehistoric volcanic forces. It is best approached from the north via the marked turn off McDonald Drive near the junction of Tatum Boulevard. From the parking lot, a well-marked path leads to the summit, a steep climb that covers 1,300 ft (390 m) in the space of a mile.

Camelback Mountain is adjacent to the Echo Canyon Recreation Area, a lovely wooded enclave with a choice of shaded picnic sites.

Pueblo Grande Museum & Archaeological Park

4619 E Washington St. ***Tel*** *(602) 495-0900.* *9am–4:45pm Mon–Sat; 1–4:45pm Sun.* *public hols.* **http://**phoenix.gov/parks/pueblo.html

Located 5 miles (8 km) east of downtown Phoenix, the Pueblo Grande Museum displays a Hohokam ruin and many artifacts, including cooking utensils and pottery. Many of these pieces come from the adjacent Archaeological Park, the site of a Hohokam settlement from the 8th to the 14th centuries. The site was originally excavated in 1887, and today has a path through the ruins. Informative signs point out the many irrigation canals once used by the Hohokam to water their crops.

Taliesin West façade, designed by Frank Lloyd Wright to blend with desert landscape

Cacti in the Desert Botanical Garden at Papago Park

Papago Park

Galvin Parkway & Van Buren St. ***Tel*** *(602) 261-8318.* **www**.phoenix.gov/parks/hikepapa.html

Papago Park is situated 6 miles (10 km) east of downtown Phoenix, and is a popular place to unwind, with a number of hiking and cycling trails, picnic areas, and fishing ponds. Many of Phoenix's top attractions are located within the rambling boundaries of Papago Park. The most famous of these is the award-winning **Desert Botanical Garden**. Covering over 145 acres (59 ha), the park displays more than 20,000 cacti and protected desert flora from around the world. The most popular part of the garden is the paved Desert Discovery Trail, which winds past half the known species of cacti in the world. Some of the rarer and more fragile specimens can be found in the nearby Cactus House and Succulent House. Of particular interest are the Sybil B. Harrington Galleries, which display examples of the remarkable varieties of cacti and succulents found around the world. The garden is prettiest in spring, when many species flower. Guided tours explain the extraordinary life cycles of the desert plants seen here. The rolling hills and lakes of **Phoenix Zoo** also occupy a large area of the Papago Park. A series of natural habitats, including the Arizona-Sonora Desert and a tropical rainforest, have been reproduced at the zoo. It is home to more than 1,300 animals from around the world; the animals' movements are controlled by banks and canals rather than fences. The Arizona Trail area of the zoo gives visitors a chance to encounter rarely seen animals that are native to Arizona's deserts and mountains. A Safari Train provides a narrated tour of the zoo.

Also in Papago Park is the **Hall of Flame Museum**, which houses an exceptional collection of fire engines and firefighting equipment, dating from 1725. The museum traces the history of organized firefighting, displaying over 130 wheeled pieces and thousands of smaller items. Arranged chronologically, the first gallery features hand- and horse-drawn fire equipment from the 18th and 19th centuries. The second gallery contains over 27 motorized fire engines from the early 20th century, while those dating from 1930 to the present are showcased in the third and fourth galleries.

Trail's End sign at Phoenix Zoo

Also part of the museum is the National Firefighting Hall of Heroes, which honors firefighters who have died in the line of duty, or been decorated for heroic service. In August 2003, the museum opened a 2,000 sq ft (186 sq m) gallery on the subject of wildland fire-fighting.

Desert Botanical Garden

1201 N Galvin Parkway. ***Tel*** *(480) 941-1225.* *8am–8pm (May–Sep: from 7am).* *major public hols.* **www**.dbg.org

Phoenix Zoo

455 N Galvin Pkwy. ***Tel*** *(602) 273-1341.* *Jan 8–May 31: 8am–5pm; Jun–Sep: 7am–2pm (to 4pm Sat & Sun); Oct 1–Nov 6: 9am–5pm; Nov 7–Jan 7: 9am–4pm.* *Dec 25.* **www**.phoenixzoo.org

Hall of Flame Museum

6101 E Van Buren St, Phoenix. ***Tel*** *(602) 275-3473.* *9am–5pm Mon–Sat; noon–4pm Sun.* *Jan 1, Thanksgiving, Dec 25.* **www**.hallofflame.org

Mystery Castle

800 E Mineral Rd. ***Tel*** *(602) 268-1581.* *Oct–May: 11am–4pm Thu–Sun.*

Mystery Castle is possibly Phoenix's most eccentric attraction. In 1927, a certain Boyce Luther Gulley came to the city hoping that the warm climate would improve his ailing health. His young daughter, Mary Lou Gulley, loved building sandcastles on the beach and, since Phoenix was so far away from the ocean, Gulley set about creating a real-life fairy-tale sandcastle for her.

He started work in 1930 and continued for 15 years, until his death in 1945. Discarded bricks, desert rock, railroad refuse, and an assortment of scrapyard junk, including old car parts, have been used to build the structure. The 18-room interior has 13 fireplaces, and can be seen on a guided tour, which explores the quirky building and its eclectic collection of antiques and furniture from around the world.

Exterior of Phoenix's unusual Mystery Castle

For hotels and restaurants in this region see pp127–30 and pp137–9

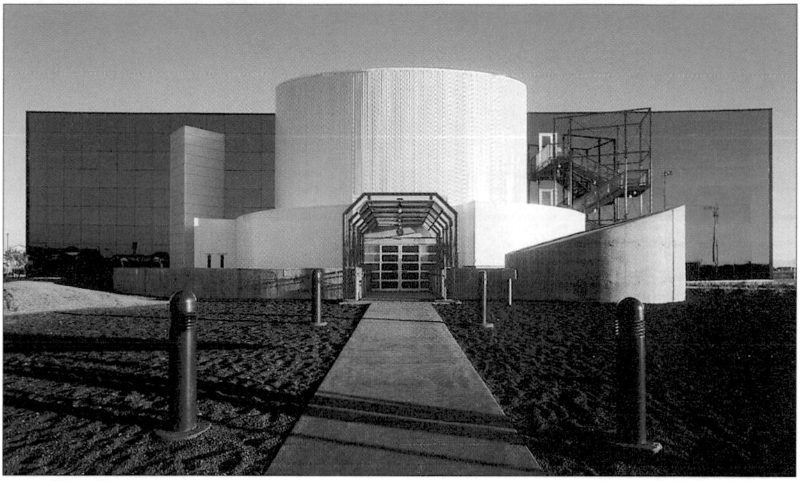
Entrance to the Challenger Space Center

Challenger Space Center

21170 N 83rd Ave, Peoria. **Tel** *(623) 322-2001.* *9am–4pm Mon–Fri; 10am–4pm Sat.* *major hols* **Public programs** *call ahead for a schedule of events.* **www**.azchallenger.org

Named in honor of the *Challenger* shuttle crew that lost their lives in the 1986 disaster, the center's mission is "to inspire, excite, and educate people of all ages about the mysteries and wonders of space, science, and the universe in which we live." Their main objective is to provide educational programs for school children. The same two-hour programs are run on Saturdays for the public, and are geared for both adults and children. Utilizing the center's multimillion dollar simulated space station and mission control center, the programs integrate teamwork, math, science, and leadership skills into exciting programs that replicate voyages to Mars or to a comet hurtling through space. There are also daily tours of the facility that include an introduction to the center's ongoing programs, and a wide variety of displays and exhibits. One of the highlights of the tour is a stroll along a floating balcony to view "A Tour of the Universe" – a breathtaking six-story tall, 27,000 sq ft (2,508 sq m) mural by official NASA space artist, Robert McCall. The mural, which depicts man's quest in space, wraps 360 degrees around the inside of the center's vast rotunda. The center also hosts star gazing and other fun, educational family programs throughout the year.

Pioneer Living History Village

3901 W Pioneer Rd. **Tel** *(623) 465-1052.* *Oct–May: 9am–5pm Wed–Sun; Jun–Sep: 8am–2pm Wed–Sun.* *major public hols and rainy days.* **www**.pioneer-arizona.com

Unlike some of Arizona's Hollywood-inspired Wild West towns, Arizona Pioneer Historical Village puts historical accuracy and education at the forefront of the experience. That doesn't stop them from staging a gunfight in the street, but at least it is a historically accurate gunfight. The village, with the help of several costumed re-enactors, re creates a frontier town from Arizona's territorial heyday circa 1860 to 1912. There are 29 buildings, 24 of which are originals moved to this site from other parts of Arizona. The remaining buildings, for instance the blacksmith's shop, are replicas of buildings that once stood in the territory – in this case a duplicate of the shop that stood in Globe in the 1870s. Also of note are the bank, sheriff's office, a ranch complex, and even an opera house that once hosted the legendary actress Lillie Langtry.

Educational tour for school children at Challenger Space Center

Apache Trail Tour ❷

The towering rocky spires and canyons of the Superstition Mountains are the setting for this loop-trail that weaves together desert beauty and Western legends. Starting at Apache Junction, the route climbs to the Tonto National Monument and the Lost Dutchman State Park. The road turns to gravel as it rises past three cool, man-made lakes, and continues to Globe. Descending, the road offers stunning views as it winds through red rock canyons to the town of Superior, and the lovely gardens and shady trails of Boyce Thompson Arboretum.

TIPS FOR DRIVERS

Tour length: *120 miles (193 km).*
Tour route: *Drive this route clockwise starting north on Route 88, from Lost Dutchman State Park to Roosevelt Dam.*
When to go: *Spring and fall are the most pleasant. Summer can be very hot, and winter can be cold with occasional snow.*

Tonto National Monument ③
These cliff dwellings were occupied by the Salado Indians from the 13th to the 15th centuries. The museum here contains fine examples of their pottery and textiles.

Lost Dutchman State Park ②
Named after the mystery mine, the park offers hiking trails through a high Sonoran Desert landscape, and great views of the surrounding mountains.

LOST DUTCHMAN MINE MYSTERY

In the 1870s, Prussian immigrant Jacob Waltz left his home in Phoenix, returning with high-grade gold ore. Drinking and spending lavishly, he often spoke of a rich mine in the Superstition Mountains. Years later, on his deathbed, he purportedly told his caregiver the location of the mine. She and countless others have since tried to find the "Lost Dutchman Mine" without success. It remains one of the most captivating mysteries of the Wild West.

Weaver's Needle peak, fabled location of the mystery mine

Superstition Mountains ①
Rising over 6,000 ft (1,829 m), this wild and rocky mountain range is 40 miles (64 km) from Phoenix. Prospectors have long sought wealth here.

Roosevelt Dam ④
Completed in 1911, it supplies water to Phoenix. The lake here is a favorite with boaters and fishermen.

Superior ⑤
Settled in 1870, the town boasts the world's smallest museum, which houses the largest Apache Tear gemstone on earth

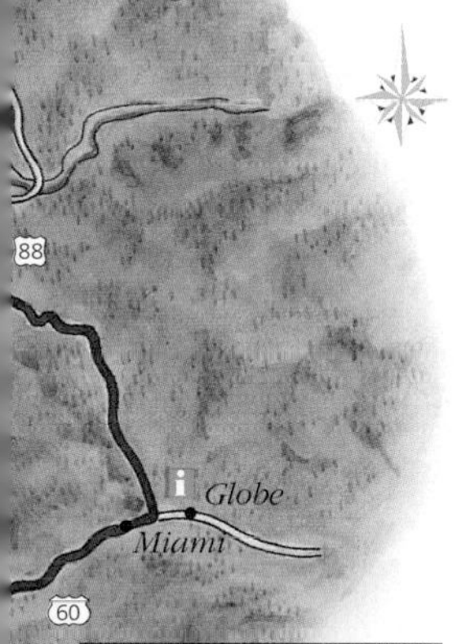

Boyce Thompson Arboretum ⑥
Dedicated to propagating desert species, the arboretum is very beautiful when the spring flowers bloom.

KEY

- Tour route
- Other roads
- Visitor information

Salt River Canyon ❸

Road map C4. *Tonto Basin Ranger District, Hwy 188, near Roosevelt, (928) 467-3200.*

The Apaches used this deep, wild canyon as a refuge from US troops in the 1800s. Today, the Salt River marks the border between the San Carlos Apache Reservation and the White Mountain Apache Reservation. The 9-mile (15-km) rim-to-rim drive on Highway 60 is truly awe-inspiring as the road drops almost 2,000 ft (610 m) in a series of hairpin turns to cross the river on a narrow bridge. Occasionally a driver forgets to pay attention, or loses control on the descent, and the resulting twisted wreckage sometimes stays for weeks at the bottom of the gorge as a visual warning to others. Numerous pullouts exist along the road for those who want to stop and admire the view. At the bottom, near the bridge, there is a parking area with interpretive signage. Several companies *(see p150)* offer single and multi-day whitewater rafting tours, which provide tremendous views of the 32,000 acre (12,950 ha) wilderness that surrounds the river.

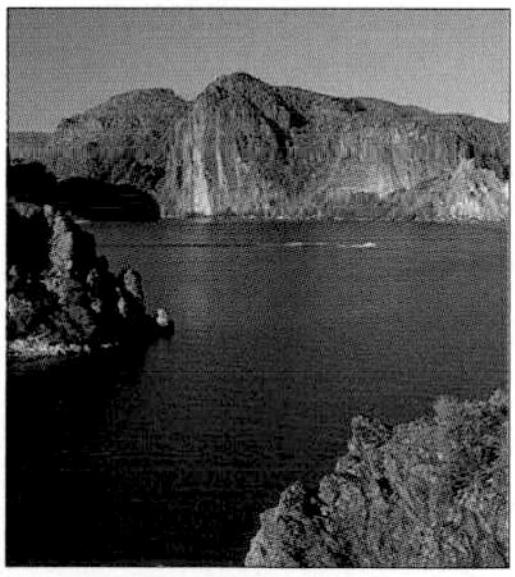

The beautiful and dramatic wilderness of Salt River Canyon

Globe ❹

Road map C4. *6,000.* *Globe Chamber of Commerce, 1360 N Broad St, (928) 425 4495.* **www**.globemiamichamber.com

The mining town of Globe lies about 100 miles (160 km) east of Phoenix in the wooded Dripping Spring and Pinal Mountains. In 1875, prospectors struck silver here, in what was then part of an Apache reservation. The silver-bearing hills were annexed from the reservation, and Globe was founded as a mining town.

It was named for a massive nugget of silver, shaped like a globe, which was unearthed in the hills nearby. The silver was quickly exhausted, but copper mining thrived until 1931, and continues today. Globe has an attractive historic district, and its history is outlined in the **Gila County Historical Museum**. On the south side of town are the Besh-Ba-Gowah Ruins, home of the Salado people in the 13th and 14th centuries.

Gila County Historical Museum
1330 N Broad St. ***Tel*** *(928) 425-7385.* *10am–4pm Mon–Fri; 11am–3pm Sat; Sun by appointment.* *Jan 1, Dec 25.*

Casa Grande Ruins National Monument ❺

Road map C4. ***Tel*** *(520) 723-3172.* *9am–5pm.* *Dec 25.* **www**.nps.gov/cagr

From around 200 BC until the middle of the 15th century, the Hohokam people farmed the Gila River Valley to the southeast of Phoenix. Among the few Hohokam sites that remain, the fortresslike structure that makes up the Casa Grande National Monument is one of the most distinctive. Built in the early decades of the 14th century, and named the "Big House" by a passing Jesuit missionary in 1694, this sturdy four-story structure has walls up to 4-ft (1.2-m) thick. The interior is out of bounds, but visitors can stroll around the exterior. The visitor center has a small museum with some interesting exhibits on Hohokam history and culture. Casa Grande is located 15 miles (24 km) east of Interstate Highway 10 (I-10) on the outskirts of Coolidge. It should not be confused with the town of Casa Grande, found to the west of I-10.

Weathered walls at Casa Grande Ruins National Monument, dating to the early 14th century ▷

Tucson 6

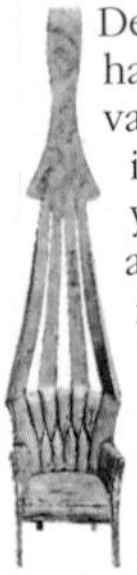
Exhibit at Arizona University

Despite being Arizona's second-largest city, Tucson has a friendly, welcoming atmosphere and a variety of interesting attractions to entertain the increasing number of visitors it receives each year. The city is located on the northern boundary of the Sonoran Desert in Southern Arizona, in a basin surrounded by five mountain ranges. When the Spanish colonizers arrived in the early 18th century they were determined to seize land from the local Tohono O'odham and Pima Native tribes, who put up strong resistance. This led the Spanish to move their regional fortress, or presidio, from Tubac to Tucson in the 1770s. The city was officially founded by Irish explorer Hugh O'Connor in 1775. Tucson's pride in its history is reflected in the careful preservation of 19th-century downtown buildings in the Barrio Historic District.

Contemporary glass skyscrapers in downtown Tuscon

Exploring Tucson

Tucson's major art galleries and museums are clustered around two central areas: the University of Arizona (UA) campus, lying between Speedway Blvd, E Sixth Street, Park, and Campbell Avenues, and the downtown area, which includes the Barrio and El Presidio historic districts. The latter contains many of the city's oldest buildings, and is best explored on foot, as is the Barrio Historic District, south of Cushing Street.

Tucson Museum of Art & Historic Block

140 N Main Ave. ***Tel*** *(520) 624-2333.* *10am–4pm Tue–Sat; noon–4pm Sun.* *public hols.* *(free on 1st Sun of month).* **www**.tucsonarts.com

The Tucson Museum of Art opened in 1975 and is located on the Historic Block, which also contains five of El Presidio's oldest dwellings – most of which are at least a 100 years old. These historic buildings form part of the art museum and house different parts of its extensive collection. The museum's sculpture gardens and courtyards also form part of the Historic Block complex.

The art museum itself displays contemporary and 20th-century European and American works. In the adobe Stevens House (1866), the museum has its collection of pre-Columbian tribal artifacts, some of which are 2,000 years old. There is the Spanish Colonial collection with some stunning pieces of religious art. The 1850s **Casa Cordova** houses *El Nacimiento*, a Nativity scene with more than 300 earthenware figurines, on display from December to March. The **J. Knox Corbett House**, built in 1907, has Arts and Crafts Movement pieces such as a Morris chair.

Both guided and self-guided walking tours of this district are available from the Tucson Museum of Art.

Pima County Courthouse

115 N Church Ave.

The courthouse's pretty tiled dome is a downtown landmark. It was built in 1927, replacing its predecessor, a one-story adobe building dating from 1869. The position of the original Presidio wall is marked out in the courtyard, and a section of the wall, 3-ft (1-m) thick and 12-ft (4-m) high, can still be seen inside the building.

El Presidio Historic District

The El Presidio Historic District occupies the area where the original Spanish Presidio, San Agustin del Tucson, was built in 1775. More than 70 of the houses here were constructed during the Territorial period, before Arizona became a state in 1912. Today, these historic buildings are largely occupied by shops, restaurants, and offices. However, archaeological excavations in the area have found artifacts from much earlier residents, the Hohokam Indians.

St. Augustine Cathedral

192 S Stone Ave. ***Tel*** *(520) 623-6351.* *Services only; call for times.* **www**.staugustinecathedral.com

Stained-glass window in the cathedral

St. Augustine Cathedral was begun in 1896 and modeled after the Spanish Colonial style of the Cathedral of Querétaro in central Mexico. This gleaming white building features an imposing sandstone façade with intricate carvings of the yucca, the saguaro, and the horned toad – three symbols of the Sonoran Desert – while a bronze statue of St. Augustine, the city's patron saint, stands above the main door.

One of many 19th-century adobe houses in the Barrio Historic District

VISITORS' CHECKLIST

Road map C5. *750,000.* *Tucson International, 10 miles (16 km) south of downtown.* *Amtrak Station, 400 E Toole Ave.* *Greyhound Lines, 471 W Congress.* *Convention & Visitors Bureau, 110 S Church Ave, (520) 624-1817, (800) 638-8350.* *9am– 5pm daily (to 4pm Sat, Sun).* *La Fiesta de los Vaqueros (late Feb).* **www**.visittucson.org

Barrio Historic District

This area was Tucson's business district in the late 19th century. Today, its streets are quiet and lined with original adobe houses painted in bright colors. On nearby Main Street is the "wishing shrine" of **El Tiradito**, which marks the spot where a young man was killed as a result of a lovers' triangle. Local people lit candles here for his soul, and still believe that if their candles burn for a whole night, their wishes will come true.

University of Arizona

Visitors' Center, 811 N Euclid Ave. ***Tel*** *(520) 621-5130.* *9am–5pm Mon–Fri.* *UA holidays.* **www**. arizona.edu/home/visiting.php

Several museums are located on or near the UA campus, about a mile (1.6 km) east of downtown. The **Arizona Historical Society Museum** traces Arizona's history from the arrival of the Spanish in 1539 to modern times. The **University of Arizona Museum of Art** focuses on European and American fine art from the Renaissance to the 20th century. Opposite the museum is the **Center for Creative Photography**, which contains the work of more than 60 of the 20th century's greatest American photographers. Visitors can also view the archives. The **Flandrau Science Center** features a range of child-friendly interactive exhibits.

One of the most renowned collections of artifacts, covering 2,000 years of Native history, is displayed by the **Arizona State Museum**, which was founded in 1893.

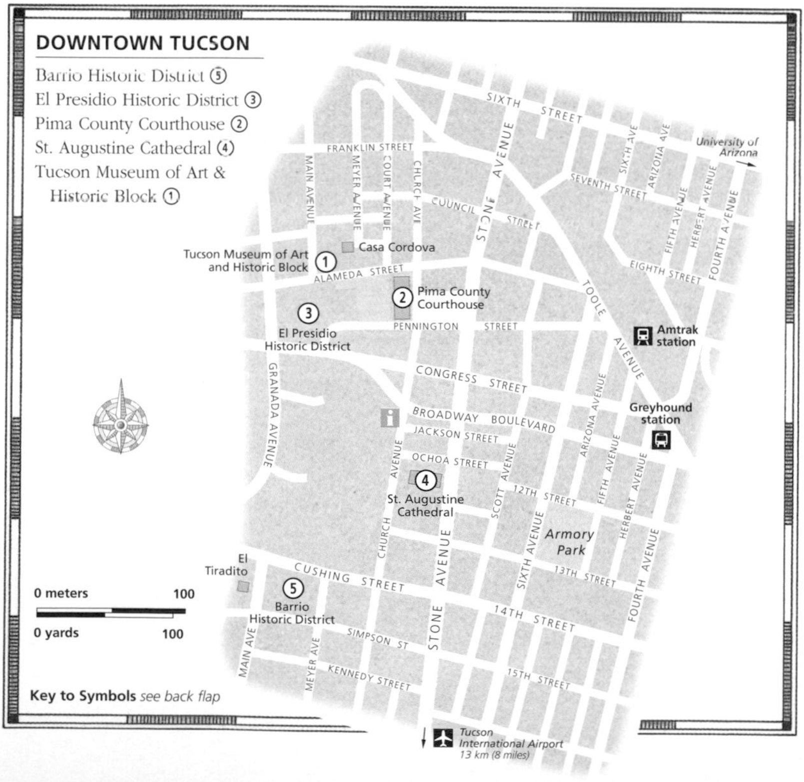

Exploring Around Tucson

Beyond downtown, Metropolitan Tucson extends north to the Santa Catalina Mountains, the foothills of which are the start of a scenic drive to the top of Mount Lemmon. To the west are the Tucson Mountains, which frame Saguaro National Park West. This park has a sister park to the east of the city. To the south lies the beautiful mission church of San Xavier del Bac, which stands out from the flat, desert landscape of the Tohono O'odham Indian Reservation.

SIGHTS AT A GLANCE

Arizona-Sonora Desert Museum ②
Mount Lemmon ⑦
Old Tucson Studios ③
Pima Air & Space Museum ⑤
Sabino Canyon Tours ⑥
Saguaro National Park (East & West) ①
San Xavier del Bac Mission *See pp92–3* ④

KEY

- Downtown Tucson
- Greater Tucson
- International airport
- Interstate
- Major highway
- Highway
- Railroad

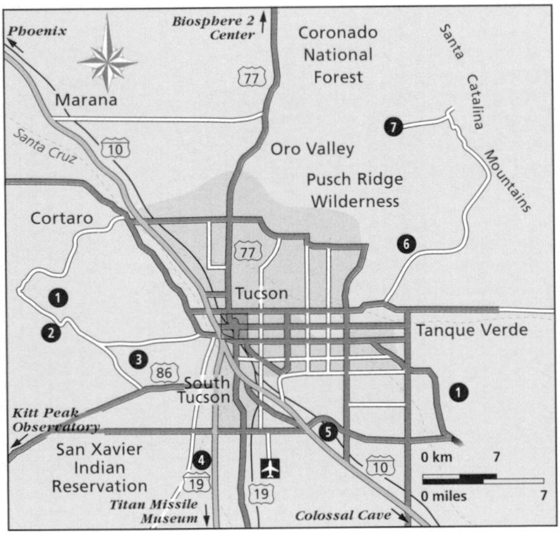

Vistas of tall saguaro cacti in Saguaro National Park

Arizona-Sonora Desert Museum

2021 N Kinney Rd. ***Tel*** *(520) 883-2702.* *Mar–May: 7:30am–5pm; Jun–Aug: 7:30am–3pm Mon–Fri, 7:30am–10pm Sat, 7:30am–5pm Sun; Sep: 7:30am–5pm; Oct–Feb: 8:30am–5pm.*
www.desertmuseum.org

This museum covers more than 21 acres (8.5 ha), and includes a botanical garden, zoo, and natural history museum, where displays describe the history, geology, and flora and fauna of the region. Outside, a walkway passes more than 1,200 varieties of plants, which provide the setting for a range of creatures, including hummingbirds, wildcats, and Mexican wolves.

One of many flowering cacti at the Arizona-Sonora Desert Museum

Saguaro National Park

3693 S Old Spanish Trail. ***Tel*** *(520) 733-5153.* *9am–5pm daily.* *Dec 25.* **www**.nps.gov/sagu

The saguaro (pronounced sa-wah-ro) cactus is unique to the Sonoran Desert. The largest cactus species in the US, it has a life span of up to 200 years. Those specimens that survive into old age may reach heights of up to 50 ft (16 m) and weigh more than 8 tons (7 kg).

Set up in 1994, the park comprises two tracts of land on the eastern and western flanks of Tucson, that together cover more than 91,000 acres (36,800 ha). The 6-mile (10-km) Bajada Loop Drive runs deep into the park on a gravel road, past hiking trails and picnic areas. One of these trails leads to Hohokam petroglyphs carved into volcanic rock. The eastern park has the oldest saguaros, which can be seen along the 8-mile (13-km) Cactus Forest Drive. There are also more than 100 miles (160 km) of hiking trails here. The park offers guided walks during the winter season.

Old Tucson Studios

201 S Kinney Rd. ***Tel*** *(520) 883-0100.* *mid-Feb–mid-Apr: 10am–6pm; mid-Apr–mid-Feb: 10am–4pm.* **www**.oldtucson.com

Modeled on a Western town of the 1860s, the studio was built as a set for a Western movie in 1939. Since then, Old Tucson Studios has formed the backdrop for some of Hollywood's most famous Westerns, such as *Gunfight at the OK Corral* (1957) and *Rio Bravo* (1958).

The popular 1970s TV series *Little House on the Prairie* was also filmed here. More recently, movies such as *The Three Amigos* (1986) and *Tombstone* (1993) were partly shot here.

Main Street's 1860s frontier atmosphere provides an authentic setting for performers in period costume, who entertain visitors with stunt shows, mock gunfights, and stagecoach rides. Visitors can also take part in such activities as panning for gold.

BIRDWATCHING IN THE CANYONS OF SOUTHERN ARIZONA

The landscape of Southern Arizona may seem dry, but this high desert environment gets about 11 in (280 mm) of rain annually. This enables vegetation to flourish which, in turn, attracts a variety of birds. In fact, the area is one of the top five birdwatching locations in the US. Just off I-19, near Green Valley, Madera Canyon plays host to some 400 bird species. Along with the more common varieties of hummingbirds, flycatchers, and warblers, many rare species, such as the brown-crested flycatcher and the black-and-white warbler, are often sighted here. Farther afield, Ramsey Canyon in the Huachuca Mountains is the country's hummingbird capital with 14 varieties of these tiny, delicate creatures.

Broad-billed hummingbird

Gunfight staged outside the mission at Old Tucson Studios

San Xavier del Bac Mission

See pp92–3.

Titan Missile Museum

1580 W Duval Mine Rd, Sahuarita. ***Tel*** *(520) 625-7736.* *8:45am–5pm.* *Thanksgiving, Dec 25.* *9am–4pm.* **www**.pimaair.org

This remote site, 25 miles (40 km) south of Tucson, is a great place to get in touch with the potential horror of the Cold War years. Built in 1963, this is one of 18 Titan II silos constructed around the Tucson area (out of 54 in the United States). This station and its single, multiple-warhead nuclear missile – the largest ever built in the US – stood ready to launch within minutes for over 20 years. Today, it is one of only two remaining Titan II missiles and launch sites left, as all the others were decommissioned by 1987. The museum tour includes a walk through the buildings and a peek down into the silo, followed by a visit to the below-ground missile launch facility and a look at the missile from within the silo.

Pima Air & Space Museum

6000 E Valencia Rd. ***Tel*** *(520) 574-0462.* *9am–5pm.* *Thanksgiving, Dec 25.* *call for times.* **www**.pimaair.org

Located nine miles (14 km) southeast of downtown Tucson, this museum contains one of the largest collections of aircraft in the world. Visitors are met with the astonishing sight of more than 275 vintage aircraft arranged in ranks across the desert.

Three presidential aircrafts are displayed – Eisenhower's, Kennedy's, and Johnson's – as well as a replica of the Wright brothers' famous 1903 aircraft. The adjacent Davis-Monthan Air Force Base displays more than 2,000 planes, including B-29s and supersonic bombers.

John Fitzgerald Kennedy's presidential plane at the Pima Air & Space Museum

Colossal Cave

Colossal Cave Mountain Park, PO Box 70, 16721 E Old Spanish Trail, Vail. ***Tel*** *(520) 647-7275.* *mid-Mar–mid-Sep: 8am–5pm daily; mid-Sep–mid-Mar: 9am–5pm daily.* **www**.colossalcave.com

The first European to discover Colossal Cave was Solomon Lick in 1879, but he was a relative latecomer. The cave was used by the Solobai people as early as 1450, and later by the Hohokam. Although opened for tours in 1923, it has never been fully explored – it took over two years to map the first two miles of the cave's estimated 39 miles (63 km) length.

Visitors today take a 50-minute guided tour that descends six stories into spaces draped in stalactites and stalagmites. The tour is only half-a-mile in length, but requires descending and climbing 363 stairs. There are longer, more energetic tours available on Saturdays.

Colossal is a "dry cave" – it is no longer being shaped by water, and its ample air supply keeps the inside temperature at a comfortable 70°F (21°C). The cave is on the grounds of La Posta Quemada (Burned Station) Ranch, named for a Southern Pacific stagecoach station, which was destroyed by a fire in 1875.

Tucson: San Xavier del Bac Mission

San Xavier del Bac is the oldest and best-preserved mission church in the Southwest. An imposing landmark as it rises out of the stark, flat landscape of the surrounding Tohono O'odham reservation, its white walls dazzle in the desert sun. A mission was first established here by the Jesuit priest Father Eusebio Kino in 1700 *(see p39)*. The complex seen today was completed in 1797 by Franciscan missionaries.

Built of adobe brick, the mission is considered to be the finest example of Spanish Colonial architecture in the US *(see p22)*. The church also incorporates other styles, including several Baroque flourishes. In the 1990s its interior was extensively renovated, and five *retablos* (altarpieces) have been restored to their original glory.

The Hill of the Cross, to the east of the mission, offering fine views

The bell tower's elegant, white dome reflects the Moorish styles that are incorporated into San Xavier's Spanish Colonial architecture.

★ Façade of the Church
The ornate Baroque façade is decorated with the carved figures of saints (although some are much eroded) including a headless St. Cecilia and an unidentifiable St. Francis, now a simple sand cone.

The mortuary chapel contains a statue of the Virgin Mary, surrounded by candles.

Stonework Detail
Over recent years the identity of the carved statues to the left of the entrance has changed. Long thought to be St. Catherine of Siena and St. Barbara, they have now been identified as St. Agatha of Catania and St. Agnes of Rome.

Painted Ceiling
On entering the church, visitors are struck by the dome's ceiling with its glorious paintings of religious figures. Vivid pigments of vermilion and blue were used to contrast with the stark white stone background.

STAR SIGHTS

- ★ Façade of the Church
- ★ Main Altar

★ Main Altar
The spectacular gold and red retablo mayor *is decorated in Mexican Baroque style with elaborate columns. More than 50 statues were carved in Mexico, then brought to San Xavier where artists gilded and painted them with brightly colored glazes.*

VISITORS' CHECKLIST

Road map C5. 1950 W San Xavier Rd, 10 miles (16 km) south of Tucson on I-19. ***Tel*** *(520) 294-2624.* *8am–5pm.* *booths selling Native American fry bread.* **www**.sanxaviermission.org

Altar Dome
The dome and high transepts are filled with painted wooden statuary and covered with murals depicting scenes from the Gospels.

The patio is closed to the public but can be seen from the museum.

The museum includes a sheepskin psalter and photographs of other historic missions on the Tohono O'odham reservation.

The shop entrance

Chapel of Our Lady
This statue is one of the church's three sculptures of Mary. Here she is shown as La Dolorosa or Sorrowing Mother.

Sabino Canyon Tours

5900 N Sabino Canyon Rd. ***Tel** (520) 749-2861. 8:30am–4:30pm.*
***Tram Tours:** Jul–mid-Dec: 9am–4pm daily (to 4:30pm Sat & Sun); mid-Dec–Jun: 9am–4:30pm daily.*
www.sabinocanyon.com

Sabino Creek began carving its way through Mount Lemmon, 13 miles (21 km) northeast of Tucson, five million years ago. The result was the lovely Sabino Canyon, with its towering rock walls and sparkling streams lined with cottonwood trees. Today, motorized trams take visitors on a 45-minute narrated trip into the canyon. Tourists can get off at one of several stops to hike on trails that range from easy to moderately difficult. Evening tram tours are also available at various times of the year.

Mount Lemmon

(520) 749-8700.

The highest peak in the Santa Catalina Mountains, standing at 9,157 ft (2,790 m), Mount Lemmon is located in the Coronado National Forest. During summer, thousands of visitors drive up on the weekends for rock climbing, hiking, camping, and fishing. A one-hour drive, beginning in the Tucson city limits and connecting to the Mount Lemmon Highway, takes visitors to the summit. The highway affords splendid vistas of the Tucson valley. There are around 150 miles (240 km) of hiking trails here, while a side road leads to the quaint resort village of Summerhaven, with shops and restaurants. At the top, the Ski Valley lift operates for a small fee most of the year, offering magnificent views.

Space Age buildings of the Biosphere 2, north of Tucson

Biosphere 2

5 miles (8 km) NE of jct of Hwys 77 & 79. ***Tel** (520) 838-6200. 9am–4pm. Thanksgiving, Dec 25.*
www.b2science.org

Biosphere 2 is a unique research facility that was set up in 1991. Eight people were sealed within a futuristic structure of glass and white steel furnished with five of the Earth's habitats: rainforest, desert, savanna, marsh, and an ocean with a living coral reef. Over a period of two years, the effect of the people on the environment as well as the effect on them were studied.

Today, there are no people living in the Biosphere, which is being used to explore and address issues of global environmental change. Visitors can take a two-hour guided tour of the facility. There are also two tours of the Biosphere, one of which incurs an additional charge.

Radio telescope at Kitt Peak

Kitt Peak Observatory

Rte 86 to 386. ***Tel** (520) 318-8726. 9am–3:45pm. Jan 1, Thanksgiving, Dec 25. donation requested. (fee) 10am, 11:30am, 1:30pm.* **www**.noao.edu/kpno/

Located 56 miles (90 km) southwest of Tucson, Kitt Peak boasts one of the largest and most diverse collections of astronomical observatories on the planet. It was established as a scientific center for the study of astronomy in 1952. Visitors can take a guided tour of the facility and get a close-up look at (but not through) several of the largest and most famous telescopes.

To actually view the cosmos, you have to sign up and pay (up to a month in advance) for nightly programs that allow you to scan the heavens through telescopes at the visitors' observatory. The guided program (Sep–mid-Jul) includes a sack dinner. Warm clothing is recommended.

Observatories at Kitt Peak in Southern Arizona

Yuma 7

Road map A4. *65,000.* *Amtrak, 2815 Gila St.* *Greyhound, 170 E 17th Place.* *Yuma Convention & Visitors' Bureau, 139 South 4th Ave, (800) 293-0071.* *May–Oct: 9am–5pm Mon–Fri, 9am–2pm Sat; Nov–Apr: 9am–5pm Mon–Fri, 9am–4pm Sat, noon–4pm Sun.* **www**.visityuma.com

Boats and watersports in the picturesque setting of Lake Yuma

Yuma occupies a strategic position at the confluence of the Colorado and Gila Rivers in Arizona's far southwestern corner. Though noted by Spanish explorers in the 16th century, it was not until the 1850s that the town rose to prominence, when the river crossing became the gateway to California for thousands of gold seekers. Later, Yuma was a supply depot as riverboats steamed up and down the Colorado to link with the Sea of Cortez. In the early 20th century, Yuma was an important stop on the first ocean-to-ocean transcontinental road that ended in San Diego. Sadly, however, for much of the 20th century, Yuma was a dusty, bypassed border town.

Yuma's hot, sunny winter climate has made it a magnet for "snowbirds" escaping the northern cold. Their swelling numbers have brought about a renaissance, as the town adds attractions, hotels, restaurants, and services.

The town's first major construction project was Yuma Territorial Prison in 1876. Arizonans were more than delighted to finally have a place to put away the growing numbers of train robbers, polygamists, murderers, and outlaws. Criminals, on the other hand, were less than thrilled, as Yuma Prison had a notorious reputation for stifling heat and brutal conditions. The prison's most famous inmate was John Swilling, sometimes called the "Father of Phoenix," who made big money selling real estate. He later tried robbing a stagecoach after falling on hard times. Visitors to the **Yuma Territorial Prison State Historic Park** can see the grounds and, in winter, take a guided tour to hear stories of the prison's famous and infamous inhabitants, guards, riots, and escapes.

Yuma's history as a crossroads is highlighted at the **Yuma Crossing State Historic Park**. It features several buildings reconstructed to their 1870s appearance, including a telegraph office and the Commanding Officer's quarters, which dates back to 1855. As the town became an important junction for supplies, the military took an interest, and built Fort Yuma in 1851, now owned by the Quechan Indians. The **Quechan Indian Museum**, housed in an 1855 adobe building, has displays on the arrival of the Spanish missionaries, the 1781 Quechan uprising, and the history of Fort Yuma.

Yuma Territorial Prison State Historic Park
1 Prison Hill Rd. ***Tel*** *(928) 783-4771.* *8am–5pm.* **www**.azstateparks.com/parks/yute

Yuma Crossing State Historic Park
201 North 4th Ave. ***Tel*** *(928) 329-0471.* *9am–5pm.* **www**.azstateparks.com/parks/yuqu

Quechan Indian Museum
Across the river from Yuma, 350 Picacho Rd, Winterhaven, CA 92283. ***Tel*** *(760) 572 0661.* *8am–noon, 1–5pm.* *major hols.*

Cell blocks at the historic, territorial prison in Yuma

Rare cacti at the Organ Pipe Cactus National Monument

Organ Pipe Cactus National Monument 8

Road map B5. ***Tel*** *(520) 387-6849.*
visitor center 8am–5pm.
major holidays.
www.nps.gov/orpi

The organ pipe is a Sonoran Desert species of cactus, which is a cousin to the saguaro *(see p90)* but with multiple arms branching up from the base, as its name suggests. The organ pipe is rare in the United States, growing almost exclusively in this large and remote area of land along the Mexican border in southwest Arizona. Many other plant and animal species flourish in this unspoiled desert wilderness, although a lot of animals, such as snakes, jackrabbits, and kangaroo rats, emerge only in the cool of the night. Other cacti such as the saguaro, the Engelmann prickly pear, and the teddy-bear cholla are best seen in the early summertime when they give their glorious displays of floral color.

Orange flowers of the barrel cactus

There are two scenic drives through the park: the 21-mile (34-km) **Ajo Mountain Drive** and the shorter 5-mile (8-km) **Puerto Blanco Drive**. The Ajo Mountain Drive takes two hours and winds through startling desert landscapes in the foothills of the mountains. The recently repaved Puerto Blanco Drive leads to a half-hour trail into Red Tanks Tinaja and the new picnic area near Pinkley Peak. A variety of hiking trails in the park range in difficulty from paved, wheelchair-accessible paths to wilderness walks.

A visitor center offers exhibits on the park's flora and fauna, as well as maps and camping permits, and there are guided walks in winter. Be aware that the park is a good two-and-a-half- to three-hour drive from Tucson one way. If you want to explore this environment in any detail, plan to camp overnight. Ajo, 34 miles (55 km) to the north, has motels and services.

Tubac 9

Road map C5. *150.*
Tubac Chamber of Commerce, (520) 398-2704. **www**.tubacaz.com

The Royal Presidio (fortress) of San Ignacio de Tubac was built in 1752 to protect the local Spanish-owned ranches and mines, as well as the nearby missions of Tumacacori and San Xavier, from attacks by local Pima Indians. Tubac was also the first stopover on the famous overland expedition to colonize the San Francisco Bay area in 1776. The trek was led by the fort's captain, Juan Bautista de Anza *(see p39)*. Following his return, the garrison moved north to Tucson, and for the next 100 years, Tubac declined. Today, the town is one of Arizona's largest art communities, with attractive shops, galleries, and restaurants lining the streets around the plaza.

Tubac's historical remains are displayed at the **Tubac Presidio State Historic Park**, which encompasses the foundations of the original presidio in an underground display, as well as several historic buildings, including the delightful Old Tubac Schoolhouse built in 1885. The Presidio Museum, which is also situated here, contains American Indian and Spanish artifacts covering over 100 years of Tubac's history. Exhibits include beautifully painted altarpieces and colonial furniture.

Mission church at Tumacacori National Historical Park near Tubac

Block of bargain stores at Nogales, a border town

Environs

Just 3 miles (5 km) south of town lies **Tumacacori National Historical Park**, with its beautiful ruined mission. The present church was built in around 1800 upon the ruins of the original 1691 mission established by Jesuit priest Father Eusebio Kino *(see p39)*. The mission was abandoned in 1848, and today its weatherbeaten ocher façade, together with its brick columns, arched entry, and carved wooden door, is an evocative reminder of former times. The cavernous interior is wonderfully atmospheric, with patches of exposed adobe brick and faded murals on the sanctuary walls. A small museum provides an excellent background on the mission builders and Pima Indians. Weekend craft demonstrations, including tortilla-making, basketry, and Mexican pottery, are held September through June. During the first weekend in December, La Fiesta de Tumacacori *(see p33)*, which celebrates the cultural heritage of the upper Santa Cruz Valley, is held on the mission grounds.

Tubac Presidio State Historic Park

Burruel St & Presidio Dr. ***Tel*** *(520) 398-2252.* *8am–5pm.* *Dec 25.*

Tumacacori National Historical Park

Tel *(520) 398-2341.* *9am–5pm.* *Thanksgiving, Dec 25.* **www**.nps.gov/tuma

Nogales ⑩

Road map C5. *19,500.* *Nogales Chamber of Commerce, 123 W Kino Park, (520) 287-3685.* **www**.thenogaleschamber.com

Mexican pottery found in Nogales

Nogales is really two towns straddling the US border with Mexico. This is a busy port of entry, handling huge amounts of freight, including 75 percent of all winter fruit and vegetables sold in North America. It attracts many visitors in search of bargains on both sides of the border. Decorative blankets, crafts, and furniture are good value.

There is a profound contrast between the US side and the ramshackle houses across the border, and visitors should be aware that the Mexican Nogales can be crowded with continuous hustle from street vendors eager for business. Still, it is a popular day-trip, and there are several good restaurants here. Visitors are advised to leave their cars on the US side, where attendants mind the parking lots, and to walk across the border. Those who drive across the border should check that their car insurance is valid in Mexico. Visas are required only for those traveling farther south than the town and for stays of more than 72 hours. US and Canadian citizens should carry a passport for identification. US dollars are accepted everywhere.

Bisbee ⑪

Road map C5. *6,500.* *Bisbee Chamber of Commerce, 1 Main St, (520) 432-5421.* **www**.bisbeearizona.com

This is one of the most atmospheric mining towns in the Southwest. The discovery of copper here in the 1880s sparked a mining rush, and by the turn of the century Bisbee was the largest city between St. Louis and San Francisco. Victorian buildings such as the landmark Copper Queen Hotel still dominate the historic town center, while attractive clusters of houses cling to the sides of the surrounding mountains.

Today, visitors can tour the mines that once flourished here, such as the deep underground Queen Mine or, a short drive south of town, the Lavender Open Pit Mine. Exhibits at the Bisbee Mining and Historical Museum illustrate the realities of mining and frontier life here.

The Victorian mining town of Bisbee

Tombstone ⓬

Road map C5. 6,500. *Chamber of Commerce, 1095 4th St, (888) 457-3929. Visitor's Center: 395 E Allen St, (520) 457-3929.* **www**.tombstonechamber.com

The town of Tombstone is a living legend, forever known as the site of the 1881 gunfight at the OK Corral between the Earp brothers and the Clanton gang *(see p27)*. The town's historic streets and buildings form one of the most popular attractions in the Southwest.

Tombstone was founded by Ed Schieffelin, who went prospecting on Apache land in 1877 despite a warning that "all you'll find out there is your tombstone." He found a mountain of silver instead, and his sardonically named shanty town boomed with the ensuing silver rush. One of the wildest towns in the Wild West, Tombstone was soon full of prospectors, gamblers, cowboys, and lawmen. In its heyday, the town was larger than San Francisco. More than $37 million worth of silver was extracted from the mines between 1880 and 1887, when miners struck an aquifer and flooded the mine shafts.

In 1962 "the town too tough to die" became a National Historic Landmark, and, with much of its historic downtown immaculately preserved, it attracts many visitors, all eager to sample the unique atmosphere. Allen Street, with its wooden boardwalks, shops, and restaurants, is the town's main thoroughfare. The **OK Corral** is preserved as a museum, and re-enactments of the infamous gunfight between the Earp brothers, Doc Holliday and the Clanton gang are staged daily at 2pm.

Re-enactment of the gunfight at the OK Corral, Tombstone

Tombstone Courthouse on Toughnut Street was the seat of justice for the county from 1882 to 1929, and is now a State Historic Site. This imposing building contains a museum featuring the restored courtroom, and many historical exhibits and artifacts, including photographs of some of the town's famous characters. Toughnut Street used to be known as "Rotten Row" as it was once lined with miners' tents, bordellos, and more than 100 bars.

Tombstone Courthouse in the town center, now a museum

Among other buildings worth looking for in the downtown area is the **Rose Tree Inn Museum**, home of what is reputedly the world's largest rosebush. There is also the **Bird Cage Theater**, once a bawdy dance hall and bordello, and so-named for the covered "crib" compartments, or cages, hanging from the ceiling, from which ladies of the night plied their trade. Nearby is the once rowdy Crystal Palace Saloon, which is still a bar.

Just north of town, the well-known **Boothill Cemetery** is full of the graves of those who perished in Tombstone, peacefully or otherwise. This evocative place is not without the occasional spot of humor. Look for the marker lamenting the death of George Johnson, hanged by mistake in 1882, which reads: "He was right, we was wrong, but we strung him up, and now he's gone."

OK Corral
Allen St. ***Tel*** *(520) 457-3456.*
9am–5pm. *Dec 25.*
www.ok-corral.com

Tombstone Courthouse
223 E Toughnut St. ***Tel*** *(520) 457-3311.* *8am–5pm.* *Dec 25.*
www.azstateparks.com

Boardwalk in Tombstone

Kartchner Caverns State Park ⑬

Road map C5. **Tel** (520) 586-4100 (info), (520) 586-2283 (reservations). ☐ 7am–6pm (cave tours 8:30am–4:30pm by reservation). ● Dec 25. ▣ ♿ ◪ obligatory. ⛺ **www.** azstateparks.com/parks/kaca

The Kartchner Caverns are one of Arizona's great natural wonders. Located in the Whetstone Mountains, the caves were discovered in 1974 when two cavers crawled through a sinkhole in a hillside that led them into 7 acres (3 ha) of caverns filled with colorful formations. Out of concern to protect the caves, they kept their discovery a secret for 14 years as they explored this wonderland of speleotherms, or cave formations, made of layers of calcite deposited by dripping or flowing water over millions of years. In 1988 the land was purchased by the state, but it took 11 years to complete the development that would allow public access while conserving the special conditions that enable these caves to continue growing.

Before entering the caves, visitors are introduced to the geology of the formations at the Discovery Center. Once inside, visitors must not touch the features, as skin oils stop their growth. Along with huge stalactites and stalagmites, there is an abundance of other types of formation such as the aptly named 21-ft (132-m) high soda straw, and the turnip shields.

Orange and white column formations at Kartchner Caverns

Amerind Foundation ⑭

Tel (520) 586-3666. ☐ 10am–4pm Tue–Sun. ● public hols. ▣ **www**.amerind.org

The Amerind Foundation is one of the most important private archaeological and ethnological museums in the country. The name Amerind is a contraction of "American Indian," and this collection contains tens of thousands of artifacts from different Native American cultures. All aspects of Native American life are shown here, with displays covering Inuit masks, Cree tools, and sculpted effigy figures from Mexico's Casas Grandes.

The adjacent Amerind Art Gallery has a fine collection of Western art by such prominent artists as William Leigh

(1866–1955) and Frederic Remington (1861–1909). The delightful pink buildings, designed in the Spanish Colonial Revival style *(see p22)*, are also of interest.

Chiricahua National Monument ⑮

Road map D5. **Tel** (520) 824-3560. ☐ 8am–4:30pm daily. ● Dec 25. ▣ ♿ ◪ ⛺ **www**.nps.gov/chir

The Chiricahua Mountains were once the homeland of a band of Apache people, and an impenetrable base from which they launched attacks on settlers in the late 1800s. This 12,000-acre (480-ha) area now preserves amazing rock formations, which were created by a series of volcanic eruptions around 27 million years ago. Massive rocks balanced on small pedestals, soaring rock spires, and enormous stone columns make up the bizarre landscape, viewed from the monument's scenic drive and hiking trails.

The nearby town of Willcox houses the intriguing **Rex Allen Arizona Cowboy Museum**, which is devoted to a native son who became a famous movie cowboy, starring in 19 films in the 1950s.

🏛 Rex Allen Arizona Cowboy Museum
155 N Railroad Ave. **Tel** (520) 384-4583. ☐ 10am–4pm. ● public hols. ▣ ♿

Massive rock spires formed by million-year-old volcanic eruptions at Chiricahua National Monument

THE FOUR CORNERS

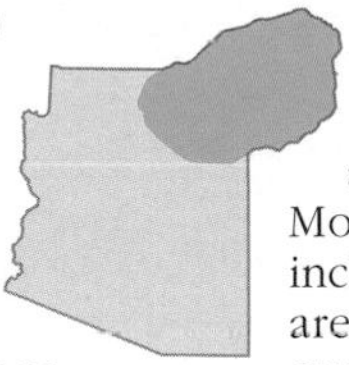

Dominated by a Navajo reservation the size of Connecticut, and presenting sweeping panoramas of mesas, canyons, and vast expanses of high desert, the Four Corners is perfect for those wanting to experience Native culture and the real West.

Although it receives less than 10 in (25 cm) of rainfall per year, this arid land has supported life since the first Paleo-Indians arrived about 12,000 years ago. The Anasazi, today known as the Ancestral Puebloan peoples, lived here from about AD 500 until the 13th century. They are responsible for the many evocative ruins found here, including those at Mesa Verde, Chaco Canyon, and Hovenweep National Monument. Their descendants include the Hopi, whose pueblos are said to be the oldest continuously occupied towns in North America. The Navajo arrived here in the 15th century and their spiritual center is Canyon de Chelly with its 1,000-ft (330-m) high red rock walls.

Monument Valley's impressive landscape has been used as a backdrop for countless movies and TV shows. The region is also popular for hiking, fishing, and whitewater rafting.

SIGHTS AT A GLANCE

Historic Towns & Cities

Aztec 15
Blanding 9
Bluff 0
Farmington 14
Ganado & Hubbell Trading Post 5
Tuba City 3
Window Rock 6

National Parks & Monuments

Canyon de Chelly National Monument 7
Chaco Culture National Historical Park 13
Four Corners Monument Navajo Tribal Park 12
Hovenweep National Monument 10
Mesa Verde National Park 17
Navajo National Monument 2

Areas of Natural Beauty

Colorado Plateau Tour 16
Monument Valley 1

Indian Reservations

Hopi Indian Reservation 4
Ute Mountain Tribal Park 11

KEY

Interstate
Major highway
Highway
Railroad
State boundary

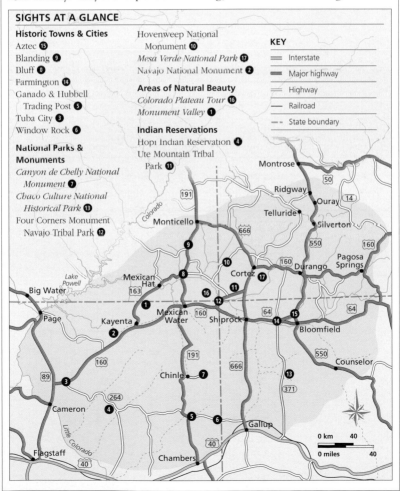

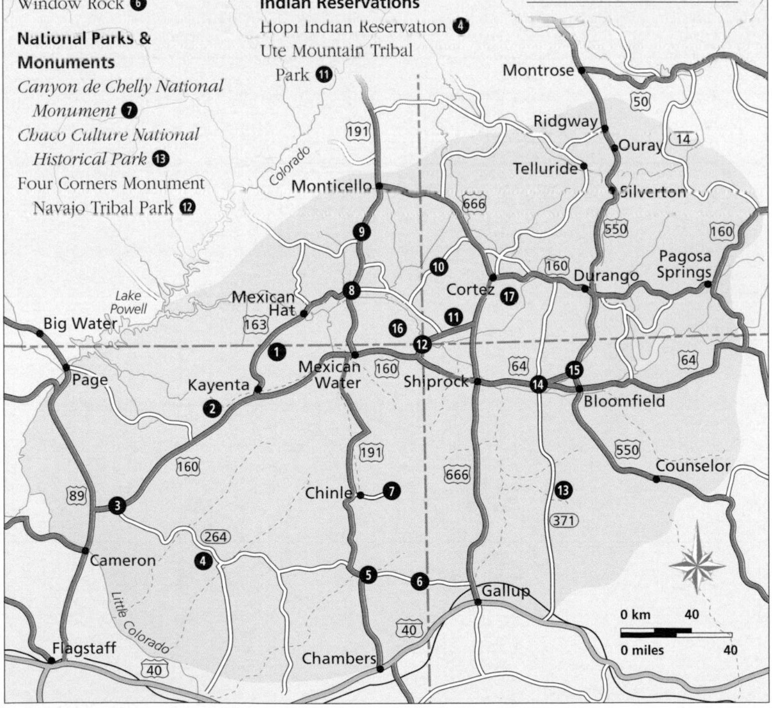

◁ **Dramatic rock formations, known as "the Mittens," in the Navajo Nation's Monument Valley**

Monument Valley ❶

From scenic Highway 163, which crosses the border of Utah and Arizona, it is possible to see the famous towering sandstone buttes and mesas of Monument Valley. These ancient rocks, soaring upward from a seemingly boundless desert, have come to symbolize the American West, largely because Hollywood has used these breathtaking vistas as a backdrop for hundreds of movies, TV shows, and commercials since the 1930s.

The area's visitor center sits within the boundary of Monument Valley Tribal Park, but many of the valley's spectacular rock formations and other sites are found just outside the park boundary.

Guided Tours
A row of kiosks at the visitor center offers Navajo-guided 4WD tours of the valley. The marketing tactics can be aggressive, but the tours offer an excellent way to see places in the park that are otherwise inaccessible.

Three Sisters
The Three Sisters are one of several distinctive pinnacle rock formations at Monument Valley. Others include the Totem Pole and the "fingers" of the Mittens. The closest view of the sisters can be seen from John Ford's Point, and is one of the most photographed sights here.

Art & Ruins
Petroglyphs such as this deer can be seen on Navajo-guided tours of rock art sites, which are dotted around the valley's ancient ruins.

EXPLORING THE VALLEY

The awe-inspiring beauty of Monument Valley's buttes and mesas can be viewed by travelers from Highway 163. Visitors can also pay a fee to travel on a 17-mile (27-km) self-guided drive along a well-marked dirt road. (Fees are collected at the visitor center.) Alternatively, Navajo guides may be hired for hiking, horseback, or 4WD tours to fascinating and less-visited parts of the valley.

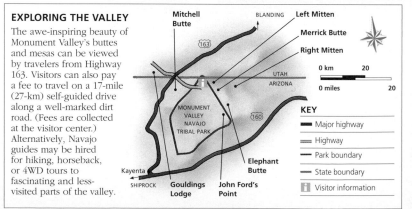

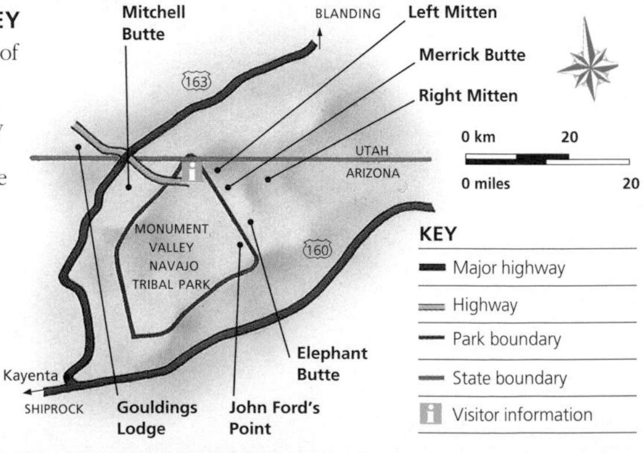

John Ford's Point
The most popular stop along the valley drive is John Ford's Point, which is said to be the film director's favorite view of the valley. Various stands offer a range of Navajo handicrafts. A nearby hogan (see p107) *serves as a gift shop where Navajo weavers demonstrate their craft.*

VISITORS' CHECKLIST

Road map C2. *PO Box 360289, Monument Valley, (435) 727-5870. sunrise–sunset. Scenic drive: 8am–4:30pm (May–Sep: 6am–8:30pm). Dec 25.* *visitor center only.* **www**.navajonationparks.org

Navajo Weaver
Navajo women are usually considered to be the finest weavers in the Southwest. One rug can take months to complete and sells for thousands of dollars. Using the natural colors of the land, the weavers often add a "spirit line" to their work to prevent their spirit being "trapped" within the rug.

MONUMENT VALLEY

Monument Valley is not really a valley. The tops of the mesas mark what was once a flat plain. Millions of years ago, this plain was cracked by upheavals within the earth. The cracks widened and eroded, until all that is left today are the formations rising from the desert floor.

Gouldings Lodge
The lodge offers accommodations, a restaurant, and guided bus tours of the valley. The original trading post is now a museum of the valley's cinematic history.

Ancestral Puebloan ruins of Keet Seel at Navajo National Monument

Navajo National Monument ❷

Road map C2. ***Tel*** *(928) 672-2700.* *end May–mid-Sep: 8am–6pm daily; mid-Sep–end May: 9am–5pm daily.* *Jan 1, Thanksgiving, Dec 25.* **www**.nps.gov/nava

Named for its location on the Navajo Reservation, this monument is actually known for its Ancestral Puebloan ruins. The most accessible ruin here is the beautifully preserved, 135-room pueblo of Betatakin, which fills a vast, curved niche in the cliffs of Tsegi Canyon. An easy one-mile (1.6-km) trail from the visitor center leads to an overlook where Betatakin is clearly visible on the far side, near the canyon floor. This is a lovely hike through piñon pines and juniper trees. From late May to early September there are daily five-hour hiking tours to Betatakin, which allow a close look at the ruins of these ancient houses.

A much more demanding 17-mile (27-km) hike leads to **Keet Seel**, a more impressive ruin. Only a limited number of permits to visit the ruin are issued each day. This hike has optional overnight camping in summer at a site with only the most basic facilities. Keet Seel was a larger and more successful community than Betatakin. Construction began on Keet Seel in about 1250, but the site is thought to have been abandoned by 1300.

These two sites are considered to mark the pinnacle of development of the area's Ancestral Puebloan people.

Tuba City ❸

Road map C2. *17,300.* *Tuba City Trading Post, (928) 283-5441.*

Named for Tuuvi, a Hopi Indian who converted to the Mormon faith, Tuba City is best known for the 65-million-year-old dinosaur tracks found just off the main highway, 5 miles (8 km) southwest of the town. Beyond that, this is the largest community in the western section of the Navajo Reservation and is a good spot from which to explore both the Navajo National Monument and the Hopi Reservation.

Hopi Indian Reservation ❹

Road map C3. *10,000.* *Hopi Cultural Center, Hwy 264, Second Mesa, (928) 734-2401.* *May–Sep: 6am–9pm; Oct–Apr: 7am–8pm.* *Jan 1, Thanksgiving, Dec 25.*

Arizona's only Pueblo Indians, the Hopi *(see pp24–5)*, are believed to be direct descendants of the Ancestral Puebloan people, or Anasazi. The Hopi Reservation is surrounded by the lands of the Navajo. The landscape is harsh and barren, yet the Hopi have cultivated the land here for a 1,000 years. They worship, through the *kachina*, the living spirits of plants and animals, believed to arrive each year to stay with the tribe during the growing season. Most of the Hopi villages are located on or near one of three mesas, or flat-topped elevations named First, Second, and Third Mesa. The artisans on each of the mesas specialize in particular crafts: on First Mesa these are carved figures representing the *kachina* spirits and painted pottery; on Second Mesa, silver jewelry and coiled baskets are made; and on Third Mesa, craftspeople fashion wicker baskets and woven rugs.

Kachina figure

Walpi, the ancient pueblo on First Mesa, was first inhabited in the 12th century. To reach Walpi, visitors drive up to the Mesa from the Pollaca settlement to the village of Sichomovi. Nearby, the Ponsi Visitor Center is the departure

Historic pueblo town of Walpi on First Mesa at Hopi Indian Reservation

A range of merchandise in the general store at Hubbell Trading Post

point for the one-hour Walpi tours. Walpi was built to be easily defended, and straddles a dramatic knife edge of rock, extending from the tip of First Mesa. In places Walpi is less than 100 ft (33 m) wide with a drop of several hundred feet on both sides. The Walpi tour includes several stops where visitors can purchase *kachina* figurines and distinctive hand-crafted pottery, or sample the Hopi *piki* bread.

Those wishing to shop further can continue on to Second Mesa, which has an array of Hopi arts and crafts. The Hopi Cultural Center is home to a restaurant *(see p141)* and the only hotel *(see p131)* for miles around, as well as a museum that has an excellent collection of photographs depicting scenes of Hopi life.

On Third Mesa, Old Oraibi pueblo, thought to have been founded in the 12th century, is of note only because of claims that it is the oldest continually occupied human settlement in North America.

Walpi
(928) 737-2262. Walking tours available. Oct–Mar: 9:30am–3:30pm; Apr–Sep: 8am–4:30pm.

Ganado & Hubbell Trading Post 5

Road map D2. *4,500.* *Hubbell Trading Post, Hwy 264, (928) 755-3254.*

A small, bustling town in the heart of the Navajo Reservation, Ganado's major attraction is the **Hubbell Trading Post National Historic Site**. Established in the 1870s by John Lorenzo Hubbell, this is the oldest continually operating trading post in the Navajo Nation. Trading posts like this one were once the economic and social centers of the reservations. The Navajo traded sheep, wool, blankets, turquoise, and other items in exchange for tools, household goods, and food. The trading posts were also a resource during times of need. When a smallpox epidemic struck in 1886, John Lorenzo helped care for the sick, using his house as a hospital.

Navajo bracelet at Hubbell Trading Post

Today, the trading post still hums with traditional trading activities. One room is a working general store, the rafters hung with frying pans and hardware, and shelves stacked with cloth, medicines, and food. Another room is filled with beautiful hand woven rugs, Hopi *kachina* dolls, and Navajo baskets. Another department has a long row of glass cases displaying an impressive array of silver and turquoise jewelry.

Visitors can tour Hubbell's restored home and view a significant collection of Southwestern art. At the visitor center Navajo women demonstrate rug weaving.

Hubbell Trading Post National Historic Site
A2264, near Ganado.
(928) 755-3475. May 27–Sep 8: 8am–6pm Mon–Sat; Sep 9–May 26: 8am–5pm Mon–Sat. public/ tribal hols.
www.nps.gov/hutr

Window Rock 6

Road map D2. *4,500* *Navajo Nation Visitor Services, Hwy 264, (928) 871-6436.*

The capital of the Navajo Nation is named for the natural arch found in the sandstone cliffs located about a mile north of the main strip on Highway 12. The **Navajo Nation Museum** located here is one of the largest Native American museums in the US. Opened in 1997, the huge *hogan*-shaped building houses displays that cover the history of the Ancestral Puebloans and the Navajo.

Navajo Nation Museum
Hwy 264 & Post Office Loop Rd. ***Tel*** *(928) 871-7941. 8am–5pm Mon; 8am–7pm Tue–Fri; 9am–5pm Sat.*

Eroded sandstone opening of Window Rock, near Highway 12

Canyon de Chelly National Monument

Flowering cactus

Few places in North America can boast a longer or more eventful history of human habitation than Canyon de Chelly. Archeologists have found evidence of four periods of Native culture, starting with the Basketmaker people around AD 300, followed by the Great Pueblo Builders, who created the cliff dwellings in the 12th century. They were succeeded by the Hopi, who lived here seasonally for around 300 years, taking advantage of the canyon's fertile soil. In the 1700s, the Hopi left the area and moved to the mesas, returning to the canyon to farm during the summer months. Today, the canyon is the cultural and geographic heart of the Navajo Nation. Pronounced "d'Shay," de Chelly is a Spanish corruption of the Native name *Tsegi*, meaning Rock Canyon.

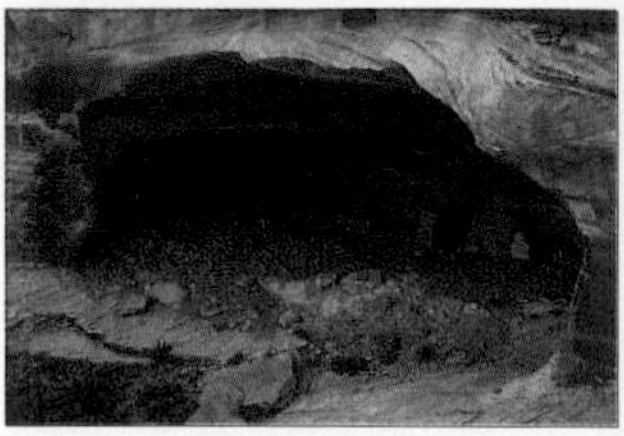

Yucca House Ruin
Perched on the mesa top, this ruin of an Ancestral Puebloan house sits in a rock hollow, precariously overhanging a sheer drop to the valley floor.

Mummy Cave Ruin
These two pueblos, separated by a central tower, were built in the 1280s by Ancestral Puebloans, who had inhabited the caves for more than 1,000 years. An overlook provides a good view of this impressive ruin.

Stone and adobe cliff dwellings were home to the Ancestral Puebloans from the 12th to the 14th centuries and were built to face south toward the sun, with cooler areas within.

Navajo Fortress
This imposing rock tower was the site of a three-month siege in 1863–64, when a group of Navajos reached the summit via pole ladders to escape Kit Carson and the US army. The persistence of Carson and starvation led them to surrender and they were marched to a camp in New Mexico (see p109).

Canyon Landscape
The sandstone cliffs of Canyon de Chelly reach as high as 1,000 ft (300 m), towering above the neighboring meadows and desert landscape in the distance. The canyon floor around the cliffs is fringed with cottonwood bushes, watered by the Chinle Wash.

VISITORS' CHECKLIST

Road map D2. 2 miles (3.5 km) east of Chinle & I-191. *PO Box 588, Chinle, (928) 674-5500.* *8am–5pm.* *Dec 25.* *partial.* *for guided tours.* **www**.nps.gov/cach

The pale walls of the White House cliff drop 550 ft (160 m) to the canyon floor.

***Hogan* Interior**
The hogan *is the center of Navajo family life. Made of horizontal logs, it has a smoke hole in the center to provide contact with the sky, while the dirt floor gives contact with the earth. A door faces east to greet the rising sun.*

WHITE HOUSE RUINS

This group of rooms, tucked into a tiny hollow in the cliff, seems barely touched by time. The dwellings were originally situated above a larger pueblo, much of which has now disappeared. The only site within the canyon that can be visited without a Navajo guide, it is reached via a steep 2.5-mile (5-km) round-trip trail that winds to the canyon floor and offers magnificent views.

MASSACRE CAVE

The canyon's darkest hour was in 1805, when a Spanish force under Lieutenant Antonio Narbona entered the area. The Spanish wanted to subdue the Navajo, claiming they were raiding their settlements. While some Navajo fled by climbing to the canyon rim, others took refuge in a cave high in the cliffs. The Spanish fired into the cave, and Narbona boasted that he had killed 115 Navajo including 90 warriors. Navajo accounts are different, claiming that most of the warriors were absent (probably hunting) and those killed were mostly women, children, and the elderly. The only Spanish fatality came when a Spaniard attempting to climb into the cave was attacked by a Navajo woman and both plunged over the cliff, gaining the Navajo name "Two Fell Over." The Anglo name is "Massacre Cave."

Pictograph on a canyon wall showing invading Spanish soldiers

Exploring Canyon de Chelly

Navajo ranger

Canyon de Chelly is startlingly different from the sparse desert landscape that spreads from its rim. Weathered red rock walls, just 30-ft (9-m) high at the canyon mouth, rise to more than 1,000-ft (300-m) high within the canyon, creating a sheltered world. Navajo *hogans* *(see p107)* dot the canyon floor; Navajo women tend herds of sheep and weave rugs at outdoor looms, and everywhere Ancestral Puebloan ruins add to the canyon's appeal. Navajo-led 4WD tours along the scenic North and South Rims are a popular way to view the site.

Antelope House Ruin
Named for a pictograph of an antelope painted by Navajo artists in the 1830s, Antelope House has ruins dating from AD 700. They can be seen from the Antelope House Overlook.

Canyon Vegetation
Within the canyon, cottonwood and oak trees line the river washes; the land itself is a fertile oasis of meadows, alfalfa and corn fields, and fruit orchards.

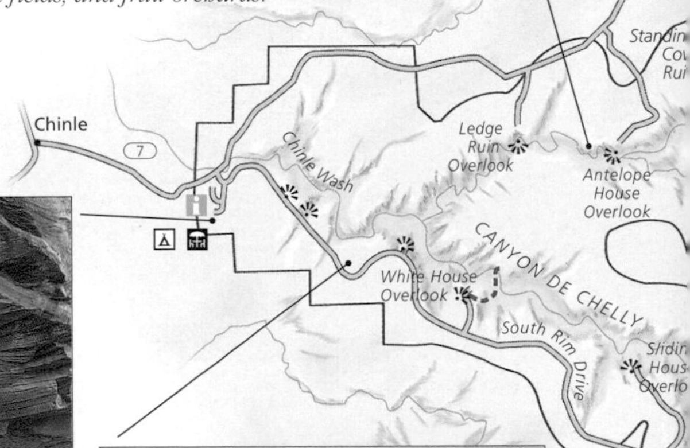

Canyon Tour
Half- and full-day tours from Thunderbird Lodge carry passengers in open flatbed or large 6WD army trucks. Of varying length and difficulty, the tours are the best way to see ruins up close.

Tsegi Overlook
This high curve along the South Rim offers good general views of the farm-studded canyon floor and surrounding landscape.

For hotels and restaurants in this region see pp130–31 and pp140–41

Hiking in the Canyon
Canyon de Chelly is a popular destination for hikers, but only the White House Ruins Trail may be walked without a guide. The visitor center (see p107) offers Navajo-guided hikes on trails of varying lengths.

KEY

═══	Highway
▬ ▪ ▬	Hiking route
Ⓐ	Campground/RV
🏕	Picnic area
ℹ	Visitor information
☀	Viewpoint
——	Park boundary

TO TSAILE
WINDOW ROCK

Massacre Cave Overlook

Mummy Cave Overlook

North Rim Drive

Canyon del Muerto

Black Rock Canyon

Spider Rock Overlook

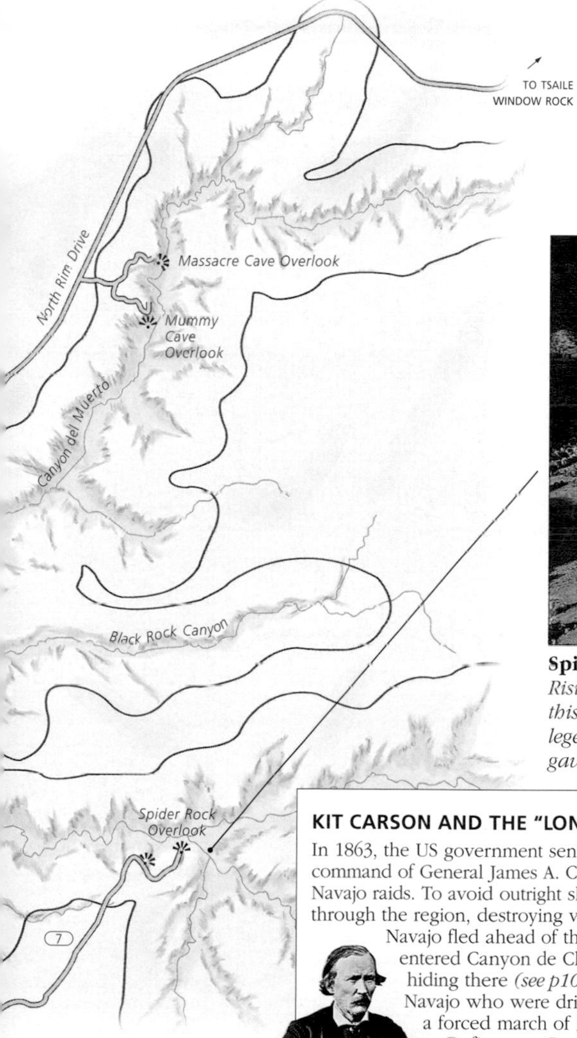

Spider Rock
Rising more than 800 ft (245 m), this is where, according to Navajo legends, Spider Woman lived and gave them the skill of weaving.

KIT CARSON AND THE "LONG WALK"

In 1863, the US government sent Kit Carson under the command of General James A. Carlton to settle the problem of Navajo raids. To avoid outright slaughter Carson led his soldiers through the region, destroying villages and livestock as the Navajo fled ahead of them. In January 1864, Carson entered Canyon de Chelly, capturing the Navajo hiding there *(see p106)*. They were among 9,000 Navajo who were driven on the "The Long Walk," a forced march of 370 miles (595 km) from Fort Defiance to Bosque Redondo in New Mexico. There, in a pitiful reservation, more than 3,000 Navajo died before the US government accepted the resettlement as a failure and allowed them to return to the Four Corners.

Fur trapper and soldier Kit Carson (1809–68)

Dramatic mesas and buttes in the Valley of the Gods near Bluff

Bluff 8

Road Map D1. 300. *Blanding Visitor Center, 12N Hwy 191, (435) 678-3662.* **www**.bluffutah.org

The charming town of Bluff was settled in 1880 by Mormons who dynamited their way through Glen Canyon's rock walls along what is now called the Hole-in-the-Rock Road. Float trips along the San Juan River include stops at Ancestral Pueblo ruins that can be reached only by boat.

Environs

About 12 miles (20 km) north is a 17 mile (27 km) dirt road through the **Valley of the Gods**. Like Monument Valley *(see pp102–3)*, it features high rock spires, buttes, and mesas, but none of the crowds. On a quiet day, visitors may have the place all to themselves and imagine what it looked like to the first settlers.

Blanding 9

Road Map D1. *3,800.* *12N Hwy 191, (435) 678-3662.* **www**.blandingutah.org

A tidy Mormon town at the base of the Abajo Mountains, Blanding is home to the **Edge of Cedars State Park** *(see pp116–17)*. The park contains modest Ancestral Puebloan ruins, including a small *kiva*, or religious chamber. The park museum has well thought-out displays on the history of these ancient people and other cultures that have inhabited the region.

Edge of Cedars State Park
Park Museum, 660 W 400 N, (435) 678-2238. *9am–5pm Mon–Sat.* *Thanksgiving, Dec 25.* **www**.stateparks.utah.gov

Hovenweep National Monument 10

Road Map D1. East of Hwy 191. ***Tel*** *(970) 562-4282.* *Apr–Sep: 8am–6pm; Oct–Mar: 8am–5pm.* *Jan 1, Thanksgiving, Dec 25.* **www**.nps.gov/hove

One of the most mysterious Ancestral Puebloan sites in the Southwest, the Hovenweep ruins lie along the rim of a shallow canyon. These well-preserved ruins, which include unique round, square, and D-shaped towers, have neither been restored nor rebuilt. Indeed, they look much as they did when W.D. Huntington, leader of a Mormon expedition, first came upon the site in 1854. The site was named in 1874, after an Ute word meaning "Deserted Valley." Little is known of the people who inhabited these ruins, and researchers have speculated that the towers at Hovenweep might have been defensive fortifications, astronomical observatories, storage silos, or the community's religious structures.

The six separate sets of ruins at Hovenweep can be visited by walking along either of the two self-guiding trails that link them.

Ute Mountain Tribal Park 11

Road Map D2. *Junction of Hwys 160 & 666, (800) 847-5485.* *Apr–Oct: 8am–3:30pm daily; Nov–Mar: 8am–3pm Wed–Sat.* *obligatory.*

The ruins of Ute Mountain Tribal Park are one of the better-kept secrets of the Southwest. The Ancestral Puebloan people first arrived here in about AD 400. They closely followed the Mesa Verde *(see pp118–19)* pattern of development, creating numerous magnificent cliff

Ancient brick tower at Hovenweep National Monument

dwellings, including the 80-room Lion House. These ruins have few visitors because of their inaccessibility. Visitors can use their own vehicles and join the tours led by local Ute guides, or pay an extra charge to be driven.

Four Corners Monument Navajo Tribal Park ⓬

Road Map D2. Junction of Hwys 160 & 41. ***Tel*** *(928) 871-6647.* *Jun–Sep: 7am–8pm; Oct–May: 8am–5pm.* *Thanksgiving, Dec 25.* **www**.navajonationparks.org

There is something oddly compelling about being able to put one foot and hand in each of four states. It is the whole premise of the Four Corners Monument – the only place in the US where four states meet at one point.

Chaco Culture National Historical Park ⓭

See pp112–13.

Farmington ⓮

Road Map D2. *40,000.* *3041 E Main St, (505) 326-7602.* **www**.farmingtonnm.org

A dusty, hard-working ranch town, Farmington is a good base for exploring the surrounding monuments. It is home to one of the most unusual museums in the Southwest. The **Bolack Museum of Fish & Wildlife** covers over 30,000 sq ft (2,800 sq m) and houses one of the largest accumulations of mounted game animals in the world. It is divided into nine themed game rooms, including African, Asian, European, and Russian. The museum's newest addition is a 10,000 sq ft (929 sq m) display of electromechanical equipment that traces America's golden age of development in electrical power generation and TV and radio broadcasting.

The **Farmington Museum** focuses on the history and geology of the area. A permanent exhibit, "From Dinosaurs to Drillbits," features a simulated ride down inside an oil well. The museum also offers popular interactive displays for adults and children.

Environs

About 25 miles (40 km) west of Farmingon is **Shiprock**, named for the spectacular 1,500-ft (457-m) rock peak that thrusts up from the valley floor about 5 miles (8 km) west of town. To the Navajo, this rock is sacred, and to early Anglo-American settlers it was a landmark that reminded them of a ship's prow. Now it is possible for sightseers to observe the peak only from the roadsides of Highways 64 or 33.

The **Salmon Ruins**, which once housed a Chaco settlement, are situated 8 miles (12 km) to the south. These ruins were protected from grave diggers by the Salmon family, who homesteaded here in the 1870s. As a result, a century later archaeologists recovered more than a million artifacts, many of which are on display in the museum at the site.

Bolack Museum of Fish &Wildlife
3901 Bloomfield Hwy. ***Tel*** *(505) 325-4275.* *9am–3pm Mon–Sat, appointment only.* *public holidays.* *obligatory.* **www**.bolackmuseum.com

Farmington Museum
3041 E Main St. ***Tel*** *(505) 599-1174.* *8am–5pm Mon–Sat.* **www**.farmingtonmuseum.org

Salmon Ruins
6131 Hwy 64. ***Tel*** *(505) 632-2013.* *8am–5pm Mon–Sat; May–Oct: 9am–5pm Sun; Nov–Apr: 9am–5pm Mon–Sat, noon–5pm Sun.* *Jan 1, Easter, Thanksgiving, Dec 25.*

Interior of the Great Kiva at Ancestral Puebloan Salmon Ruins

Aztec ⓯

Road Map D2. *6,000.* *110 North Ash St, (505) 334-9551.* *Mon–Fri (Jun–Aug: also Sat & Sun).*

This small town was named for its ruins, which are Ancestral Puebloan and not Aztec as originally believed. Preserved as a National Monument, the site's 500-room pueblo was a flourishing settlement in the late 1200s. Visitors can look inside a rebuilt *kiva (see p36).*

Aztec Ruins National Monument
N of Hwy 516 on Ruins Rd. ***Tel*** *(505) 334-6174.* *8am–5pm daily (to 6pm May–Sep).* *Jan 1, Thanksgiving, Dec 25.* **www**.nps.gov/azru

The spectacular red peak of Shiprock near Farmington

Chaco Culture National Historical Park ⓭

Arrowhead at Chaco Museum

Chaco Canyon is one of the most impressive cultural sites in the Southwest, reflecting the sophistication of the Ancestral Puebloan civilization *(see pp36–7)* that existed here. With its six "great houses" and many lesser sites, the canyon was once the political, religious, and cultural center for settlements that covered much of the Four Corners. At its peak during the 11th century, Chaco was one of the most impressive pre-Columbian cities in North America. Despite its size, it is thought that Chaco's population was small because the land could not have supported a larger community. Archaeologists believe that the city was mainly used as a ceremonial gathering place, with a year-round population of less than 3,000. Probably the social elite, the inhabitants supported themselves largely by trading.

Architectural Detail
Chaco's skilled builders had only stone tools to work with to create this finely wrought stonework.

The many *kivas* here were probably used by visitors arriving for religious ceremonies.

PUEBLO BONITO
Pueblo Bonito is an example of a "great house." Begun around AD 850, it was built in stages over the course of 300 years. This reconstruction shows how it might have looked, with its D-shaped four-story structure that contained more than 650 rooms.

Chetro Ketl
A short trail from Pueblo Bonito leads to another great house, Chetro Ketl. Almost as large as Pueblo Bonito, at 3 acres (2 ha), Chetro Ketl has more than 500 rooms. The masonry used to build the later portions of this structure is among the most sophisticated found in any Ancestral Puebloan site.

Casa Rinconada
Also known as a great kiva, *Casa Rinconada is the largest religious chamber at Chaco, measuring 62 ft (19 m) in diameter. It was used for spiritual gatherings.*

Pueblo Alto
Pueblo Alto was built atop the mesa at the junction of several ancient Chacoan roads. Reaching the site requires a two-hour hike, but the views over the canyon are well worth it.

VISITORS' CHECKLIST

Road map D2. 3 miles (5 km) SE of Nageezi off US 550.
Chaco Culture Visitor Center (505) 786-7014.
8am–5pm. *public hols.*
www.nps.gov/chcu

This great house was four stories high.

Hundreds of rooms within Pueblo Bonito show little sign of use and are thought to have been kept for storage or for guests arriving to take part in ceremonial events.

Early Astronomers at Fajada Butte
Measurement of time was vital to the Chacoans for crop planting and the timing of ceremonies. A spiral petroglyph, carved on Fajada Butte, is designed to indicate the changing seasons through the shadows it casts on the rock.

EXPLORING CHACO

The site is accessed via a 13-mile (21-km) dirt road that is affected by flash floods in wet weather. Drivers can follow the paved loop road that passes several of Chaco's highlights. There is parking at all major sites. From the visitor center, a trail leads to Una Vida and the petroglyphs.

KEY

- Highway
- Unpaved road
- Hiking route
- Campground/RV
- Picnic area
- Visitor information
- Park boundary

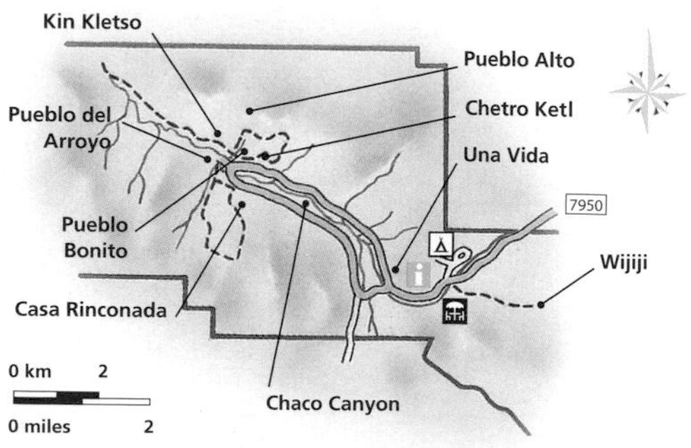

Totem Pole Rock at Monument Valley Navajo Tribal Park ▷

Colorado Plateau Tour (16)

The haunting beauty of the high plateau country, with its deep canyons and ancient, mysterious ruins, is the star of this tour, which follows some of the loneliest but loveliest roads in America. This area is very popular with hiking, mountain biking, river paddling, and 4WD enthusiasts. The plateau rises from around 2,000 ft (610 m) in elevation near Monument Valley to over 7,000 ft (2,134 m) at Monticello, Utah. The area is dotted with the ruins of the Ancient Puebloan civilization. Some, such as Hovenweep and Mesa Verde, were large complex towns, while others, for instance the ruins at Edge of Cedars State Park on a vast plain below the snowcapped Abajo Mountains, were small outposts.

Bluff (3)
This appealing small town was founded by hardy Mormon pioneers in 1880. Today, it makes a great base for exploring the region, and is the starting point for rafting tours of the San Juan River *(see p151)*.

Valley of the Gods (4)
A 17-mile (27-km) long dirt road winds through this valley of eroded red rock spires. Recommended for high-clearance vehicles, this road presents the remote beauty of the Southwest that existed before modern roads were built.

Goosenecks State Park (5)
A set of incredibly tight switchbacks on the San Juan River give this overlook its name. The viewpoint is 1,500 ft (457 m) above the sinuous curves of the river, which travels 6 miles (9.7 km) to move 1.5 miles (2.4 km) forward.

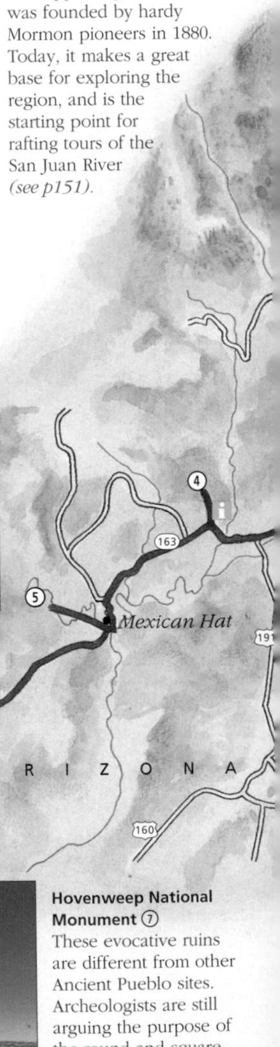

Monument Valley (6)
Made famous through Western movies, the valley's buttes and bluffs were once ground level, before wind and water sculpted the landscape *(see pp102–3)*.

Hovenweep National Monument (7)
These evocative ruins are different from other Ancient Pueblo sites. Archeologists are still arguing the purpose of the round and square towers built along this canyon *(see p110)*.

Edge of Cedars State Park ②
These small, well-preserved ruins are dwarfed by the surrounding high plateau. The park museum has a superb collection of Ancient Pueblo pottery and artifacts *(see p110)*.

TIPS FOR DRIVERS

Tour length: *290 miles (467 km).*
When to go: *Spring and fall. Snow in winter is a possibility.*
Stopping-off points: *The best bets for restaurants and accommodations are Bluff and Cortez.*
Note: *This route can be driven in either direction. There are long distances, up to 50 miles (80 km), without services, so fill up the gas tank, and review desert driving safety* (see p160).

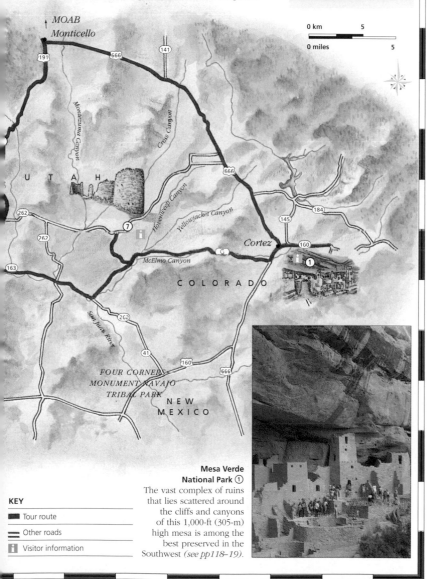

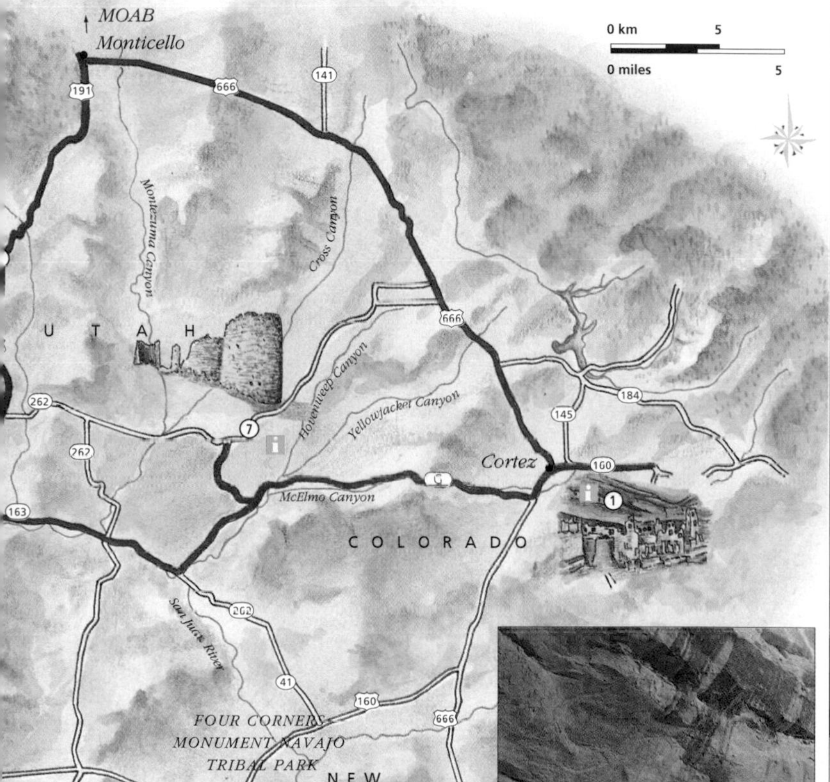

Mesa Verde National Park ①
The vast complex of ruins that lies scattered around the cliffs and canyons of this 1,000-ft (305-m) high mesa is among the best preserved in the Southwest *(see pp118–19)*.

KEY

Tour route

Other roads

Visitor information

Mesa Verde National Park ⑰

This high, forested mesa overlooking the Montezuma Valley was home to the Ancestral Puebloan people *(see pp36–7)* for more than 700 years. Within canyons that cut through the mesa are some of the best preserved and most elaborate cliff dwellings built by these people. Mesa Verde, meaning "Green Table," was a name given to the area by the Spanish in the 1700s, but the ruins were not widely known until the late 19th century. This site provides a fascinating record of these people from the Basketmaker period, beginning around AD 550, to the complex society that built the many-roomed cliff dwellings between 1000 and 1250. Displays at the Far View Visitor Center and the Chapin Mesa Museum provide a good introduction.

Spruce Tree House
Tucked into a cliff niche, these three-story structures were probably home to as many as 100 people.

Guided Tours
Ranger-led tours give visitors a chance to actually enter the ruins and get a feel of the daily lives of these ancient people.

CLIFF PALACE

With 150 rooms, this is the largest Ancestral Puebloan cliff dwelling found anywhere, and is the site that most visitors focus on. The location and symmetry suggest that architecture was important to the builders. Begun around 1200, it was vacated around 1275.

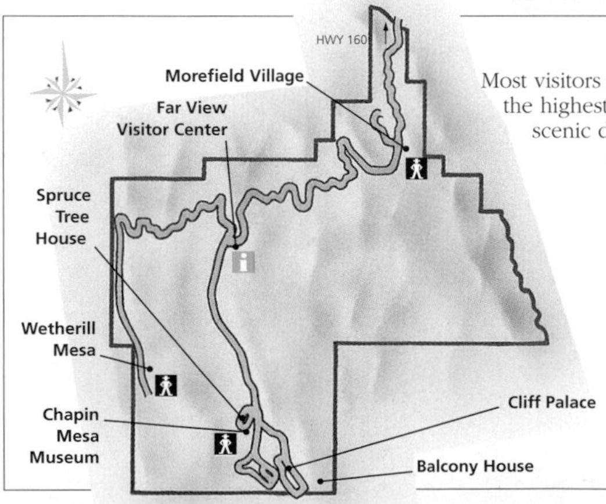

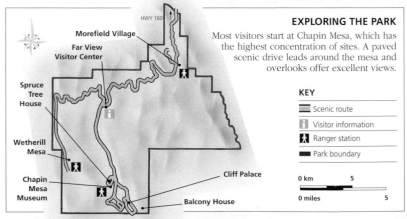

EXPLORING THE PARK

Most visitors start at Chapin Mesa, which has the highest concentration of sites. A paved scenic drive leads around the mesa and overlooks offer excellent views.

Balcony House
Possibly built for defense, Balcony House could not be seen from above, and access was (and still is) difficult. Visitors on tours must climb three ladders high above the canyon floor, then crawl through an access tunnel.

VISITORS' CHECKLIST

Road Map D2. *PO Box 8, Mesa Verde, (970) 529-4465.* Cortez. *Far View Visitor Center: early Apr–mid-Oct: 8am–5pm; Chapin Mesa Archaeological Museum: 8am–6:30pm Apr–Sep & 8am–5pm Oct–Mar.* **www**.nps.gov/meve

Towers were probably used for signaling or as lookouts for defense.

Square Tower House
Early cowboys named this ruin for the prominent, tower-like central structure, which was actually a vertical stack of rooms that was once surrounded by other rooms. It may have been used as a dwelling or for ceremonial purposes.

The 23 *kivas* or religious rooms at this site are thought to indicate that at least 23 clans lived here at various times.

Wetherill Mesa Long House
A scenic 12-mile (17-km) drive on a winding mountain road leads to Wetherill Mesa, named for the local rancher Richard Wetherill, who found Cliff Palace in the 1880s. Two cliff dwellings here, Step and Long houses, are open to visitors.

DRINK
Coca-Cola
JOE & AGGIE
ROUTE
66
OPEN
MEXICAN & AMERICAN
FOOD
Free PARKING IN REAR of CAFE

TRAVELERS' NEEDS

WHERE TO STAY

Arizona has a long history of hospitality that is reflected in the wide variety of places to stay. From lavish five-star resorts to simple rustic lodges, there is a wealth of options for visitors. You can choose modern or historic hotels, cozy bed-and-breakfasts, inns, convenient motels, or fully equipped apartments. For those seeking Western-style adventure, there are dude ranches, many of which provide luxurious lodgings with horseback riding and outdoor activities.

Weatherford Hotel sign in Flagstaff

Accommodations in all price categories usually offer private bathrooms in addition to clean, comfortable rooms. Historic hotels provide a glimpse into Arizona's early, pioneering years, and the lobby areas of these impressive hotels are worth a visit even when staying elsewhere.

Hotel prices in the region tend to vary according to season. The listings provided on pages 124–31 recommend places in all price ranges, each representing the best of their kind for that area.

Teepees at the Wigwam Motel on Route 66 in Holbrook, Arizona *(see p125)*

HOTEL CLASSIFICATIONS

The tourist industry throughout Arizona is recognized for quality lodgings. A guideline for travelers is the diamond rating system of the American and Canadian Automobile Associations (AAA and CAA). Visit www.aaa.com and www.caa.ca for more information. Every establishment, from the one-diamond motel to the five-diamond resort hotel, is rated for service, cleanliness, and the facilities offered. AAA members also benefit from discounts when they book in advance.

TAXES

Accommodation tax varies across the region as it is charged by both state and city or county governments. Expect to pay between 10 and 14 percent of the room price in tax. Prices given for hotels in this book include taxes.

LUXURY HOTELS

In Arizona, hotels come in every shape and size, including historic showplaces, such as the Grand Canyon's El Tovar *(see p125)*, which was originally built to impress East Coast investors and prove that the Southwest was an exciting tourist destination. Today, some of the most lavish hotels in Arizona are large resort hotels located in the Scottsdale and Phoenix area. A prime example is the Fairmont Scottsdale Princess in Scottsdale *(see p128)*, with its two championship 18-hole golf courses, spa facilities, and gourmet dining. The areas around Sedona, Phoenix, and Tucson are famous for both luxury health spas and golf resorts. Small, independently owned "boutique" hotels offer opulent facilities combined with an intimate atmosphere and attentive service.

There are also many hotels aimed specifically at business travelers, offering weekly rates, and computer and fax outlets in rooms, although these services are now available in a range of hotels.

CHAIN HOTELS & MOTELS

For the most part, you can count on efficient service, moderate prices, and comfortable (if bland) surroundings at a chain hotel. The most popular chains include **Holiday Inn**, **Comfort Inn**, **Best Western**, **Ramada Inns**, **Econolodge**, and **Super 8**. Particularly good value are suite hotels, such as **Country Inn and Suites** and **Embassy Suites**, which offer living rooms and kitchenettes for little more than the cost of a basic hotel room. Chain hotels also offer central reservation systems that can help you find a room at peak times. Motels provide rooms that are usually accessible from the parking area. They are often the only option in remote areas, and can vary from nostalgic Route 66 places *(see pp28–9)* to such bargain lodgings as Motel 6.

A hotel in the Best Western chain

◁ **One of the oldest establishments on Route 66 – Joe & Aggies Cafe in Holbrook**

Exterior view of the Peaks Resort and Golden Door Spa, Telluride *(see p131)*

HISTORIC INNS & BED-&-BREAKFASTS

There are hundreds of excellent inns, and bed-and-breakfasts located throughout Arizona. Generally, inns are larger, with more spacious public areas and a dining room. Bed-and-breakfast establishments tend to be smaller and more homey. Both inns and bed-and-breakfasts may be found in restored or reconstructed historic buildings, and many are located in charming Victorian houses in historic towns. These lodgings pride themselves on providing a warm welcome and friendly service. For bookings, contact **Arizona Association of Bed & Breakfast Inns**, **Arizona Trails Bed & Breakfast Reservation Service**, and **Mi Casa Su Casa**.

WESTERN HOTELS & DUDE RANCHES

If you have ever wanted to indulge your "Wild West" fantasies, there are plenty of historic hotels in which to do so. Between 1880 and 1920, Western towns gained a reputation for the quality and grandeur of their hotels, and many boasted extravagantly ornate decor. Today, several of them have been restored to their original splendor and offer great settings for a vacation. Prescott's Hotel St. Michael *(see p126)*, for example, with its grand lobby and attractive rooms, is both a historic hotel and an oasis for a relaxing, pampered stay.

Dude ranches offer visitors the chance to experience Western life. They first appeared in the 1920s – the name "dude" is a colloquialism meaning "a city dweller unfamiliar with life on the range". Choices range from relaxing vacations that include leisurely horseback rides to working ranches where you participate in such activities as cattle roundups. Meals, accommodations, and horses are usually included in the price. Arizona has a **Dude Ranch Association** to help you find the perfect Western vacation.

The pretty hacienda-style Lodge on the Desert, Tucson *(see p130)*

CAMPGROUNDS & RV PARKS

Campgrounds for both tents and RVs (recreational vehicles) are found all over Arizona, and are especially popular in the national parks. The **National Forest Service** provides information on forest campgrounds, which range from extremely basic to those with running water and limited RV hookups.

DIRECTORY

CHAIN HOTELS

Best Western
Tel (800) 528-1234.

Comfort Inn
Tel (800) 221-2222.

Country Inn & Suites
Tel (800) 456-4000.

Econolodge
Tel (800) 424-4777.

Embassy Suites
Tel (800) 362-2779.

Holiday Inn
Tel (800) 465-4329.

Ramada Inns
Tel (800) 272-6232.

Super 8
Tel (800) 800-8000.

HISTORIC INNS & BED-&-BREAKFASTS

Arizona Association of Bed & Breakfast Inns
www.arizona-bed-breakfast.com

Arizona Trails Bed & Breakfast Reservation Service
Box 18998, Fountain Hills, AZ 85269. *Tel (888) 799-4284.*
www.arizonatrails.com

Mi Casa Su Casa
Box 950, Tempe, AZ 85280.
Tel (800) 456-0682.
www.azres.com

DUDE RANCHES

Arizona Dude Ranch Association
Box 603, Cortaro, AZ 85652.
www.azdra.com

CAMPGROUNDS & RV PARKS

National Forest Service
333 Broadway SE,
Albuquerque, NM 87102.
Tel (877) 444-6777.
www.recreation.gov

Choosing a Hotel

Hotels have been selected across a wide price range for facilities, good value, and location. All rooms have private bath, TV, and air conditioning, and they are wheelchair accessible unless otherwise indicated. Most have Internet access; fitness facilities may be offsite. The hotels are listed by area. For map references, see the *Back endpaper*.

PRICE CATEGORIES
Price categories are for a standard double room per night, inclusive of service charges and any additional taxes:

Ⓢ Under $100
ⓈⓈ $100–$150
ⓈⓈⓈ $150–$200
ⓈⓈⓈⓈ $200–$250
ⓈⓈⓈⓈⓈ Over $250

GRAND CANYON AND NORTHERN ARIZONA

CAMP VERDE Camp Verde Comfort Inn Ⓢ
340 N Goswick Way, AZ 86322 **Tel** *(928) 567-9000* **Fax** *(928) 567-1828* **Rooms** *85* **Map** *B3*

A clean, chain motel with an outdoor heated pool, the Comfort Inn is located on I-17 in the Verde River Valley, just 3 miles (5 km) from Montezuma Castle and other local sights. It offers a less pricey alternative to hotels in nearby Sedona and Jerome. Try the make-your-own waffles at their complimentary breakfast. **www.choicehotels.com**

CAMP VERDE Camp Verde Super 8 Ⓢ
1550 W. Hwy 260, AZ 86322 **Tel** *(928) 567-2622* **Fax** *(928) 567-9520* **Rooms** *44* **Map** *B3*

Convenient to the interstate, this tidy two-story motel has a large indoor swimming pool and video library and offers a complimentary breakfast. Guest rooms are neat and clean, with comfortable beds, a microwave and refrigerator. **www.super8.com**

COTTONWOOD Best Western Cottonwood Inn ⓈⓈ
993 S Main St, AZ 86326 **Tel** *(928) 634-5575* **Fax** *(928) 634-5576* **Rooms** *78* **Map** *B3*

At the base of Mingus Mountain, this chain hotel is in the heart of the Verde River Valley, a few miles from Tuzigoot National Monument and the Dead Horse Ranch State Park. Amenities include comfortable rooms with fridges; a heated pool, which is open most of the year; and a Continental breakfast. **www.bestwesterncottonwoodinn.com**

FLAGSTAFF Hotel Weatherford Ⓢ
23 N Leroux St, AZ 86001 **Tel** *(928) 779-1919* **Fax** *(928) 773-8951* **Rooms** *10* **Map** *C3*

Just a block from the Santa Fe Railroad Station, this 1897 sandstone building, with a wraparound veranda, was once a refuge for passing politicians, authors, and gunslingers. Reasonably priced, its restored rooms are decorated with antiques, but most have no telephone or TV. A few have shared baths. **www.weatherfordhotel.com**

FLAGSTAFF Arizona Mountain Inn ⓈⓈ
4200 Lake Mary Rd, AZ 86001 **Tel** *(928) 774-8959 or (800) 239-5236* **Fax** *(928) 774-8837* **Rooms** *20* **Map** *C3*

It's all about the great outdoors at this collection of 16 chalet-style cottages scattered amid tall pines just outside Flagstaff. An ideal base for exploring this corner of the Southwest, the chalets are fully stocked for romantic getaways or family gatherings. Many have fireplaces, but no TV, phone, or air conditioning. **www.arizonamountaininn.com**

FLAGSTAFF Hilton Garden Inn ⓈⓈ
350 W Forest Meadows St, AZ 86001 **Tel** *(928) 226-8888* **Fax** *(928) 556-9059* **Rooms** *90* **Map** *C3*

Hikers and bikers appreciate the indoor pool, sauna, and whirlpool spa of this hotel, located near downtown and Northern Arizona University. Rooms are equipped with microwave ovens and refrigerators, phone, and free Internet. Take advantage of a Stay-Fit Kit – mat, ball, and dumbbells – for an in-room workout. **www.hiltongardeninn.com**

FLAGSTAFF Hotel Monte Vista ⓈⓈ
100 N. San Francisco St, AZ 86001 **Tel** *(928) 779-6971 or (800) 545-3068* **Fax** *(928) 779-2904* **Rooms** *50* **Map** *C3*

This 1926 four-story brick hotel boasts an illustrious past. Rooms are named for the celebrities who stayed here, from Bob Hope to John Wayne, and more recently, rock star Jon Bon Jovi. There's a long list of resident ghosts, too. The Monte Vista is close to the railroad, so you might need to ask for earplugs. **www.hotelmontevista.com**

FLAGSTAFF Little America Hotel ⓈⓈⓈ
2515 E Butler Ave, AZ 86004 **Tel** *(928) 779-2741* **Fax** *(928) 779-7983* **Rooms** *247* **Map** *C3*

Head straight for the pool, surrounded by ponderosa pines, at this attractive hotel just minutes from downtown. Save time for a walk along the Coconino Forest Trail, or enjoy family fun time in a game of horseshoe, volleyball, or croquet. Rooms are comfortably decorated with French Provençal furniture. **www.littleamerica.com/flagstaff**

FLAGSTAFF Radisson Woodlands Hotel Flagstaff ⓈⓈⓈ
1175 W Route 66, AZ 86001 **Tel** *(928) 773-8888* **Fax** *(928) 773-0597* **Rooms** *183* **Map** *C3*

Take advantage of the treadmill and other machines at this upscale chain hotel located near downtown, off Route 66 and just minutes from Sunset Crater and the Native American ruins at Wupatki. Upgrade to a room with a Sleep Number Bed, which adjusts mattress comfort at the touch of a button. **www.flagstaffwoodlandshotel.com**

Key to Symbols *see back cover flap*

FLAGSTAFF Starlight Pines Bed & Breakfast $$$

3380 E Lockett Rd, AZ 86001 **Tel** *(928) 527-1912 or (800) 752-1912* **Rooms** *4* **Map** *C3*

The Victorian-style Starlight Pines is accessed via a wraparound porch with white wicker furniture. The B&B features a crackling fire and rooms filled with fresh flowers, antiques, and Tiffany lamps. Start the day with a whiff of the pine-scented air mixed with the aroma of the Grand Marnier French toast. **www.starlightpinesbb.com**

GRAND CANYON Phantom Ranch $

Grand Canyon, AZ 86023 **Tel** *(303) 297-2757 or (888) 297-2757* **Fax** *(303) 297-3175* **Rooms** *40* **Map** *B2*

Few visitors to the Grand Canyon are given the opportunity to stay in the beautiful Phantom Ranch, far below the Canyon rim. The rustic lodge and timber cabins are reached by rafting the Colorado River, by hiking, or by mule. Accommodation is dormitory-style, in bunk beds. Book very early. **www.grandcanyonlodges.com**

GRAND CANYON Best Western Grand Canyon Squire Inn $$$

Hwy 64, AZ 86023 **Tel** *(928) 638-2681 or (800) 622-6966* **Fax** *(928) 638-2782* **Rooms** *250* **Map** *B2*

This showplace member of the Best Western chain features bright, clean rooms that are decorated in an attractive Southwestern motif. A family fun center offers bowling and billiards. The hotel's greatest advantage, however, is its location: just outside the south entrance to the Grand Canyon. **www.grandcanyonsquire.com**

GRAND CANYON (NORTH RIM) Jacob Lake Inn $

Hwy 89A and AZ-67, AZ 86022 **Tel** *(928) 643-7232* **Fax** *(928) 643-7235* **Rooms** *56* **Map** *B2*

Nestled in the woods just off the highway leading to the North Rim of the Grand Canyon, accommodations in this inn range from rustic cabins to modern motel rooms. There is an onsite restaurant, which serves burgers, steaks, and trout; a gift shop; and a bakery offering freshly-baked cookies. **www.jacoblake.com**

GRAND CANYON (NORTH RIM) Grand Canyon Lodge $$

Grand Canyon, AZ 86052 **Tel** *(480) 377-1320* **Rooms** *205* **Map** *B2*

The drive from the South Rim to the North Rim is over 200 miles (320 km), but it is worth it to stay in this traditional mountain lodge right on the edge of the canyon. Accommodation is either in motel-style rooms, rustic mountain cabins, or more luxurious log cabins. The lodge is open seasonally, and reservations are a must. **www.grandcanyonlodges.com**

GRAND CANYON (SOUTH RIM) Maswik Lodge $

Grand Canyon Village, AZ 86023 **Tel** *(303) 297-2757* **Fax** *(303) 297-3175* **Rooms** *278* **Map** *B2*

This family-friendly lodge, consisting of two buildings sitting among ponderosa pines, is a quarter-mile south of the Canyon rim. The south-facing rooms have all the basics but no air conditioning; the more spacious north rooms have modern facilities. The rustic cabins can be booked only during the summer. **www.grandcanyonlodges.com**

GRAND CANYON (SOUTH RIM) Bright Angel Lodge $$

Grand Canyon Village, AZ 86023 **Tel** *(303) 297-2757* **Fax** *(303) 297-3175* **Rooms** *89* **Map** *B2*

Make bookings well in advance to get one of the edge-of-the-canyon cabins, priced well below similar lodgings at El Tovar *(see below)*. Designed by Mary Elizabeth Colter in 1935, this historic log-and-stone lodge is very popular. Low-priced motel-like rooms and cabins also got spruced up. **www.grandcanyonlodges.com**

GRAND CANYON (SOUTH RIM) Yavapai Lodge $$

Grand Canyon Village, AZ 86023 **Tel** *(303) 297-2757* **Fax** *(303) 297-3175* **Rooms** *358* **Map** *B2*

Those making late reservations are likely to find rooms at the Yavapai, near the Market Village, a half-mile from the Canyon rim and the visitors' center, and conveniently located near a general store, bank, and post office. East-facing rooms are air conditioned; west rooms have fans and vaulted ceilings. **www.grandcanyonlodges.com**

GRAND CANYON (SOUTH RIM) El Tovar Hotel $$$

Grand Canyon Village, AZ 86023 **Tel** *(303) 297-2757* **Fax** *(303) 297-3175* **Rooms** *78* **Map** *B2*

Located on the South Rim, this historic landmark lodge celebrated its centennial in 2005. Renowned for luxury in its heyday, when it was visited by the likes of Albert Einstein and Elizabeth Taylor, El Tovar is still the premier lodge in the park. Its distinctive design includes natural stone and Douglas fir. **www.grandcanyonlodges.com**

GRAND CANYON (SOUTH RIM) Thunderbird and Kachina Lodges $$$

Grand Canyon Village, AZ 86023 **Tel** *(303) 297-2757* **Fax** *(303) 297-3175* **Rooms** *140* **Map** *B2*

Right on the Canyon rim, these two lodges have very comfortable family rooms featuring large picture windows and amenities such as a refrigerator, a safe, and full baths. Partial canyon views can be seen from half the rooms in each lodge, for a slightly higher price. Restaurants are within walking distance. **www.grandcanyonlodges.com**

HOLBROOK Wigwam Village Motel $

811 West Hopi Dr, AZ 86025 **Tel** *(928) 524-3048* **Rooms** *15* **Map** *C3*

This Route 66 hotel features rooms shaped like Native American teepees made out of concrete. Built in 1950, the hotel is a prime example of the roadside kitsch that was an icon of the postwar era, and rooms here are enormously popular with nostalgia fans. The retro theme means no three-pronged plugs or phones, but there is cable TV.

JEROME Ghost City Inn Bed & Breakfast $$

541 Main St, AZ 86331 **Tel** *(928) 634-4678 or (888) 634-4678* **Rooms** *6* **Map** *B3*

Nestled among Jerome's ghosts and galleries, this 1890s copper miners' boarding house has been made into a tasteful inn. Perched high atop Cleopatra Hill, with views over the Verde River Valley, it has individually decorated rooms. Breakfast is served in the drawing room or on the back patio, next to a waterfall. **www.ghostcityinn.com**

KINGMAN Best Western A Wayfarer's Inn & Suites $$

2815 E Andy Devine Ave/Route 66, AZ 86401 **Tel** *(928) 753-6271* **Fax** *(928) 753-9608* **Rooms** *101* **Map** *A3*

A comfortable chain hotel with a seasonal outdoor pool and an indoor spa. A Wayfarer's Inn is located a short drive from the Powerhouse Museum, which exhibits Route 66 memorabilia, and the Kingman Army Airfield Museum, displaying World War II airplanes. **www.bestwesternarizona.com**

LAKE HAVASU CITY Hampton Inn $$

245 London Bridge Rd, AZ 86403 **Tel** *(928) 855-4071* **Fax** *(928) 855-2379* **Rooms** *162* **Map** *A3*

The Hampton Inn has become one of the most popular hotels in town. Just a quarter-mile from the lake, it has many rooms with balconies and lake views. All the rooms also have refrigerators and microwaves. Guests can try their skill at the horseshoe pit, or take the walking trail to the beach. **www.hamptoninn.com**

LAKE HAVASU CITY Heat $$$$

1420 Mcculloch Blvd, AZ 86403 **Tel** *(888) 898-4328* **Fax** *(928) 854-1130* **Rooms** *17* **Map** *A3*

This trendy boutique hotel, with stylish contemporary design and European accents, is a stone's throw from London Bridge and a welcome addition to the town. The plush rooms have beautiful views of the bridge and the Bridgewater Channel. The inn places a big emphasis on service. **www.heathotel.com**

PAGE Best Western Arizonainn $$

716 Rim View Dr, AZ 86040 **Tel** *(928) 645-2466 or (800) 826-2718* **Fax** *(928) 645-2053* **Rooms** *103* **Map** *C2*

This Best Western offers clean, modern rooms, many with panoramic views of Lake Powell and the Glen Canyon area. The hotel also features high-speed Internet access and fitness facilities, and offers a wide range of excursions, including boating on Lake Powell and trips to the Grand Canyon. **www.bestwesternarizona.com**

PAGE Best Western at Lake Powell $$

208 N Lake Powell Blvd, AZ 86040 **Tel** *(928) 645-5988* **Fax** *(928) 645-2578* **Rooms** *132* **Map** *C2*

In the heart of Page, with views of Glen Canyon Dam and the Vermillion Cliffs, this reliable chain hotel decorated in Southwestern desert colors is within walking distance of shops, restaurants, tour outfitters, and the John Wesley Powell Museum. It has a large outdoor pool and extensive parking facilities. **www.bestwesternarizona.com**

PAGE Courtyard by Marriott $$$

600 Clubhouse Dr, AZ 86040 **Tel** *(928)-645-5000* **Fax** *(928) 645-5004* **Rooms** *150* **Map** *C2*

Surrounded by the lush green fairways of the 18-hole Lake Powell National Championship Golf Course, the Courtyard features luxurious rooms in a beautiful Southwestern-style building. Lounge by the pool, book a golf package, see the nearby Glen Canyon Dam, or spend your day on Lake Powell. **www.courtyard.com**

PAGE Lake Powell Resort $$$

100 Lakeshore Dr, AZ 86040 **Tel** *(928) 645-2433 or (888) 896-3829* **Fax** *(928) 645-1031* **Rooms** *350* **Map** *C2*

This lakeside hotel is the flagship of Lake Powell's premier resort, which also includes restaurants, houseboat rentals, a marina, and tour facilities. The rooms are clean and bright, and many offer views of the lake. The pretty pool also overlooks the lake, but for the best views, sign up for one of the resort's boat tours. **www.visitlakepowell.com**

PRESCOTT Hotel St. Michael $

205 W Gurley St, AZ 86301 **Tel** *(928) 776-1999 or (800) 678-3757* **Fax** *(928) 776-7318* **Rooms** *72* **Map** *B3*

Built in 1901, this historic hotel counts among its customers Theodore Roosevelt, author Zane Grey, and early Western movie star Tom Mix. The clean, simple rooms are decorated in Western style. Located downtown, the hotel also features a historic saloon and shops offering antiques, fashions, and baked goods. **www.stmichaelhotel.com**

SEDONA Star Motel $

295 Jordan Rd, AZ 86336 **Tel** *(928) 282-3641* **Rooms** *11* **Map** *B3*

Located right in the center of uptown Sedona, this small, unassuming motel is a real find for budget-minded families. Rooms might be short on romance or atmosphere, but they are spotlessly clean. The Star Motel's main advantage is that it is close to everything, and it even has views of Sedona's beautiful red rocks.

SEDONA Cozy Cactus B&B $$$

80 Canyon Circle Dr, AZ 86351 **Tel** *(928) 284-0082 or (800) 788-2082* **Fax** *(928) 284-4210* **Rooms** *5* **Map** *B3*

The family-friendly Cozy Cactus is attractively furnished with Southwestern accents that complement its stunning view of Bell Rock, Courthouse Butte, and Castle Rock. Relax on the terrace and listen for the call of the coyotes. After breakfast, lace up your boots and hike on unofficial trails from right outside the back gate. **www.cozycactus.com**

SEDONA Amara Resort and Spa $$$$$

310 N Hwy 89A, AZ 86336 **Tel** *(928) 282-4828* **Fax** *(928) 282-4825* **Rooms** *100* **Map** *B3*

This boutique resort, just steps from uptown, has stylish furnishings and vibrant colors. The ambience emphasizes comfort and service. Take a swim in the saltwater pool, or indulge your senses at the Amara Spa. Spend the evening stargazing with a glass of wine, on a comfy cushion next to the fire pit. **www.amararesort.com**

SEDONA Enchantment Resort $$$$$

525 Boynton Canyon Rd, AZ 86336 **Tel** *(928) 282-2900* **Fax** *(928) 282-9249* **Rooms** *236* **Map** *B3*

Hidden among the red rocks of Boynton Canyon, the Enchantment pulls out all the stops for luxury and pampering. Its adobe casitas have typically Southwestern interiors. The leisure activities on offer include hiking, biking, croquet, and tennis, plus a full-service spa. Camp Coyote offers a program for children. **www.enchantmentresort.com**

Key to Price Guide *see p124* **Key to Symbols** *see back cover flap*

WAHWEAP Lake Powell Resort $$

100 Lakeshore Dr, AZ 86040 ***Tel*** *(928) 645-2433* ***Fax*** *(928) 645-1031* ***Rooms*** *348* ***Map*** *C2*

This resort sits right on the edge of Lake Powell, overlooking Wahweap Marina. Its upscale rooms, each with a balcony or patio, are located in eight two-story buildings. Half of them boast lake views. Activities available at the hotel and at the Glen Canyon National Recreation Area include boat rentals and cruises. **www.lakepowell.com**

WILLIAMS Mountain Side Inn Grand Canyon $

642 E Route 66, AZ 86046 ***Tel*** *(928) 635-4431 or (800) 462-9381* ***Fax*** *(928) 635-2292* ***Rooms*** *96* ***Map*** *B3*

Tucked away among the tall pines of Kaibab National Forest, the unpretentious Mountain Side Inn is convenient for travelers on their way to the Grand Canyon and is a good base for long walks. Those looking for more entertainment will enjoy the karaoke in the Route 66 Lounge. **www.mountainsideinngrandcanyon.com**

WILLIAMS Grand Canyon Railway Hotel $$$

235 N Grand Canyon Blvd, AZ 86046 ***Tel*** *(928) 635-4010* ***Fax*** *(928) 635-2180* ***Rooms*** *297* ***Map*** *B3*

This elegant hotel adjoins the railway terminus that has seen visitors depart by train to the Grand Canyon for a century. The stylish lobby is reminiscent of yesteryear's grand railway hotels. In winter, the crackling fireplace provides a warm welcome. A nearby pet resort has rooms for dogs and custom condos for cats. **www.thetrain.com**

WINSLOW La Posada $$

303 E 2nd St (Route 66), AZ 86047 ***Tel*** *(928) 289-4366* ***Fax*** *(928) 289-3873* ***Rooms*** *37* ***Map*** *C3*

Built in 1930, and billing itself as "America's last great railway hotel," La Posada was considered the masterpiece of architect Mary Colter. A 1997 renovation brought Colter's vision back to life. Today the hotel offers elegant rooms on lush, landscaped grounds, all within an easy drive of Northern Arizona's top attractions. **www.laposada.org**

PHOENIX AND SOUTHERN ARIZONA

APACHE JUNCTION Best Western Apache Junction Express Inn $$

1101 W Apache Trail, AZ 85220 ***Tel*** *(480) 982-9200* ***Fax*** *(480) 671-6183* ***Rooms*** *40* ***Map*** *C4*

East of Phoenix, and convenient to the Apache Trail, this chain hotel has striking views of Superstition Mountain, site of the legendary Lost Dutchman Goldmine. Featuring a Southwestern theme throughout, the small hotel offers comfortable, clean rooms, an outdoor pool, and a deluxe complimentary breakfast. **www.bestwestern.com**

BISBEE Shady Dell $

1 Old Douglas Rd, AZ 85603 ***Tel*** *(520) 432-3567* ***Rooms*** *11* ***Map*** *C5*

High up in the Mule Mountains, close to the Mexican border, the Shady Dell offers a truly unique experience. Step back in time to the 1950s and spend the night in a vintage trailer, such as a sleek aluminum 1949 Airstream or a 1950 Spartanette, while listening to old rhythm-'n'-blues cassette tapes. **www.theshadydell.com**

BISBEE Bisbee Grand Hotel $$$

61 Main St, AZ 85603 ***Tel*** *(520) 432-5900 or (800) 421-1909* ***Fax*** *(520) 432-9113* ***Rooms*** *13* ***Map*** *C5*

A major restoration in 1986 brought this elegant Victorian hotel back to life. Every room in this Old West gem is furnished with period antiques. Located in the heart of Bisbee's historic center, the Grand Hotel is within easy walking distance of antiques shops, galleries, and other attractions. **www.bisbeegrandhotel.com**

BISBEE Copper Queen Hotel $$$

11 Howell Ave, AZ 85603 ***Tel*** *(520) 432-2216* ***Fax*** *(520) 432-3819* ***Rooms*** *53* ***Map*** *C5*

With its rolltop desk at reception and antique-filled rooms decorated with period wallpaper, the Copper Queen is an early 1900s establishment that welcomed dignitaries in the city's long-gone boomtown days. Today, visitors can cool off in a claw-foot tub (some rooms only), or take a dip in the second-floor pool. **www.copperqueen.com**

DOUGLAS The Gadsden Hotel $

1046 G Ave, AZ 85607 ***Tel*** *(520) 364-4481* ***Fax*** *(520) 364-4005* ***Rooms*** *130* ***Map*** *C5*

Enter one of the most opulent lobbies in the West at the historic Gadsden, where Eleanor Roosevelt, Lee Marvin, and Shelley Winters once stayed. Prices are reasonable at this hotel with a majestic marble staircase, marble columns topped in gold leaf, and an authentic 42 ft- (13 m-) long Tiffany stained-glass mural. **www.hotelgadsden.com**

DRAGOON Triangle T Guest Ranch $$$

I-10 exit 318, Dragoon Rd, AZ 85609 ***Tel*** *(520) 586-7533* ***Fax*** *(520) 586-4476* ***Rooms*** *10* ***Map*** *C5*

Situated in the cool Dragoon Mountains in the Texas Canyon, the Triangle T is close to the Kartchner Caverns, Tombstone, and the Amerind Foundation. Its rustic cabins are just steps away from fields with gigantic boulders, an area popular with birdwatchers, hikers, and artists. Horseback riding is also available. **www.triangletguestranch.com**

GREEN VALLEY Best Western Green Valley $$

111 S La Cañada Drive, AZ 85614 ***Tel*** *(520) 625-2250* ***Fax*** *(520) 625-0215* ***Rooms*** *108* ***Map*** *C5*

Located mere minutes from the "white dove of the desert," – the San Xavier del Bac church, this reliable chain hotel has comfortable rooms and attractive landscaping. Save some time for a swim in the pool after birdwatching at the nearby Madera Canyon, part of a migratory corridor for over 300 bird species. **www.bestwesterngreenvalley.com**

PHOENIX Best Western Central Phoenix Inn & Suites $$

1100 N Central Ave, AZ 85004 ***Tel*** *(602) 252-2100* ***Fax*** *(602) 252-2100* ***Rooms*** *107* ***Map*** *B4*

As its name implies, this hotel is centrally located, within walking distance of the city's famous museums and Copper Square. It has an outdoor pool and hot tub, and a dry sauna in which to relax after using the fitness center. There are beautiful views of downtown from the rooms on the upper floors. **www.bestwesterncentralphoenix.com**

PHOENIX Quality Inn & Suites $$

202 E McDowell Rd, AZ 85004 ***Tel*** *(602) 955-6600* ***Fax*** *(602) 258-7259* ***Rooms*** *48* ***Map*** *B4*

A good downtown base for visiting the Phoenix Art Museum, the Quality Inn chain hotel is also only a few blocks from the Heard Museum and offers a free weekday shuttle to Copper Square and the Convention Center. In the summer months, you can escape the hot weather in the outdoor pool. **www.choicehotels.com**

PHOENIX Hotel San Carlos $$$

202 N Central Ave, AZ 85004 ***Tel*** *(602) 253-4121 or (866) 253-4121* ***Fax*** *(602) 253-6668* ***Rooms*** *128* ***Map*** *B4*

This historic hotel is full of character and charm. Despite some small rooms, it is reasonably priced and very nostalgic. Its legendary guest roster includes the likes of Mae West, Clark Gable, and Marilyn Monroe, plus, of course, the obligatory resident ghost. A rooftop pool and a sidewalk café complete the picture. **www.hotelsancarlos.com**

PHOENIX Radisson Hotel Phoenix City Center $$$

3600 N 2nd Ave, AZ 85031 ***Tel*** *(602) 604-4900* ***Fax*** *(602) 604-4901* ***Rooms*** *274* ***Map*** *B4*

A breath of fresh air in the city, the upscale Radisson boasts a lovely gazebo garden and two outdoor pools with a massive rock waterfall, plus a rooftop pool, tennis courts, a putting green, and a children's playground. Visitors can also take advantage of the complimentary parking. **www.radisson.com/phoenixaz_citycenter**

PHOENIX Arizona Biltmore Resort & Spa $$$$$

2400 E Missouri Ave, AZ 85016 ***Tel*** *(602) 955-6600* ***Fax*** *(602) 381-7600* ***Rooms*** *738* ***Map*** *B4*

This legendary 1930s resort is heralded for its Frank Lloyd Wright-inspired architecture. Enjoy afternoon tea and experience the same luxuries as royalty and statesmen, in the lush surroundings where Irving Berlin penned "White Christmas." Play lawn chess or golf, or order your pet a meal through room service. **www.arizonabiltmore.com**

PHOENIX Arizona Grand Resort $$$$$

7777 S Pointe Parkway, AZ 85044 ***Tel*** *(602) 438-9000* ***Fax*** *(602) 431-6535* ***Rooms*** *640* ***Map*** *B4*

This family-friendly resort offers golf, tennis, horseback riding, and a spa. Its pièce de résistance, exclusive to guests, is The Oasis, a waterpark with a slide, a wave pool, and the "Zuni River". Each balcony suite has a living room and a wet bar. There are miles of hiking trails in the adjacent South Mountain Preserve. **www.arizonagrandresort.com**

PHOENIX Clarendon Hotel and Suites $$$$$

401 W Clarendon Ave, AZ 85013 ***Tel*** *(602) 252-7363* ***Fax*** *(602) 274-9009* ***Rooms*** *105* ***Map*** *B4*

The trendy Clarendon has an interior inspired by Art Deco design, and cutting-edge lighting: undulating cobalt-blue and salmon-red lights glow late into the night at its chic French-fusion Camus restaurant. The hotel is located in the city's business district and offers perks such as free nationwide calling and free parking. **www.theclarendon.net**

PHOENIX Embassy Suites Phoenix-Biltmore $$$$$

2630 E Camelback Rd, AZ 85016 ***Tel*** *(602) 955-3992* ***Fax*** *(602) 955-6479* ***Rooms*** *232* ***Map*** *B4*

An exquisite towering atrium filled with tall palms, the sound of waterfalls, and exotic Japanese koi-carp ponds greet visitors at this all-suite hotel. Start the day with a complimentary cooked-to-order breakfast, then visit the exclusive Biltmore Fashion Park adjacent to the hotel. **www.phoenixbiltmore.embassysuites.com**

PHOENIX Hyatt Regency Phoenix $$$$$

122 2nd St, AZ 85004 ***Tel*** *(602) 252-1234 or (800) 233-1234* ***Fax*** *(602) 254-9472* ***Rooms*** *696* ***Map*** *B4*

Located in the heart of Phoenix, across from the Convention Center, this 712-room urban resort puts you in the perfect place to sample the best of downtown. Offering a full range of exercise and business facilities, the hotel is also renowned for the award-winning Compass Restaurant *(see p138)*. **www.phoenix.hyatt.com**

PHOENIX Ritz-Carlton Hotel $$$$$

2401 E Camelback Rd, AZ 85016 ***Tel*** *(602) 468-0700* ***Fax*** *(602) 468-0793* ***Rooms*** *281* ***Map*** *B4*

Standing 11 stories tall, the Ritz-Carlton has refined, elegant decor throughout and far-reaching views of the downtown Phoenix skyline, Camelback Mountain, and Squaw Peak. Store your golf bag here and you will get a complimentary shine for your grassy golf shoes. There are additional fees for valet parking. **www.ritzcarlton.com**

PHOENIX The Wigwam Resort $$$$$

300 Wigwam Blvd, Litchfield Pk, AZ 85340 ***Tel*** *(623) 935-3811* ***Fax*** *(623) 935-3737* ***Rooms*** *331* ***Map*** *B4*

This sprawling resort west of downtown was once an Egyptian-cotton plantation in the Sonoran Desert; parts of the agricultural area are now occupied by three magnificent golf courses. Oversized, elegant casita-style rooms provide a sense of privacy. Guests can relax at the brand-new Elizabeth Arden Red Door Spa. **www.wigwamresort.com**

SCOTTSDALE Fairmont Scottsdale Princess $$$$$

7575 E Princess Dr, AZ 85255 ***Tel*** *(480) 585-4848* ***Fax*** *(480) 585-0091* ***Rooms*** *651* ***Map*** *B4*

This relaxed resort features Spanish Colonial architecture, with a tiled roof, arches, pink stucco, and fountains. Rooms are spacious, luxurious, and decorated in earthy accents, with many amenities. The Princess is noted for its two Tournament Players Club golf courses, Willow Stream spa, and kids' club. **www.fairmont.com/scottsdale**

SCOTTSDALE Hotel Valley Ho $$$$$

6850 E Main St, AZ 85251 **Tel** *(480) 248-2000* **Rooms** *194* **Map** *B4*

Once a playground for the likes of Bogart and Monroe, the Valley Ho became fashionable again when it reopened after major renovations in 2004. Retro-chic rooms have glass walls opening onto balconies with views to Camelback Mountain. Also available are a yoga-Pilates studio, 24-hour fitness and room service, and tubs for two. **www.HotelValleyHo.com**

SCOTTSDALE Hyatt Regency Scottsdale Resort and Spa at Gainey Ranch $$$$$

7500 E Doubletree Ranch Rd, AZ 85258 **Tel** *(480) 444-1234* **Fax** *(480) 483-5550* **Rooms** *490* **Map** *B4*

This elegant resort with exquisite modern decor is close to the Old Town. With ten pools, a sandy beach, and tall palms, it's truly a water playground. The spacious rooms, full of deluxe amenities, all have views. Activities include championship golf, a spa, and the fascinating Native American Learning Center. **www.scottsdale.hyatt.com**

SCOTTSDALE The Phoenician $$$$$

6000 E Camelback Rd, AZ 85251 **Tel** *(480) 941-8200* **Fax** *(480) 947-4311* **Rooms** *647* **Map** *B4*

From the art collection to the enchanting cactus garden and the spa's Meditation Atrium, The Phoenician is a place where lavish opulence mixes with nature's beauty. The graceful rooms have muted tones, marble bathrooms, and selected artworks. Championship golf is also on offer, along with a pampering spa. **www.thephoenician.com**

SHOW LOW Best Western Paint Pony Lodge $

581 W Deuce of Clubs, AZ 85901 **Tel** *(928) 537-5773* **Fax** *(928) 537-5766* **Rooms** *50* **Map** *C3*

Located in the tall pine country of Show Low, this hotel is a good notch above other chain hotels. Tastefully decorated rooms come equipped with a microwave oven, fridge, and cable TV. Guests can enjoy a complimentary hot breakfast in the morning and freshly baked cookies in the afternoon. **www.bestwesternarizona.com**

TOMBSTONE Silver Nugget Bed & Breakfast $

520 E Allen St, AZ 85638 **Tel** *(520) 457-9223* **Fax** *(520) 457-3471* **Rooms** *4* **Map** *C5*

Located in notorious bandit town, Tombstone, the character filled Silver Nugget B&B boasts the only balcony overlooking historic Allen Street. Sit outside and view the scene of the 1881 shootout involving Wyatt Earp and Doc Holliday, relax in the comfortable common area, or visit the adjacent ice cream parlour. **www.tombstone1880.com/silvernugget**

TOMBSTONE Tombstone Boarding House $

108 N 4th St, AZ 85638 **Tel** *(520) 457-3716 or (877) 225-1319* **Rooms** *5* **Map** *C5*

This B&B is located in two side-by-side historic adobe homes in Tombstone, the town that was "too tough to die." Rooms are decorated with period antiques and quilts, and the honeymoon suite features a large clawfoot bathtub. The 1880s dining room houses a full-service restaurant. **www.tombstoneboardinghouse.com**

TOMBSTONE Best Western Lookout Lodge $$

801 N Hwy 80 W, AZ 85638 **Tel** *(520) 457-2223* **Fax** *(520) 457-3870* **Rooms** *40* **Map** *C5*

Within walking distance of the Boothill Graveyard, where the OK Corral gunslingers were laid to rest, the Lookout Lodge is a good base for seeing the sights of Tombstone, while escaping the hustle and bustle of Allen Street. All rooms have views of the Dragoon Mountains, and the hotel is very pet-friendly. **www.bestwesternarizona.com**

TUCSON El Presidio Bed & Breakfast Inn $$

297 N Main Ave, AZ 85701 **Tel** *(520) 623-6151 or (800) 349-6151* **Fax** *(520) 623-3860* **Rooms** *4* **Map** *C5*

Close to Old Town Artisans and the Tucson Museum of Art, this Victorian adobe inn, an American Territorial-style home from 1886, is located in a neighborhood of elegant mansions known as Snob Hollow. Filled with antiques, it has a lush and shady courtyard garden and offers fine gourmet breakfasts. **www.bbonline.com/az/elpresidio**

TUCSON Windmill Suites at St. Philip's Plaza $$$

4250 N Campbell Ave, AZ 85718 **Tel** *(520) 577-0007* **Fax** *(520) 577-0045* **Rooms** *122* **Map** *C5*

Located on the northern edge of Tucson, at the foot of the Santa Catalina Mountains, the Windmill is part of a pleasant plaza with shops, galleries, and restaurants. It offers spacious accommodation in its two-room suites, guest use of bicycles, a lending library, and a complimentary breakfast. The hotel is good value for money. **www.windmillinns.com**

TUCSON Arizona Inn $$$$

2200 E Elm St, AZ 85719 **Tel** *(520) 325-1541* **Fax** *(520) 881-5830* **Rooms** *95* **Map** *C5*

This historic pink-stucco boutique inn is in the heart of Tucson. The individually decorated rooms are in casitas spread throughout the lush gardens. Guests are made to feel welcome with complimentary high tea, fireside drinks in the library in winter, and in summertime, ice creams poolside. Clay tennis courts are also available. **www.arizonainn.com**

TUCSON Hacienda del Sol Guest Ranch Resort $$$$

5601 N Hacienda del Sol Rd, AZ 85718 **Tel** *(520) 299-1501* **Fax** *(520) 299-5554* **Rooms** *30* **Map** *C5*

At the foot of the Santa Catalina Mountains, the Hacienda del Sol once housed a school attended by the rich and famous. It is now a relaxing luxury resort with exquisite rooms decorated in warm Southwestern tones and Spanish Colonial design. Go horseback riding, or get a jade-stone massage at the spa. **www.haciendadelsol.com**

TUCSON Royal Elizabeth Bed & Breakfast Inn $$$$

204 S Scott Ave, AZ 85701 **Tel** *(520) 670-9022 or (877) 670-9022* **Fax** *(928) 833-9974* **Rooms** *6* **Map** *C5*

The meticulously restored 1878 Victorian adobe mansion is located in a historic downtown district. Affectionately known as "The Liz," it is richly appointed with original antiques and beautiful woodwork. The list of amenities includes a heated pool, hot tub, garden, and delicious gourmet breakfasts. **www.royalelizabeth.com**

TUCSON Lodge on the Desert $$$$$

306 N Alvernon Way, AZ 85711 **Tel** *(520) 325-3366* **Fax** *(520) 327-5834* **Rooms** *103* **Map** *C5*

In operation since 1936, this is an urban oasis near the University of Arizona, with views of the Santa Catalina Mountains. Lodging is in hacienda-style rooms, many with high, wood-beamed ceilings, fireplaces, and tiled patios. Towering palm trees preside over the pool, surrounded by lush desert gardens. **www.lodgeonthedesert.com**

TUCSON Tanque Verde Guest Ranch $$$$$

14301 E Speedway Blvd, AZ 85748 **Tel** *(520) 296-6275* **Fax** *(520) 721-9426* **Rooms** *74* **Map** *C5*

At the base of the Rincon Mountains, next to Saguaro National Park, this ranch was founded in 1868. With weekly barbecues featuring Western singalongs, cowboy-style breakfasts, and morning horseback rides, it is a great place for families wishing to enjoy nature and outdoor living. **www.tanqueverderanch.com**

TUCSON White Stallion Ranch $$$$$

9251 W Twin Peaks Rd, AZ 85743 **Tel** *(520) 297-0252* **Fax** *(520) 744-2786* **Rooms** *45* **Map** *C5*

In the Sonoran Desert, this working ranch allows city slickers to see longhorn cattle and weekly rodeos. Guests can ride Western-style among the saguaro cacti, and take hayrides to cookouts. The Southwestern-style rooms are very comfortable. Great for families, with outdoor games, a petting zoo, and a pool. **www.wsranch.com**

YUMA La Fuente Inn & Suites $$

1513 E 16th St, AZ 85365 **Tel** *(928) 329-1814 or (800) 841-1814* **Fax** *(928) 343-2671* **Rooms** *97* **Map** *A4*

This clean, modern hotel features rooms and suites that are spacious and reasonably priced. The inviting pool is shaded by palm trees, and guests can enjoy a complimentary full buffet breakfast every morning. The inn is located near the historic Yuma Prison and other attractions. **www.lafuenteinn.com**

THE FOUR CORNERS

BLUFF Recapture Lodge $

Hwy 191, UT, 84512 **Tel** *(435) 672-2281* **Fax** *(435) 672-2284* **Rooms** *26* **Map** *D1*

A favorite place for kayaking and rafting, the Recapture Lodge is on the San Juan River. Shuttles to the river can be arranged, and the lodge has regular speakers and slide shows on local geology and archaeology. Children can play on the jungle gym with monkey bars and swings. Rooms are simple but clean. **www.recapturelodge.com**

BLUFF Desert Rose Inn $$

701 W Hwy 191, UT, 84512 **Tel** *(435) 672-2303 or (888) 475-7673* **Fax** *(435) 672-2217* **Rooms** *36* **Map** *D1*

The best thing about this modern inn is its location in the charming town of Bluff, along the sparkling San Juan River, surrounded by the natural splendor of the Colorado Plateau. The rooms are bright, clean, and decorated in nouveau-rustic style, with tasteful Southwestern art and quilted wood-framed beds. **www.desertroseinn.com**

CAMERON Cameron Trading Post $$

Route 89, AZ 86020 **Tel** *(928) 679-2231* **Fax** *(928) 679-2501* **Rooms** *66* **Map** *C2*

Located at a crossroads with routes to Lake Powell, the Grand Canyon, and the Four Corners, this Native American hotel and trading post offers reasonable rates and a large Native art gallery. Balconies overlook a desert garden or the Little Colorado River Gorge, with the old 1911 swayback suspension bridge. **www.camerontradingpost.com**

CHINLE Best Western Canyon de Chelly Inn $

100 Main St, AZ 86503 **Tel** *(928) 674-5875* **Fax** *(928) 674-3715* **Rooms** *99* **Map** *D2*

In a region where dependable accommodation is scarce, the predictable quality of this Best Western hotel can be very welcome. Billing itself as the only Chinle hotel with a hot tub, sauna, and indoor pool, the Canyon de Chelly Inn offers rooms that are clean and airy. **www.bestwesternarizona.com**

CHINLE Thunderbird Lodge $$

Canyon de Chelly Navajo Route 7, AZ 86503 **Tel** *(928) 674-5841* **Fax** *(928) 674-5844* **Rooms** *74* **Map** *D2*

A century ago, this lovely establishment right at the mouth of Canyon de Chelly was a small trading post with bungalows. Now a pleasant chain motel, it's a pink adobe-style building nestled among mature cottonwoods. Tours by experienced Navajo guides in six-wheel-drive vehicles can be arranged at the lodge. **www.tbirdlodge.com**

CORTEZ Holiday Inn Mesa Verde Cortez $$

2121 E Main St, CO, 81321 **Tel** *(970) 565-6000* **Fax** *(970) 565-3438* **Rooms** *100* **Map** *D1*

A reliable member of the Holiday Inn chain, this hotel offers colorful desert-inspired decor, wireless Internet, a complimentary Continental breakfast, and a well-appointed gym. It is just 9 miles (14.5 km) from Mesa Verde National Park and 20 miles (32 km) from the Four Corners National Monument. **http://www.coloradoholiday.com**

CORTEZ Kelly Place Bed & Breakfast $$

14663 Rd G, CO, 81321 **Tel** *(970) 565-3125 or (800) 745-4885* **Fax** *(970) 564-9440* **Rooms** *11* **Map** *D1*

Near the Canyons of the Ancients, this family retreat is nestled among the orchards in McElmo Canyon, at the foot of Sleeping Ute Mountain. The estate contains numerous ancient Puebloan sites to explore, including a thousand-year-old *kiva* and pueblo just steps from the lodge. Archaeologist-guided hikes are available. **www.kellyplace.com**

Key to Price Guide *see p124* **Key to Symbols** *see back cover flap*

DURANGO The Rochester Hotel $$$

721 E Second Ave, CO, 81301 ***Tel*** *(800) 664-1929* ***Fax*** *(970) 385-1967* ***Rooms*** *15* ***Map*** *D1*

Within walking distance of the major Durango attractions, this beautifully restored 1892 hotel is attractively decorated with Old West and cowboy decor. The spacious guestrooms are comfortable, with 1890s-style furnishings and Western art. A full gourmet breakfast is served in the lobby. **www.rochesterhotel.com**

DURANGO Strater Hotel $$$

699 Main Ave, CO, 81301 ***Tel*** *(970) 247-4431* ***Fax*** *(970) 259-2208* ***Rooms*** *93* ***Map*** *D1*

Built in 1887, this gorgeous red-and-white gingerbread Victorian building has a rich history and is a prominent landmark in downtown Durango. The rooms are all uniquely decorated and filled with period antiques. Honky-tonk ragtime plays in the Diamond Belle Saloon. **www.strater.com**

FARMINGTON Best Western Inn at Farmington $$

700 Scott Ave, NM, 87401 ***Tel*** *(505) 327-5221* ***Fax*** *(505) 327-1565* ***Rooms*** *192* ***Map*** *D2*

Guests can walk or jog along the banks of the Animas River, just behind this dependable chain hotel. A full hot breakfast is included in the price, and an indoor pool is located in a handsome plant-filled atrium. The hotel has a sports bar with billiards, Rookies Lounge, and dining at the Riverwalk Patio & Grille. **www.bestwestern.com**

MESA VERDE NATIONAL PARK Far View Motor Lodge $$

Mile Marker 15, Mancos, CO, 81328 ***Tel*** *(602) 331-5210* ***Fax*** *(970) 564-4311* ***Rooms*** *150* ***Map*** *D2*

The views from the balconied rooms at this adobe-style lodge stretch clear over the Montezuma Valley. It is a quiet, yet modern retreat near the park's visitors' center, but away from the crowds touring the cliff dwellings. The lodge houses the excellent Metate Room restaurant *(see p141)* and a shop. Closed in winter. **www.visitmesaverde.com**

MEXICAN HAT Valley of the Gods Bed and Breakfast $$

Valley of the Gods Rd, UT, 84531 ***Tel*** *(970) 749-1164* ***Rooms*** *4* ***Map*** *C2*

Relax on the long porch of this solar- and wind-powered rustic but comfortable home, with a stunning view towards the Valley of the Gods and the Belle's Butte monolith. Staying here is truly a memorable experience. A full breakfast is served daily, but you should bring your own dinner supplies. **www.valleyofthegods.cjb.net**

MONUMENT VALLEY Goulding's Lodge $$$

1000 Main St, off Hwy 163, UT, 84536 ***Tel*** *(435) 727-3231* ***Fax*** *(435) 727-3344* ***Rooms*** *78* ***Map*** *C2*

Originally a trading post, the Goulding's Lodge is tucked into a mesa just opposite the entrance to Monument Valley. It has a bustling restaurant and superb views of the park buttes from its balconied rooms. The small museum on site displays memorabilia from famed movies by director John Ford. **www.gouldings.com**

MONUMENT VALLEY The View Hotel $$$

Hwy 163, Monument Valley Tribal Park, UT 84536 ***Tel*** *(435) 727-5555* ***Fax*** *(435) 727-4545* ***Rooms*** *95* ***Map*** *C2*

Inside Monument Valley, and with amazing views of the monuments, this modern hotel is furnished in contemporary style. The comfortable guestrooms have private balconies with views of the monuments, and the third floor rooms are great for star-gazing. Be sure to watch the sunrise over Monument Valley. **www.monumentvalleyview.com**

SECOND MESA, HOPI RESERVATION Hopi Cultural Center Inn $

Route 264, AZ 86043 ***Tel*** *(928) 734-2401* ***Fax*** *(928) 734-6651* ***Rooms*** *33* ***Map*** *C2*

When you get to Second Mesa, you step back more than 1,000 years in time. This adobe, pueblo-style inn, the only one for miles around, has clean, basic rooms, and is an excellent base for touring all three mesas. Expect high-desert windy days in spring, and breathtaking views. Reserve in advance. **www.hopiculturalcenter.com**

TELLURIDE The Victorian Inn $$$

401 W Pacific Ave, CO, 81435 ***Tel*** *(970) 728-6601* ***Fax*** *(970) 728-3233* ***Rooms*** *33* ***Map*** *D1*

The Victorian Inn is just blocks from the historic downtown district of Telluride. In an area where hotels tend to be pricey, this is a supremely affordable option. Ask for a quiet room, and be aware that some lodgings are a bit small. Continental breakfast is served, and the dry sauna is open during the winter months. **www.TheVictorianInn.org**

TELLURIDE New Sheridan Hotel $$$$$

231 W Colorado Ave, CO, 81435 ***Tel*** *(970) 728-4351* ***Fax*** *(970) 728-5024* ***Rooms*** *32* ***Map*** *D1*

Built in 1891, the small but historic New Sheridan lacks no luxury. Its rooms are furnished with period antiques, and some come with mountain views. A complimentary breakfast awaits guests in the morning; there is a well-stocked library; and avid skiers can store their equipment securely. On the roof are two hot tubs. **www.newsheridan.com**

TELLURIDE The Peaks Resort & Golden Door Spa $$$$$

136 Country Club Dr, CO, 81435 ***Tel*** *(970) 728-6800* ***Fax*** *(970) 728-6175* ***Rooms*** *174* ***Map*** *D1*

If you're looking for luxury and spectacular Rocky Mountains views, the place to be is the Peaks Resort in Mountain Village close to Telluride. This is the spot for ski access in winter, golf in summer, and the magnificent Golden Door Spa, open all year round. **www.thepeaksresort.com**

WINDOW ROCK Quality Inn Navajo National Capital $

48 W Hwy 264, AZ 86515 ***Tel*** *(928) 871-4108 or (800) 662-6189* ***Fax*** *(928) 871-5466* ***Rooms*** *56* ***Map*** *D2*

Close to the governmental center of the Navajo Nation, and next door to the tribal-controlled Community College, the Navajo National Museum, and the zoo, this hotel offers rooms with Southwestern decor. As well as a business center, it has an on-site restaurant where a complimentary breakfast is served. **www.qualityinnwindowrock.com**

WHERE TO EAT

As well as offering high quality and top-class regional cusine, Arizona offers an exciting range of eating experiences, especially in its larger cities. Phoenix, Scottsdale, Tucson, and Sedona rival any city in the United States for the quality of ingredients and variety of cuisine available, with ambiences ranging from rustic to romantic. In keeping with its newly-acquired international status, Southwestern cuisine is served in a growing number of casual but stylish cafés. Steakhouses, too, abound in this region.

Pub sign in Flagstaff

Local restaurants usually serve the best Mexican food, and there are also eateries with a cowboy or Mexican theme, where one can get an inexpensive meal and great entertainment. In small towns, the best dishes are served in hotel restaurants. The establishments on pages 134–41 have been chosen for their quality, location, and good value. Some typical Mexican dishes available in Arizona are shown in the box at the bottom of this section.

PRICES & TIPPING

Eating out in Arizona is very reasonable, and even expensive restaurants offer good value. Light meals in cafés and diners usually cost under $10, while chain restaurants serve complete dinners for under $15. Mexican restaurants offer combination plates, which generally include rice, beans, tacos, and some sort of meat for $8–$12. At finer restaurants, dinner entrées range from $15 to $30, and diners can still buy a three-course meal, excluding wine, for under $50.

The standard tip is 15 percent of the cost of the meal. However, leave up to 20 percent if the service is good. Sales tax is not shown on the menu and will add around 5–7 percent to the cost of a meal.

A tortilla and bean stall at Tumacacori, Southern Arizona

TYPES OF FOOD & RESTAURANTS

Dining establishments in Arizona range from small and friendly diners and cafés, offering hearty burgers and snacks, to gourmet restaurants that serve the latest Southwestern and fusion cuisine, to lavish dining rooms in the top-class and upscale resorts found in and around Phoenix, Scottsdale, and Tucson.

Starting at the lower end of the scale, fast food is a way of life throughout the state, and a string of outlets such as McDonald's, Burger King, Wendy's, and Arby's are found along the main strips of most towns in the state. They all serve the usual inexpensive variations of burgers, fries, and soft drinks. Chains such as Applebee's and Denny's offer more variety, with soups, salads, sandwiches, meals, and desserts. These are generally good value, but the quality varies from one establishment to the next. Pizza chains are also ubiquitous in the region.

Mid-range eating places can include a range of ethnic cuisine such as Italian, Greek,

REGIONAL DISHES AND SPECIALTIES

Avocados

Southwestern food reflects the region's strong Hispanic and Native cultures. Mexican food and its more refined cousin, Southwestern cuisine, enjoy a following around the globe. One of the pleasures of a visit to Arizona is discovering the great variety of restaurants that serve dishes made with the freshest ingredients, and cooked with great expertise. The chile pepper is at the heart of Southwestern cuisine, and some pack a powerful bite, but there are other milder varieties that add flavor without heat. Most menus in restaurants frequented by tourists provide an explanation of the dishes, and friendly staff offer advice. The region's other great staple is beef, and there is no shortage of good steaks and burgers in most areas.

Enchiladas *are rolled tortillas filled with cheese, chicken, or beef, topped with a red chile sauce and melted cheese.*

Chinese, Japanese, and Indian. Many good restaurants that fall into this category can be found in shopping malls.

Native American food is found throughout the state, especially on reservations, and is generally reasonably priced. Fry bread forms the base of many meals, and is often topped with meat, beans, cheese, lettuce, and tomatoes.

Steakhouses serving steaks, mesquite barbecue, and ribs are found across Arizona in a wide variety of price ranges. Some of these restaurants also serve fresh mountain-trout and seafood, and provide live Western-style entertainment.

Mexican restaurants are popular and are located all over the state. They vary from roadside stands and snack bars to upscale restaurants. New Mexican cuisine, inspired by the cooking methods of the Pueblo culture, is widespread. The distinctive taste of the dishes comes from the use of piñon pine nuts, nopales (the fruit of the prickly pear cactus), and the chayote, which is similar to zucchini.

Southwestern cuisine is a fusion of Native American, Hispanic, and international influences, and is increasingly showcased in Arizona's finest restaurants. The most important ingredients are chiles, corn, beans, cilantro, tomatillos, and pine nuts. Restaurants visited by locals tend to server hotter chiles than those catering to tourists, but if you are unsure many places will serve a little dish on the side.

A colorful restaurant housed in a massive teepee along Route 66

VEGETARIAN

Southwestern cuisine is largely meat based. Vegetarians may not be able to find much variety outside the larger cities and resorts. However, salad bars are available everywhere, from fine restaurants to fast food chains. Salads can be a complete meal as they often come with meat and seafood, but vegetarian orders are usually accommodated. Many fast food chains now serve salads, soups, or baked potatoes to cater to the more health-conscious customer.

The more expensive restaurants, and those affiliated with hotels, are usually willing to provide vegetarian meals on request when they have the ingredients. It is a good idea to phone ahead.

DISABLED FACILITIES

Restaurants are required to provide wheelchair access and a ground-level restroom by law, but check with older places in advance.

ALCOHOL

Beer, particularly the many kinds of *cervezas* imported from Mexico, is the most popular drink in the region. Typical brands include San Miguel and Corona. Arizona has a growing brew-pub and micro-brewery industry as well. Wine and other alcoholic drinks are also available throughout the state, except on Native reservations. The finer restaurants usually serve a wide variety of beverages. Visitors must be 21 to buy alcohol. Make sure you carry ID as you may be requested to show it.

Margarita cocktail

Huevos rancheros, *fried eggs on a soft tortilla with chile, cheese, and refried beans, are eaten at breakfast.*

Tacos *are crisp-fried tortillas filled with ground beef, beans, cheese, and salad, and served with guacamole*

Chile relleno *is a whole green chile stuffed with cheese, meat, or rice, dipped in light batter and then deep-fried.*

Choosing a Restaurant

The restaurants in this section have been selected across a wide range of price categories for their exceptional food, good value, or interesting location. Entries are listed by region, in alphabetical order within price category, starting with the least expensive. For map references, see the *Back endpaper*.

PRICE CATEGORIES
Price categories include a three-course meal for one, a glass of house wine, and all unavoidable extra charges, including tax:
$ Under $25
$$ $25–$35
$$$ $35–$50
$$$$ $50–$70
$$$$$ Over $70

GRAND CANYON AND NORTHERN ARIZONA

FLAGSTAFF Downtown Diner $$
7 E Aspen Ave, AZ 86001 ***Tel*** *(928) 774-3492* ***Map*** *C3*

If you are having an early start, join the locals at Downtown Diner, near Heritage Square: it opens at 5:30am and stays open until 9pm (on Sundays, it opens from 7:30am until 6pm). Enjoy a hearty breakfast, or a burger, sandwich, or fresh trout from the nearby Oak Creek. There are large photos on the walls and booth seating. No alcohol is served.

FLAGSTAFF San Felipe's Cantina $$
103 N Leroux St, AZ 86001 ***Tel*** *(928) 779-6000* ***Map*** *C3*

Just off Route 66, San Felipe's is a Baja-style cantina serving Mexican food "with an attitude." Try the grilled *mahi mahi*, Mango Tango, or Mango Chicken, each topped with a zesty mango salsa. Sip a margarita or taste the delicious Choco Taco, filled with ice cream. Blues musicians perform here on Sundays, and there is a kid's menu too.

FLAGSTAFF Black Bart's Steak House $$$
2760 E Butler Ave, AZ 86004 ***Tel*** *(928) 779-3142* ***Map*** *C3*

Named for an 1870s stagecoach robber, Black Bart's offers oak-fire-grilled steaks and seafood. There is also a selection of appetizers including mushrooms dipped in Bart's secret batter, token vegetarian and salad options, and deserts such as the Devilicious Chocolate Cake. A nightly musical review features old standards and showtunes.

FLAGSTAFF Charly's Pub & Grill $$$
23 N Leroux St, AZ 86001 ***Tel*** *(928) 779-1919* ***Map*** *C3*

Popular for people-watching at its sidewalk tables, Charly's serves Navajo tacos, fresh soups, and delicious pies, as well as posole steaks and vegetarian dishes. Late at night, diners can expect varied music acts, from blues to jazz. Located in the Hotel Weatherford *(see p124)*, which offers a selection of bars and restaurants on each floor.

FLAGSTAFF Pasto $$$
19 E Aspen Ave, AZ 86001 ***Tel*** *(928) 779-1937* ***Map*** *C3*

A casual, busy downtown restaurant, Pasto serves a range of Italian dishes. Two lifesize statues carry vases filled with fresh flowers, and the decor is complemented by photos of Italy. Under a painted copper ceiling or, weather permitting, in the garden, you can enjoy creamed-bacon crostini, followed by rabbit *cacciatore*.

FLAGSTAFF Cottage Place Restaurant $$$$$
126 W Cottage Ave, AZ 86001 ***Tel*** *(928) 774-8431* ***Map*** *C3*

Dine in an airy, bungalow-style residence-turned-restaurant with tables dressed in pink linen. The menu offers dishes such as pan-seared tenderloin filet topped with Gorgonzola and served with a Port demi-glaze. A good selection of seafood and vegetarian dishes is also available, and there is an extensive wine list. Closed Mon, Tue.

GRAND CANYON Phantom Ranch Canteen $$
Grand Canyon, AZ 86023 ***Tel*** *(928) 638-2631 or (888) 297-2757* ***Map*** *B2*

Adventurers traveling to the canyon bottom – by raft, mule, or on foot – must be early risers. Dinner tends to be an early affair, too. Breakfast and dinner are at specific times here, and reservations are a must; email in advance, along with any lodging requests *(see p125)*. Choose steak, Hiker's Stew, or a vegetarian dish. A sack lunch is also available.

GRAND CANYON Coronado Room $$$
SR64, AZ 86023 ***Tel*** *(928) 638-2681* ***Map*** *B2*

This fine dining room attached to the Best Western Grand Canyon Squire Inn hotel *(see p125)* offers a traditional menu of prime-rib steaks and seafood. The menu also includes a blend of dependable European- and Southwestern-inspired dishes – from escargot to spinach enchiladas and sizzling fajitas.

GRAND CANYON Canyon Star Restaurant $$$$
SR64, AZ 86023 ***Tel*** *(928) 638-3333* ***Map*** *B2*

This family-friendly hotel restaurant is open all day and features nightly entertainment ranging from Native dancers to local entertainer "Banjo Paul." The menu relies heavily on grilled steaks, but it also has Southwestern dishes such as chile rellenos and enchiladas, as well as seafood specialties, including salmon.

Key to Symbols *see back cover flap*

GRAND CANYON (NORTH RIM) Grand Canyon Lodge $$$

Grand Canyon, AZ 86052 ***Tel*** *(928) 638-2611 ext.160* ***Map*** *B2*

This beautiful, remote restaurant offers astounding views of the Kaibab Plateau through two large windows. Dining is more sophisticated than one would imagine, with dishes such as crab cakes in a chipotle sauce, or chicken breasts sautéed in Dijon cream sauce. In high season, reservations should be made a month or two in advance.

GRAND CANYON (SOUTH RIM) Maswik Cafeteria $

Grand Canyon Village, AZ 86023 ***Tel*** *(928) 638-2631* ***Map*** *B2*

For families on the go, the self-service cafeteria at the Maswik Lodge *(see p125)* is an excellent choice. Several types of food are sold at various stations – with burgers, traditional meals, and Mexican fare as firm favorites among the diners. A well-portioned meal here is both inexpensive and filling.

GRAND CANYON (SOUTH RIM) Bright Angel Restaurant $$$

Grand Canyon Village, AZ 86023 ***Tel*** *(928) 638-2631* ***Map*** *B2*

The Bright Angel offers family-style casual dining and Southwestern fare named for the people who helped build the lodge. Try the Colter Quesadilla (for the architect who designed the building in 1935) or a Harvey House Steak. Seating is on a first-come, first-served basis, but in high season you can put your name on a waiting list.

GRAND CANYON (SOUTH RIM) El Tovar $$$$

Grand Canyon Village, AZ 86023 ***Tel*** *(928) 638-2631 ext. 6432* ***Map*** *B2*

Unquestionably, the best dining in the park can be found at El Tovar, where the menu offers a mix of classic and Southwestern flavors. The impressive dining room has a few window tables overlooking the Grand Canyon – meals are pricier in this section, and you must reserve in advance. For views and a light meal, head for the veranda.

JEROME Flatiron Café $

416 N Main St, AZ 86331 ***Tel*** *(928) 634-2733* ***Map*** *B3*

If you travel the tortuous road up to Jerome, a one-time copper boomtown, you can't miss the tiny Flatiron Café, facing downhill where the road splits. Order chicken quesadilla with blue cheese, spinach and home-made cilantro pesto, followed by an exceptionally strong espresso. Be sure not to slip on the café's slanted floors.

JEROME Asylum Restaurant $$$

200 Hill Street, AZ 86331 ***Tel*** *(928) 639-3197* ***Map*** *B3*

This cozy restaurant in the Jerome Grand Hotel has great views of the Verde Valley. The menu features New American cuisine, including Pacific King Salmon with prickly pear barbecue sauce, and grilled pork tenderloin with chipotle apricot sauce. The wine list is excellent.

KINGMAN Mr D'z Route 66 $

105 E Andy Devine Ave, AZ 86401 ***Tel*** *(928) 718-0066* ***Map*** *A3*

Decked out in a kitsch pink and teal color-scheme, this gas-station-turned-diner is filled with 1950s memorabilia of the Elvis and Marilyn kind. Even Oprah Winfrey stopped by for a burger and onion rings. Try a frothing, home-made root beer or munch on sweet-potato fries while admiring vintage vehicles at the hot-pink picnic tables outside.

LAKE HAVASU CITY Shugrue's $$$

1425 McCulloch Blvd, AZ 86403 ***Tel*** *(928) 453-1400* ***Map*** *A3*

Shugrue's atrium has open views of London Bridge and the English Village across the boat channel. A second room offers booth seating and a scenic mural. Halibut baked in a Dijon garlic crust with jumbo sea scallops is just one of the many favorites among regular diners. Book a table at sunset for unbeatable views.

LAKE HAVASU CITY Mudshark Brewing Co $$$$

210 Swanson Ave, AZ 86403 ***Tel*** *(928) 453-2981* ***Map*** *A3*

Named for a local beach, Mudshark is a popular spot for handcrafted beer on tap. Its varied menu includes burgers, sandwiches, and slow-cooked pork chops. Try the Margarita Shrimp Pizza, with tomato, garlic, and feta cheese, and chase it with a glass of Scorpion Amber Ale. Huge, eye-catching wall murals add to the pleasant ambience.

PAGE Dam Bar and Grille $$$

644 N Navajo Dr, AZ 86040 ***Tel*** *(928) 645-2161* ***Map*** *C2*

Fine dining based on steak, seafood, and pasta is mixed with a lively, contemporary atmosphere here; there is also a separate sports bar. An elegant, 30 ft- (9 m-) long etched-glass wall celebrates the nearby Glen Canyon Dam. Diners can sit on the sidewalk patio, while they enjoy their meal and watch the sun go down.

PAGE The Rainbow Room $$$

Lake Powell Resort, Lakeshore Drive, UT, 86040 ***Tel*** *(928) 645-1162* ***Map*** *C2*

The Rainbow Room is the fine-dining establishment at the Lake Powell Resort. The restaurant offers intriguing takes on old favorites, including a smoked sirloin steak with sundried cranberry demi-glaze or chargrilled lamb chops with a prickly pear sweet-pepper jelly. Floor-to-ceiling windows present a panoramic view of Lake Powell.

PRESCOTT Murphy's $$$

201 N Cortez St, AZ 86301 ***Tel*** *(928) 445-4044* ***Map*** *B3*

Housed in Prescott's historic 1890 Gardner Building, this popular restaurant specializes in slow-roasted prime rib and fresh seafood dishes, including Halibut Rockefeller and mesquite-grilled shrimp brochette on a bed of pilaf rice. Murphy's also offers an extensive wine list and more than 60 brands of beers.

PRESCOTT The Palace $$$

120 S Montezuma St, AZ 86301 ***Tel*** *(928) 541-1996* **Map** *B3*

When the original Palace Saloon, which had served the likes of Wyatt Earp and Doc Holliday, burned down in the Whisky Row Fire in 1900, patrons saved the historic, ornate Brunswick bar. Today it still serves thirsty visitors, who can also dine on the saloon's excellent and subtly crafted variations on traditional steaks, ribs, and seafood.

SEDONA Black Cow Café $

229 N Hwy 89A, AZ 86336 ***Tel*** *(928) 203-9868* **Map** *B3*

If there's one word for the home-made ice cream at Black Cow, it's decadence – the Belgian vanilla is particularly indulgent. Decorated like an old-time ice-cream parlor, with photos from Sedona in the 1940s and 1950s, this café also serves filling sandwiches and pastries, coffee, and smoothies. Located in uptown Sedona.

SEDONA El Rincon Restaurante Mexicano $$$

Tlaquepaque Village, 336 S Hwy 179, Suite A112, AZ 86336 ***Tel*** *(928) 282-4648* **Map** *B3*

Arched doorways and Spanish-style furnishings bring the Tlaquepaque charm indoors, or you can dine al fresco on the patio. The Arizona-style Mexican cuisine at El Rincon offers everything from burritos to tamales, always with a touch of Navajo Indian influence. Finish the meal with the fruit-filled dessert chimichanga à la mode.

SEDONA Fournos Restaurant $$$

3000 W Hwy 89A, AZ 86336 ***Tel*** *(928) 282-3331* **Map** *B3*

This restaurant is so small you practically have to go through the kitchen to get to the ten tables in the back. Authentic Greek dishes include handmade *dolmades* (vine leaves wrapped around rice and meat), flaming shrimp with feta cooked in ouzo, and the signature Cephalonian roast lamb shanks. Two seatings per night. Open Thu–Sat.

SEDONA Oaxaca Restaurante & Rooftop Cantina $$$

321 N Hwy 89A, AZ 86336 ***Tel*** *(928) 282-4179* **Map** *B3*

Admire the stunning scenery or a pretty sunset through the archways in the seasonally open rooftop cantina in this lively and long-running restaurant in uptown Sedona. Oaxaca is owned by a dietician, so you can expect to find a heart-healthy menu. The specialty appetizer is marinated and grilled nopalitos cactus in a zesty sauce.

SEDONA Takashi Japanese Restaurant $$$

465 Jordan Rd, AZ 86336 ***Tel*** *(928) 282-2334* **Map** *B3*

Take a vacation from Southwestern cuisine and treat your taste buds to sushi and other Japanese specialties at Takashi, near uptown Sedona. Adorned with oriental lanterns and simple wooden furniture, the restaurant offers a broad and enticing menu, with soft-shell crabs, teriyaki, sukiyaki, tempura, and teppanyaki dishes. Closed Mon.

SEDONA Dahl & Diluca Ristorante Italiano $$$$

2321 W Hwy 89A, AZ 86336 ***Tel*** *(928) 282-5219* **Map** *B3*

Enjoy the romance of old Italy among rich fabrics, warm colors, and tables dressed in white linen, in what seems like a Tuscan villa. A varied menu includes deep-fried cheese-filled olives and linguine with wild mushrooms in a creamy ragout sauce *(linguine con funghi)*. There is also an excellent wine selection to choose from.

SEDONA The Heartline Café $$$$

1610 W Hwy 89A, AZ 86336 ***Tel*** *(928) 282-0785* **Map** *B3*

Colorful blooms from an organic garden are used in cooking and decorating at the Heartline Café. Dine in a casual, contemporary atmosphere on a mix of Asian, European, and Mediterranean food. Try the portobello mushroom tortilla sandwich, or the Game Trio for dinner, with fennel-mustard marinade and garlic mashed potatoes.

SEDONA Shugrue's Hillside Grill $$$$$

Hillside Courtyard, 671 Hwy 179, AZ 86336 ***Tel*** *(928) 282-5300* **Map** *B3*

It's all about the views in Sedona, and Shugrue's lofty floor-to-ceiling windows provide just that. They also have a large outdoor viewing terrace. Considered by many to have great steaks, the restaurant is also known for grilled, sautéed, or blackened seafood, such as blackened shrimp and sambuca sauce with fried saganaki cheese.

SHOW LOW Branding Iron Steakhouse $$$

1261 Deuce of Clubs, AZ 85901 ***Tel*** *(928) 537-5151* **Map** *C3*

If you're heading through the tall pines of the White Mountains and get a hankering for a thick, grilled steak, you can satisfy your hunger at the Branding Iron Steakhouse. This classic Western steakhouse offers all your favorite cuts of beef and an exceptionally well stocked salad bar.

WILLIAMS Twisters Soda Fountain & The Route 66 $

417 E Route 66, AZ 86046 ***Tel*** *(928) 635-0266* **Map** *B3*

With its black-and-white checkerboard floor and red vinyl-topped soda-fountain chairs, Twisters transports you back to the 1950s, aided by its selection of retro music and delectable banana splits. They serve burgers, sandwiches, chile dogs, and more. You can also shop for Route 66, Elvis, and Coca-Cola collectibles while there. Closed Sun.

WILLIAMS Red Raven Restaurant $$

135 W Route 66, AZ 86046 ***Tel*** *(928) 635-4980* **Map** *B3*

This is an unexpected gem of a restaurant for such a remote area. Creative, yet simple, the menu offers a great selection of Southwest-inspired steaks, salads, soups, and pasta dishes, served in a casual, relaxed atmosphere. There is a selection of quality wines and beers on offer, and the desserts are excellent.

Key to Price Guide *see p134* **Key to Symbols** *see back cover flap*

WILLIAMS Miss Kitty's Steakhouse & Saloon $$$

Mountainside Inn, 642 E Route 66, AZ 86046 ***Tel*** *(928) 635-4431* ***Map*** *B3*

Miss Kitty's is fun on week-nights, but it really gets going on the weekend, with country singers or the rhythmic sounds of ragtime bringing the gathered crowds to their feet. Designed like a Wild West saloon, the place offers juicy steaks, prime rib, and barbecue ribs – all at reasonable prices.

WILLIAMS Rod's Steak House $$$

301 E Route 66, AZ 86046 ***Tel*** *(928) 635-2671* ***Map*** *B3*

Look for a glowing-red neon sign of Domino the Steer, the restaurant's mascot and a landmark for more than 50 years on Route 66 in Williams. Then, once you get to Rod's Steak House, let the slow-cooked prime rib melt in your mouth. The whole joint is a tribute to Domino and even the menu is a die-cut in the shape of a steer. Closed Sun.

PHOENIX AND SOUTHERN ARIZONA

APACHE JUNCTION Mining Camp Restaurant & Trading Post $$

6100 E Mining Camp St, AZ 85217 ***Tel*** *(480) 982-3181* ***Map*** *C4*

Diners sit at long wooden tables, family-style, in this authentic version of an old-time miners' shanty built of rough-sawn ponderosa pine. Heaping platters of roast chicken, oven-baked ham, and barbecue ribs are accompanied by big bowls of coleslaw and baked beans, and Prospector's Cookies for the kids. A long-standing favorite. Closed Jun–Oct.

GLOBE Chalo's Casa Reynoso $

902 E Ash St, AZ 85501 ***Tel*** *(928) 425-0515* ***Map*** *C4*

This local hangout is known for its traditional home cooking and family atmosphere. It is a cozy place where everyone knows each other's name. The interior is sparse, and rumor has it that Chalo's has the prettiest waitresses in the area. Take your choice of either spicy or mild Mexican *sopaipillas* generously filled with pork and beef.

GLOBE Jerry's Restaurant $

699 E Ash St, AZ 85501 ***Tel*** *(928) 425-5282* ***Map*** *C4*

Brightly lit and with a casual atmosphere, Jerry's is a favorite with locals, who come for American classics, friendly service, and large portions. The menu features comfort food, such as burgers, ham and cheese sandwiches, Reuben sandwiches, chicken, steak, and cornbread. Group bookings are welcome.

NOGALES La Roca Restaurant $$$

Calle Elias 91, Nogales, Mexico ***Tel*** *(520) 375-5750* ***Map*** *C5*

For authentic Mexican food, why not cross the border to Nogales? You can dine in a romantic, Spanish Colonial atmosphere on Sonoran cuisine in this century-old hacienda built right into the rocks. Take note of the Mayan and Mexican paintings while eating shrimp *ceviche* or grilled changarro beef tenderloin. Bring your passport.

PHOENIX Matt's Big Breakfast $

801 N 1st St, AZ 85004 ***Tel*** *(602) 254-1074* ***Map*** *B4*

Matt's uses only grain-fed meats, organic produce, and cage-free eggs. During the week, it is busy with office workers ordering sandwiches and salads; at weekends, people come for a salami scramble, waffles, and freshly squeezed orange juice. Decorated with 1950s dinette tables, a bright-orange counter, and vintage artwork. Closed Mon.

PHOENIX Aunt Chilada's at Squaw Peak $$$

7330 N Dreamy Draw Dr, AZ 85020 ***Tel*** *(602) 944-1286* ***Map*** *B4*

Casual, rustic, and spilling over with flowers, this out-of-the-way Mexican restaurant's patio offers pleasant al fresco dining. In the late 19th century, it was a general store serving the local mercury miners. Select the chicken-breast mole with sesame seeds, and enjoy it with a cool margarita. Colorful murals complement the atmospheric decor.

PHOENIX Café at Heard Museum $$$

Heard Museum, 2301 N Central Ave, AZ 85004 ***Tel*** *(602) 252-8848 ext. 5085* ***Map*** *B4*

Stop here for salads, gourmet sandwiches, and baked tarts, or push the boat out and order the house specialty: *posole* (spicy corn stew) with roasted pork and all the trimmings. Save room for the tuxedo cake, topped with white and dark chocolate ganache. Before or after lunch, see the Heard Museum's collection of Native American artworks.

PHOENIX Pizzeria Bianco $$$

623 E Adams St, AZ 85004 ***Tel*** *(602) 258-8300* ***Map*** *B4*

Located in a historic brick-faced building with large picture windows, this small eatery offers a simple menu of wood-fired pizzas of coveted award quality – they are rated by locals as the best in town. The toppings on the Wiseguy pizza are wood-roasted onion, fresh house-smoked mozzarella, and fennel sausage – delicious. Closed Mon, Sun.

PHOENIX Sam's Café $$$

2566 E Camelback Rd, AZ 85016 ***Tel*** *(602) 954-7100* ***Map*** *B4*

Inside Biltmore Fashion Park, Sam's Café provides affordable home-made specialties with a Southwestern twist. A delicious entrée is lightly smoked Atlantic salmon with spicy pecans, served over sautéed spinach and mashed sweet potatoes, and topped with a red papaya-and-cilantro sauce. They are also proud of their margaritas.

PHOENIX Rustler's Rooste $$$$

Arizona Grand Hotel, 7777 S Pointe Pkwy W, AZ 85044 **Tel** *(602) 431-6474* **Map** *B4*

High on a butte overlooking Pointe South's golf courses and the twinkling lights of Phoenix, Rustler's Rooste is a sawdust-floored, cowboy-themed steakhouse. The fun begins at the mine-like entrance, where guests can opt to ride the slide down to the dining room. Generous portions are served. Try the crispy rattlesnake appetizer.

PHOENIX Arizona Kitchen $$$$$

Wigwam Resort, 300 Wigwam Blvd, Litchfield Pk, AZ 85340 **Tel** *(623) 935-3811* **Map** *B4*

This restaurant specializes in Arizona cuisine prepared in a glistening exhibition kitchen with a wood-burning oven. Indigenous flavors make the difference in dishes like the chile-rubbed maple-leaf duck with yellow mole sauce, sweet potato, and roasted corn hash. For dessert, the chile-spiked ice cream is served in a bowl of hardened sugar.

PHOENIX Compass Restaurant $$$$$

Hyatt Regency, 122 N 2nd St, AZ 85004 **Tel** *(602) 440-3166* **Map** *B4*

Located high above Phoenix in the Hyatt Regency *(see p128)*, Compass, the city's only revolving restaurant, boasts splendid views. Decorated with black and red accents, it has a modern feel. On the menu are American regional selections, such as achiote-paste-rubbed pork chop with braised fennel. Sunday brunch is also delicious.

PHOENIX Vincent's on Camelback $$$$$

3930 E Camelback Rd, AZ 85018 **Tel** *(602) 224-0225* **Map** *B4*

Since the 1980s, Vincent's has set the standard for fine dining, with an inventive menu that blends Southwestern ingredients with a Provençal flair. Start with the corn ravioli with white-truffle oil, followed by poached organic chicken with wild mushrooms, leeks, and thyme broth. Attentive service and an extensive wine list. Closed Sun.

PINETOP-LAKESIDE Charlie Clark's Steakhouse $$$

1701 E White Mountain Blvd, AZ 85935 **Tel** *(928) 367-4900* **Map** *C3*

This charming restaurant located amid apple orchards was a secluded mountainside speakeasy during the Prohibition years. Today it is renowned for producing some of the area's finest mesquite-grilled steaks. The menu also includes chicken, fish, venison steaks, mesquite-grilled quail on wild rice, and buffalo ribeye steaks.

SCOTTSDALE Frank & Lupe's $$

4121 N Marshall Way, AZ 85251 **Tel** *(480) 990-9844* **Map** *B4*

This small, minimally-decorated restaurant serves New Mexican favorites, including mole enchiladas, tamales and tacos, with red or green chile sauce, charro beans, fresh salsa, and crispy home-made chips. Beer and mixed drinks are available to complement the food.

SCOTTSDALE Roaring Fork $$$

4800 N Scottsdale Rd, Ste. 1700, AZ 85251 **Tel** *(480) 947-0795* **Map** *B4*

Creative Southwestern entrées include filet mignon with green-chile macaroni, fish tacos, cedar planked salmon, and Big-A burgers with roasted green chiles. Lamb, pork, and fresh fish dishes are also on the menu, and the wood-fired oven turns out delicious pizzas. Service is very friendly.

SCOTTSDALE Cowboy Ciao $$$$$

7133 E Stetson Dr, AZ 85251 **Tel** *(480) 946-3111* **Map** *B4*

Desserts are listed at the top of the menu (for those who just can't wait) at Cowboy Ciao, on Restaurant Row, in Scottsdale's arts district. Inventive dishes such as Parmesan burritos and calamari chimichanga can be accompanied by a range of unusual global wines. The welcoming decor, defined as "Border Baroque," includes camp cherubs.

SCOTTSDALE Ruth's Chris Steakhouse $$$$$

7001 N Scottsdale Rd, AZ 85253 **Tel** *(480) 991-5988* **Map** *B4*

This chain is famed for its corn-fed, aged US prime beef and for its warm hospitality. Steaks are tender and cooked to perfection. The menu also features chicken and seafood dishes. Located in the Seville Shopping Center, the restaurant offers splendid mountain views and seasonal patio dining.

SCOTTSDALE Sassi $$$$$

10455 E Pinnacle Peak Pkwy, AZ 85255 **Tel** *(480) 502-9095* **Map** *B4*

Designed as a southern Italian-style villa, Sassi has an enclosed garden terrace and outdoor patios. Located at the base of Pinnacle Peak, with excellent views, it is a good place to visit with a group of friends, since several specialties are available to share. On the menu are pasta dishes, seafood, and poultry. The tasting menu has five courses.

SUPERIOR Buckboard City $

1111 Hwy 60, AZ 85273 **Tel** *(520) 689-5800* **Map** *C4*

This fun place is located next to the World's Smallest Museum. Delicious, hearty, and very affordable fare is their specialty. Breakfast ranges from light, fluffy pancakes to huge omelettes – including a monster appropriately called "The Hog". A lunch favorite is the Sky High Decker, a super-sized club with cheddar cheese and home-baked chicken.

TOMBSTONE Big Nose Kate's $

417 E Allen St, AZ 85638 **Tel** *(520) 457-3107* **Map** *C5*

Named for Tombstone's original harlot (allegedly) and Doc Holliday's girlfriend, Big Nose Kate's was built as a hotel in 1881. These days, the bustling saloon is filled with Western memorabilia, steer heads, and stained glass. The Goldie's Over-Stuffed Reuben Sandwich has corned beef, sauerkraut, and Swiss cheese. Live country music daily.

Key to Price Guide *see p134* **Key to Symbols** *see back cover flap*

TOMBSTONE OK Café $

3rd & Allen Streets, AZ 85638 **Tel** *(520) 457-3980* **Map** *C5*

Locals rub elbows at this tiny café, appropriately located just opposite the famous OK Corral. Enjoy the standard omelette and coffee for breakfast, and great soups for lunch, but bear in mind that this place is billed as the "Home of the Buffalo Burger." It also serves more exotic meats, such as charbroiled emu and ostrich burgers.

TUCSON La Cocina $$

Old Town Artisans, 201 N Court Ave, AZ 85701 **Tel** *(520) 622-0351* **Map** *C5*

La Cocina is situated in the one-time stables of the 18th-century El Presidio. You can dine al fresco – on the patio or in the charming, shaded courtyard – or inside the cantina, surrounded by sculptures and artwork from the Old Town Artisans. Try a chicken enchilada with a green-chile cream sauce. Closed Sun.

TUCSON La Parilla Suiza $$

5602 E Speedway Blvd, AZ 85712 **Tel** *(520) 747-4838* **Map** *C5*

The long-standing La Parilla Suiza is the place for those who want a break from Sonoran cuisine. The family recipes here are firmly rooted in Mexico City. Tacos, meat, and cheese dishes are charcoaled or grilled. The Bistek Tacos consists of diced, charbroiled beef served on two corn tortillas with lettuce, refried beans, and rice.

TUCSON Café Poca Cosa $$$

110 E Pennington St, AZ 85701 **Tel** *(520) 622-6400* **Map** *C5*

This casual-chic bistro serves creative Nuevo Mexican cuisine prepared with fresh ingredients. Your server presents you with a chalkboard menu in English and Spanish; this is changed twice daily. The *plato de poca cosa* – a chicken, beef, and vegetarian sample of the day's entrées – highlights typically regional flavors.

TUCSON El Charro Café $$$

311 N Court Ave, AZ 85701 **Tel** *(520) 622-1922* **Map** *C5*

The famous El Charro, located in the El Presidio historic district downtown, serves superb Mexican food prepared from ancient family recipes. No one should leave without trying the much sought-after *carne seca* – shredded sun-dried Angus beef marinated in fresh garlic and lime juice, and grilled with fresh green chile, tomatoes, and onions.

TUCSON El Corral $$$

2201 E River Rd, AZ 85718 **Tel** *(520) 299-6092* **Map** *C5*

An affordable steakhouse located in a historic Territorial ranch house north of downtown, El Corral has a warm ambience with its fireplaces, flagstone floors, and wood-beamed ceilings. Prime rib is the specialty here, but steaks and chicken are also served. Come early, since there can be a line of people waiting for tables.

TUCSON Feast $$$

4122 E Speedway Blvd, AZ 85712 **Tel** *(520) 326-9363* **Map** *C5*

This "foodies" restaurant has a Wine Country feel about it, with red-brick walls, floor-to-ceiling glass windows facing the Santa Catalina Mountains, and a wine wall filled with boutique labels. The food has a Mediterranean and Eastern influence, and the menu changes monthly. The entire menu is available for takeout. Closed Mon.

TUCSON Li'l Abner's Steakhouse $$$$

8500 N Silverbell Ave, AZ 85743 **Tel** *(520) 744-2800* **Map** *C5*

A Tucson legend, Li'l Abner's is one of those great local steakhouses that have been around forever. No frills, just great steaks, chicken, and seafood – much of it off the big mesquite grill out back. The walls are covered in graffiti from happy customers. Locals flock there on Friday and Saturday nights, when a country-and-western band plays.

TUCSON The Grill $$$$$

Hacienda del Sol, 5601 N Hacienda del Sol Rd, AZ 85718 **Tel** *(520) 529-3500* **Map** *C5*

Dine in understated elegance at the esteemed Grill restaurant, where fresh ingredients are handpicked from the hacienda's lush gardens. The lobster gazpacho is a popular appetizer, followed by grilled Tasmanian sea trout on a purée of purple Peruvian potatoes. There is also an extensive wine list, and live music Thursdays to Sundays.

TUCSON Janos $$$$$

Westin La Paloma Resort, 3770 E Sunrise Dr, AZ 85718 **Tel** *(520) 615-6100* **Map** *C5*

At this much-celebrated fine-dining restaurant, Janos Wilder creates Southwestern dishes with a French twist and presents them with imaginative decorative touches. In addition to beautiful views of Tucson and an extensive wine list, there's also a prix-fixe menu with wine pairings. Closed Sun.

TUMACACORI Wisdom's Café $

1931 Frontage Rd, AZ 85640 **Tel** *(520) 398-2397* **Map** *C5*

Look for two huge roadside white chickens. At the family-run Wisdom Café, recipes have been passed on from one generation to the next, and there are also murals and paintings by aunts and uncles. When a jam-filled tortilla fell into cooking oil, their famous fruit burro was born; it is now served with apples, cherries, peaches, or blueberries.

YUMA The Garden Café $

250 Madison Ave, AZ 85364 **Tel** *(928) 783-1491* **Map** *A4*

This three-season restaurant (not open in summer) is very popular with locals. Diners sit in a multi-tiered patio set among lush gardens. Menu favorites include the Southwestern-inspired lunches featuring chicken taco salad, tortilla soup, quiche, seasoned steak, fresh salads, and tempting desserts. Closed Jun–Sep.

THE FOUR CORNERS

BLUFF Twin Rocks Café $

913 E Navajo Twins Dr, UT, 84512 **Tel** *(435) 672-2341* **Map** *D1*

A pair of sandstone pillars stands huddled together high above the cliffs at the Twin Rocks Café. The menu offers a wide variety of moderately priced sandwiches, salads, and dinner entrées, in addition to the unique Navajo pizza, based on fry bread topped with the usual pizza ingredients. Take time to pay a visit to the trading post.

BLUFF Cottonwood Steakhouse $$$

Main & 4th West St, Hwy 191, UT, 84512 **Tel** *(435) 672-2282* **Map** *D1*

The cottonwood tree outside this roadside steakhouse is almost bigger than the building and provides some cool shade over the picnic tables around the outdoor barbecue pit. Sizable portions of steak, chicken, ribs, shrimp, or even catfish are served with plenty of green salad. Wash them down with beer and malt coolers.

CAMERON Cameron Trading Post $$

Route 89, AZ 86020 **Tel** *(928) 679-2231* **Map** *C2*

Located at a convenient Four Corners crossroads, the Trading Post has windows looking out all the way to the Little Colorado River Gorge. Fine Native American artworks adorn the walls up to the pressed-tin ceiling. The house specialty is the Navajo taco, but a variety of American, Mexican, and Native dishes are also served.

CHINLE Chinle Junction Restaurant $

100 Main St, AZ 86503 **Tel** *(928) 674-5875* **Map** *D2*

This restaurant in Chinle's Best Western Hotel *(see p130)* serves up classic Native American-inspired dishes, including savory beef stew and a pretty good version of Navajo fry bread. Don't look for low-cholesterol dishes, but do look for hearty helpings of serious comfort food. Other favorites include pizza and big ice-cream sundaes.

CHINLE Thunderbird Lodge $

Canyon de Chelly, Navajo Route 7, AZ 86503 **Tel** *(928) 674-5841* **Map** *D2*

Located on the Navajo reservation at Canyon de Chelly, on the site of an 1896 trading post, this pleasant place serves classic American and Continental dishes, from cafeteria-style breakfast through to dinner. Portions are generous, with different items each day. The Navajo rugs and artworks decorating the walls can be purchased.

CHINLE Garcia's Restaurant $$$

Garcia Trading Post at Canyon de Chelly, Navajo Route 7, AZ 86503 **Tel** *(928) 674-5000* **Map** *D2*

On the site of the old Garcia Trading Post, adjoining the Holiday Inn, is Garcia's Restaurant. Decorated in light colors with white furniture, it serves classic Southwestern dishes, along with Native and Mexican specialties, including fajitas and a marinated sirloin steak. Kids eat free if they are guests at the hotel. Limited opening hours in winter.

DURANGO Carver Brewing Co. $$$

1022 Main Ave, CO, 81301 **Tel** *(970) 259-2545* **Map** *D1*

Considered a Durango institution by the locals, Carver has been brewing beer for two decades, from light lagers to hardy oatmeal stouts. Selections from its diverse menu include Southwest Ravioli, made with ancho chile, and seared sesame ahi stir-fry, served with a ginger-and-peanut sauce. There is a covered beer garden at the back.

DURANGO Ariano's $$$$

150 E College Drive, CO, 81301 **Tel** *(970) 247-8146* **Map** *D1*

Dine in an intimate, candlelit atmosphere in a turn-of-the-20th-century building in downtown Durango. Paintings of northern Italy hang on the walls in this split-level restaurant, which is considered one of the best in town. Among the specialties is the *pollo al cartoccio* – chicken with prosciutto and herbs baked in parchment paper. Closed Mon.

DURANGO Red Snapper $$$$

144 E 9th St, CO, 81301 **Tel** *(970) 259-3417* **Map** *D1*

This haven for seafood lovers is housed in a turn-of-the-20th-century downtown building. Chefs prepare fried red snapper in a tamarind sauce, or bake it in tarragon Mornay sauce. Fresh fish is flown in daily. The menu also includes a "landfood" section for meat eaters. The atmosphere is casual, with a huge illuminated aquarium.

FARMINGTON Clancy's Pub $$

2703 E 20th St, NM, 87402 **Tel** *(505) 325-8176* **Map** *D2*

Housed in an adobe-style building, Clancy's is known as an "Irish cantina" because it is a slice of Ireland in New Mexico. It serves typical Southwestern and Mexican fare but is perhaps better known for its massive burgers. The extraordinary menu also includes a full sushi selection.

GREY MOUNTAIN Anasazi $

Hwy 89, Grey Mountain Trading Post, Grey Mountain, AZ 86016 **Tel** *(928) 679-2203* **Map** *C2*

East of the Grand Canyon's South Rim, on the border of the Navajo Reservation, this convenient roadside restaurant serves up an authentic Navajo fry bread, as well as Mexican and American fare. Its decor probably comes from the adjacent Curio, a shop filled with Navajo arts, crafts, pottery, and trinkets.

Key to Price Guide *see p134* **Key to Symbols** *see back cover flap*

KAYENTA Amigo Café $

Hwy 163, AZ 86033 ***Tel*** *(928) 697-8448* ***Map*** *C2*

Far from the busy city life, on the Navajo Reservation, the Amigo Café is frequented by locals and tourists alike. They serve up a very inexpensive combo plate ($9), which is a great way to sample Mexico cuisine, with chimichangas, tacos, tamales, tostados, and more. Takeout is also available. Closed Sun.

MESA VERDE NATIONAL PARK Spruce Tree Terrace Café $

Mile Marker 15, Mancos, CO, 81328 ***Tel*** *(970) 529-4444* ***Map*** *D2*

Housed in a historic stone building opposite the Chapin Mesa Museum, deep inside the park, the Spruce Tree is open for cafeteria service or takeout. Navajo tacos are a favorite on the expansive menu, and prices are reasonable. Dine inside, or pick a table under a white umbrella on the patio for a cool beer. Open all year round.

MESA VERDE NATIONAL PARK Metate Room $$$$

Mile Marker 15, Mancos, CO, 81328 ***Tel*** *(970) 529-4422* ***Map*** *D2*

The extremely remote, Metate Room will delight visitors with its adventurous cuisine based on sustainable staples used by the Ancestral Puebloans. From the cactus nopalitos dip or the blue-corn trout, to quail stuffed with fig and chorizo, or the pepper-and-coriander-crusted elk, the menu never fails to surprise. Local wines are on the menu. Closed mid-Oct to Apr.

MONUMENT VALLEY The View Hotel Restaurant $$

Hway 163 Monument Valley Tribal Park, UT 84536 ***Tel*** *(435) 727-5555* ***Map*** *C2*

Dine in a spacious restaurant decorated with Navajo art and with a spectacular view of Monument Valley. The menu features Navajo specialties, such as mutton stew with fry bread, as well as classic American dishes, such as grilled salmon and steaks. A local flute player often plays for diners.

MONUMENT VALLEY Stagecoach Dining Room $$$

Goulding's Lodge, UT, 84536 ***Tel*** *(435) 727-3231* ***Map*** *C2*

Located high on a hill, the Stagecoach provides a large dining room to cater for the many tourists visiting Monument Valley, just down the road. There's the standard T-bone steak and salad bar, and a more interesting Navajo taco sampler appetizer. Come here for the stunning panorama views from every table.

OURAY Backstreet Bagel & Deli $

524 Main St, CO, 81427 ***Tel*** *(970) 325-0550* ***Map*** *E1*

Catering to the climbing community, Backstreet will placate any sweet-tooth needs, as well as any requirement for an energy boost, with its home-made pastries, pies, and phenomenal cheesecake. The three-cheese bagels are popular, as are the sandwiches, soups, and special frozen coffees – try the Bailey's milkshake.

OURAY Bon Ton Restaurant $$$$

St. Elmo Hotel, 426 Main St, CO, 81427 ***Tel*** *(970) 325-4951* ***Map*** *E1*

Located in the basement of the historic St. Elmo, Bon Ton offers a cozy atmosphere and upscale Italian fare. The grilled Angus beef wrapped in pastry and the scampi served in a sherry-cream sauce over fettuccine are some of the favorites. For dessert, try the Black Nasty, a decadent chocolate pie. There is an award-winning wine list and a martini bar.

SECOND MESA, HOPI RESERVATION Hopi Cultural Center Restaurant $

Route 264, AZ 86043 ***Tel*** *(928) 734-2402* ***Map*** *C3*

Steaming mutton stew, fired on a hot stone, with hominy and roasted green chiles, is one of the traditional Hopi specialties served at this restaurant. Piki bread, made of blue corn, is parchment-paper-thin. Mexican and American dishes, and an excellent salad bar, are also available at this popular restaurant.

TELLURIDE Excelsior Café $$$$

200 W Colorado Ave, CO, 81435 ***Tel*** *(970) 728-4250* ***Map*** *D1*

Open only for dinner, the Excelsior has a contemporary decor, with large windows and a sidewalk patio that is great for people-watching. Highlights on the Italian-influenced menu include wild-mushroom risotto with white-truffle oil, and ruby-red Rocky Mountain trout. The menu is moderately priced and there are several fine Italian wines.

TELLURIDE 221 South Oak $$$$$

221 South Oak, CO, 81435 ***Tel*** *(970) 728-9507* ***Map*** *D1*

This restaurant occupies two rooms in a historic house. There are comfortable couches in the entry room and an overall homey atmosphere, with golden walls, candlelight, and white linens. Among the eclectic dishes on the menu are sautéed soft-shell crabs with red-peppercorn sauce. Summertime dining can be enjoyed on the garden patio.

TUBA CITY Hogan Restaurant $$

Main St and Moenave Rd, AZ 86045 ***Tel*** *(928) 283-5260* ***Map*** *C2*

Adjacent to the historic Tuba Trading Post and shaped like a hogan dwelling (hence the name), this restaurant is in the heart of the Navajo tribal lands, near scenic desert landscapes and the Grand Canyon. Traditional mutton stew and Navajo tacos can be found on the menu, as well as a variety of Mexican and American dishes.

WINDOW ROCK Diné $

Quality Inn, 48 W Hwy 264, AZ 86515 ***Tel*** *(928) 871-4108* ***Map*** *D2*

Located near the governmental buildings of the Navajo Nation's capital, Diné is especially busy at lunchtime, when it attracts politicians and businessmen. The restaurant is decorated with Navajo art, and serves traditional mutton stew, Navajo fry bread, and Navajo tacos, in addition to Mexican and American fare.

SHOPPING IN ARIZONA

With such an exciting range of Native American, Hispanic, and Anglo-American products, shopping in Arizona is a cultural adventure. Native crafts, including rugs, jewelry, and pottery, top the list of things that people buy. The Southwest is also known as a center for the fine arts, with Scottsdale *(see p80)* and Sedona *(see p68)* famous for their many galleries, selling everything from Arizona-inspired landscapes and the latest contemporary work, to kitsch bronze sculptures of cowboys and Indians.

Chile-shaped pot

Across the state, specialty grocery stores and supermarkets stock a range of Southwestern products from hot chile sauces to blue corn tortilla chips. Western clothing, including boots, hats, and belts can be found in shops across the state. In the major cities, there is a choice of chic fashion districts, usually situated in air-conditioned, landscaped malls. Phoenix and Scottsdale rank shopping among their top attractions, and themed malls and boutique shopping areas attract hundreds of thousands of visitors each year.

WESTERN CLOTHING

Among the most popular souvenirs bought in Arizona are hand-tooled cowboy boots, cowboy hats, and decorative leather belts. Western clothing is made to high standards throughout the Southwest. Phoenix is well-known as a center for cowboy clothes. **Az-Tex Hats** of Scottsdale has the largest selection of cowboy hats in the Southwest, while **Saba's Western Store** has been outfitting customers in Western fashions since 1927. **Bacon's Boots & Saddles**, which is located in the historic mining town of Globe *(see p85)*, is owned by craftsman Ed Bacon who has been making fine boots and saddles for more than 50 years. **Sheplers** is another famous store, and kids as well as grown-ups are catered for with cute mini hats, spurs, and toys.

Typical Southwestern boots and hats on sale in Phoenix

Chile peppers hanging from a wooden cart

REGIONAL FOOD

Arizonans are proud of their Southwestern cuisine, and in most shopping areas you will find grocery stores and specialty shops selling an array of Arizona-made sauces, salsas, dips, and gourmet food items. Many of these foods are chile based, ranging from the mild jalapeño to the super-hot habañero peppers. The mesquite-smoked jalapeño pepper, known as *chipotle*, is medium hot and has a smoky flavor. Salsa is a popular condiment made from tomatoes, chile, garlic, and cilantro.

Farmers' markets are another good source of local produce, and usually stock a range of dried chile strings, known as *ristras*. Several companies have websites where you can order such regional gourmet foods as handmade corn tortillas, chile-stuffed olives, hot-spiced microwave popcorn, mesquite bean candy, chile peanut butter, and prickly pear jam.

A large number of bookstores and shops offer a variety of cookbooks with recipes on Arizonan and Southwestern cuisine, from easy-to-prepare dishes to traditional and fusion recipes using all the favorite ingredients.

GEMS & MINERALS

With Arizona's fascinating geology and long mining history, it is not surprising to find glittering gems and minerals on display in shops across the state. Rock shops and museum shops, such as the shop in the **Arizona**

Cut stones on display during the Tucson Gem & Mineral Show

Typical Route 66 souvenir shop, on the Arizona-New Mexico border

Mining & Mineral Museum in Phoenix, provide reasonably priced and beautiful minerals such as turquoise, azurite, and malachite, quartz crystals of varied shapes and sizes, and gold and silver. The staff in these shops are usually knowledgable and enjoy talking about Arizona's minerals and geology. The Sleeping Beauty Mine in Globe is Arizona's largest source of turquoise, and its retail shop, **True Blue Jewelry & Gift Shop**, offers turquoise jewelry, tumbled nuggets, and rough turquoise. **Tucson Mineral & Gem World** carries a large selection of both Arizonan and other minerals and crystals for novices and collectors alike. **Ramsey's Fine Jewelry & Minerals** in Sedona specializes in making custom jewelry using Arizona gemstones, as well as quality gemstones and minerals from every corner of the globe, and offers an eye-catching array of colorful crystals, minerals, and fossils.

Besides shopping, Arizona hosts two of the world's largest gems and minerals shows during January and February each year in Quartzsite and Tucson *(see p33)*. Rockhounds, gem and mineral dealers and enthusiasts from around the world are known to gather in Arizona for these shows.

ROUTE 66 MEMORABILIA & TOURIST KITSCH

Memories, memorabilia, kitsch, and souvenirs from the golden age of the automobile can be found in shops all along Arizona's Route 66. The **Historic Route 66 Association of Arizona** in Kingman is a non-profit corporation that is dedicated to the preservation, promotion, and protection of Route 66 and its memories. The association's gift shop offers books, videos, and souvenirs all about the road. **Route 66 Roadworks**, located in Winslow, carries Harley Davidson, Burma Shave, and other memorabilia of the era. In Williams, **The Route 66 Place** provides Route 66 information and mementos, including T-shirts, jackets, vests, and signs and shields, as well as Coca-Cola, John Deere, Betty Boop, and 1950s memorabilia.

ANTIQUES

Antiques, and especially those that evoke memories of the Wild West, are very popular in Arizona. Western, Native and cowboy antiques include saddles, hats, spurs, badges, Navajo rugs, silver and turquoise jewelry. In addition you can also buy lanterns and wagon wheels.

In the Phoenix area, the **Old Towne Shopping District** in downtown Glendale is the main antiques district, with more than 50 antiques shops and specialty stores. Arizona's largest collector's show, the **Phoenix Fairgrounds Antique Market**, is held at the Arizona State Fairgrounds six times a year.

Prescott is also known for its antiques shops, many of which are located in the central town square area of downtown Prescott. In Tucson, the Fourth Avenue shopping district has several antiques stores between 4th and 7th Streets.

Shopkeeper stands among the varied collectibles in his antiques store near Prescott

Outside view of Scottsdale's El Pedregal Festival Marketplace

FLEA MARKETS

Across the state, flea markets offer everything Arizonan and much more. Flea markets are usually open on weekends, and sometimes on Fridays or other weekdays. Advertised as the largest open-air flea market in the Southwest, **Phoenix Park 'n Swap** in Phoenix offers a broad range of products, from clothing, tools, and jewelry, to furniture, luggage, and athletic footwear. **Mesa Market Place Swap Meet** features 1,600 booths filled with new and used items, antiques, home furnishings, clothing, jewelry, toys, and food products. In Tucson, 800 vendors at the **Tanque Verde Swap Meet** flea market sell antiques and collectibles, fresh produce, Southwestern crafts, and coins and stamps. **Peddler's Pass** of Prescott Valley has a range of antiques and collectibles, plus clothing, crafts, and fresh produce. Quartzsite has more than a dozen festive flea markets from November to March, including the **Main Event** in January, which sells gems and minerals.

MALLS

Southern Arizona has some of the most stunning malls in the US, featuring air conditioning, plant-filled atriums, and fine restaurants. The largest of these is Phoenix's **Metrocenter**, with more than 200 stores. Large department stores such as Neiman Marcus can be found at the **Scottsdale Fashion Square**. Phoenix's **Biltmore Fashion Park** offers Chico's, Cole Hann, and Saks Fifth Avenue, and has some of the best dining options in town.

Themed malls are abundant in the region. **Borgata of Scottsdale** is styled as a 14th-century Italian village with medieval courtyards. The Arizona Center in Phoenix has restaurants and shops set among gardens, fountains, and a waterfall. The **El Pedregal Festival Marketplace** in Scottsdale has a festive Moroccan atmosphere with 25 boutique shops.

Tucson has several large shopping malls, including one of the largest in the state, **Tucson Mall** with over 200 stores. **El Con Mall** has a great selection of department and specialty stores.

ART GALLERIES

Arizona has a vibrant artistic tradition with skilled artists and numerous galleries across the state displaying works of art that reflect the unique colors, light, and landscapes of the Southwest. Scottsdale is Arizona's premier fine art center. It has over a 100 galleries that stock the works of internationally recognized artists in many disciplines. The popular **Scottsdale ArtWalk**, which takes place on Thursday evenings, features special exhibits and artist receptions in the galleries.

The downtown area of Tucson is home to over 40 art galleries. **Old Town Artisans** houses eight distinctive galleries and shops that display the arts and crafts of hundreds of local and regional artists.

Sedona has an active art scene, and Western art can be found in 40 galleries in the city. **Tlaquepaque** is a small art village in Spanish Colonial style with courtyards and gardens, offering primarily Southwestern and Native art. Tubac, Bisbee, and Jerome all have galleries and craft shops, many of which display the work of emerging artists.

ONE-OF-A-KIND SHOPS

Arizona-style independence and creativity have created unique products that go beyond the expected. Part of the delight of shopping in Arizona is finding shops such as **Poisoned Pen**, one of the country's largest mystery books' store. Traveling mystery buffs can browse through 15,000 titles, and appreciate the special events and talks given by authors.

Architect Paolo Soleri built Arcosanti, the experimental town in the high desert of Arizona *(see p81)*, to the north of Phoenix. **Cosanti Originals**, located in the town, offers unique, one-of-a-kind Soleri sculptures in the form of windbells, and their sales help fund research into alternative living.

Paintings and drawings on adobe walls at DeGrazia Gallery in Tucson

DIRECTORY

WESTERN WEAR

Az-Tex Hats
3903 N Scottsdale Rd, Scottsdale, AZ 85251.
Tel *(800) 972-2116, (480) 481-9900.*
www.aztexhats.com

Bacon's Boots & Saddles
290 N Broad St, Globe, AZ 85501.
Tel *(928) 425-2681.*

Saba's Western Store
3965 N Brown Ave, Scottsdale, AZ 85251.
Tel *(877) 342-1835, (480) 947-7664.*
www.sabas westernwear.com

Sheplers
829 N Dobson Road, Mesa, AZ 85201.
Tel *(480) 668-1211.*
www.sheplers.com

GEMS & MINERALS

Arizona Mining & Mineral Museum
1502 W Washington St, Phoenix, AZ 85007.
Tel *(602) 771-1611.*
www.admmr. state.az.us.

Ramsey's Fine Jewelry & Minerals
150 Hwy 179, Suite #6, Sedona, AZ 86339.
Tel *(928) 204-2075.*
www.ramseyssedona.com

True Blue Jewelry & Gift Shop
200 N Willow St, Globe, AZ 85501.
Tel *(928) 425-7625, (888) 425-7698.*
www.sbturquoise.com

Tucson Mineral & Gem World
2801 S Kinney Rd, Tucson, AZ 85735.
Tel *(520) 883-0682.*
www.tucson mineral.com

ROUTE 66 MEMORABILIA & TOURIST KITSCH

Historic Route 66 Association of Arizona
120 W Andy Devine Ave, Kingman, AZ 86401.
Tel *(928) 753-5001.*
www.azrt66.com

The Route 66 Place
417 E Route 66, Williams, AZ 86046.
Tel *(928) 635-0266.*
www.route66place.com

Route 66 Roadworks
101 W Second St, Winslow, AZ 86047.
Tel *(928) 289-5423.*
www.roadworks route66.com

ANTIQUES

Old Towne Shopping District
East of 59th Avenue, Glendale, AZ 85308.
Tel *(877) 800-2601.*

Phoenix Fairgrounds Antique Market
Arizona State Fairgrounds
Tel *(623) 587-7488, (602) 717-7337.*
www. azantiqueshow.com

FLEA MARKETS

Main Event
PO Box 2801, Quartzsite, AZ 85346.
Tel *(928) 927-5213.*
www.ci.quartzsite.az.us

Mesa Market Place Swap Meet
10550 E Baseline, Mesa, AZ 85212.
Tel *(480) 380-5572.*
www.mesamarket.com

Peddler's Pass
6201 E Hwy 69, Prescott Valley, AZ 86314.
Tel *(928) 775-4117.*
www.peddlerspass.com

Phoenix Park 'n Swap
3801 E Washington St, Phoenix, AZ 85034.
Tel *(800) 772-0852.*
www. americanparknswap.com

Tanque Verde Swap Meet
4100 S Palo Verde Rd, Tucson, AZ 85714.
Tel *(520) 294-4252.*
www.tanqueverde swapmeet.com

MALLS

Biltmore Fashion Park
2502 Camelback Rd, Phoenix, AZ 85016.
Tel *(602) 955-8400.*
www.shopbiltmore.com

Borgata of Scottsdale
6166 N Scottsdale Rd, Scottsdale, AZ 85253.
Tel *(602) 953-6538.*
www.borgata.com

El Con Mall
3601 E Broadway Blvd, Tucson, AZ 85701.
Tel *(520) 795 9958.*

El Pedregal
34505 N Scottsdale Rd, Scottsdale, AZ 85251.
Tel *(480) 488-1072.*
www.elpedregal.com

Metrocenter
9617 Metro Parkway, Phoenix, AZ 85051.
Tel *(602) 997-2641.*

Scottsdale Fashion Square
7014 E Camelback Rd, Scottsdale, AZ 85251.
Tel *(480) 941-2140.*
www.fashionsquare.com

Tucson Mall
4500 N Oracle Rd, Tucson, AZ 85705.
Tel *(520) 293-7330.*
www.tucsonmall.com

ART GALLERIES

Old Town Artisans
201 N Court Ave, Tucson, AZ 85701.
Tel *(520) 623-6024.*
www.oldtown artisans.com

Scottsdale Arts District & ArtWalk
Scottsdale, AZ 85251.
Tel *(480) 421-1004.*
www.scottsdale galleries.com

Tlaquepaque
336 Hwy 179, Sedona, AZ 86351.
Tel *(928) 282-4838.*
www.tlaq.com

ONE-OF-A-KIND SHOPS

Cosanti Originals
6433 E Doubletree Ranch Rd, Paradise Valley, AZ 85253.
Tel *(800) 752-3187.*
www.cosanti.com

Poisoned Pen
4014 N Goldwater Blvd, Suite 101, Scottsdale, AZ 85251.
Tel *(888) 560-9919.*
www.poisonedpen.com

NATIVE ARTS & CRAFTS

Cameron Trading Post
Highway 89, Cameron, AZ 86020.
Tel *(928) 679-2231.*
www.camerontrading post.com

Heard Museum Shop
2301 N Central Ave, Phoenix, AZ 85004-1323.
Tel *(800) 252-8344, (602) 252-8844.*
www.heardmuseum shop.com

Hopi House
Main St, Grand Canyon, AZ 86023.
Tel *(928) 638-2631.*

Hubbell Trading Post
Highway 264, Ganado, AZ 86505.
Tel *(928) 755-3254.*
www.nps.gov/hutr

Sewell's Indian Arts
7087 5th Ave, Scottsdale, AZ 85251.
Tel *(480) 945-0962.*

Shopping for Native Arts & Crafts

Pottery

One of the most rewarding parts of a trip to Arizona is shopping for Native arts and crafts *(see pp20–21)*. Now valued as collectors' items, many modern crafts, such as pottery and basket-making, can trace their history to centuries-old tribal life. There is intense competition between Native artisans, and the quality of traditional arts continues to be high. At the same time, a new wave of Native artists are successfully blending traditional art with modern media and styles from around the world.

Whether shopping in trading posts, art galleries, or museum shops *(see p145)*, a skillful eye can result in bargains. Purchasing work from Native artists offers the bonus of possible new friendships.

Rug-making *is practiced by the Navajo. A large rug created by a master weaver can fetch thousands of dollars.*

TRADING POSTS

The Cameron Trading Post and the Hubbell Trading Post originated in the mid-1800s, and are thriving Native arts and crafts centers today. Trading posts are classic middlemen. They benefit the tribes by nurturing Native artists and offering a ready market for their work. For visitors, they provide advice and a generous variety of crafts for comparison shopping.

Basket-making *is one of the oldest Native American crafts, dating back over a 1,000 years. Virtually all tribes in Arizona practice basket-making, but the baskets of the Apache and the Hopi are particularly refined.*

Pottery *is practiced by many tribes, but Hopi pottery is considered to be the best. Made from local clays, it features both contemporary and traditional designs, many taken from nature, with names such as "birdwing," "dragonfly," "hummingbird," or "rain."*

Silverwork, *often with turquoise arrays, has been produced by Navajo, Zuni, and Hopi peoples for centuries. Since the mid-19th century, Navajo jewelers have incorporated Spanish styles. Hopi and Zuni silver is different, with an intricate overlay process that has raised silver patterns against a dark background.*

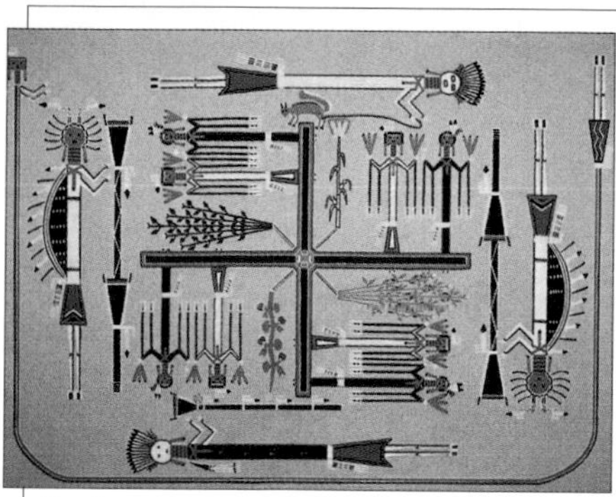

Navajo sand painting showing abundant crops

GALLERIES & MUSEUMS

Some of the very best traditional and contemporary Native art can be found in fine art galleries and museum shops, such as **Hopi House** at the Grand Canyon or the **Heard Museum Shop**. Prices in these shops tend to be higher, but careful shopping can still result in bargains. These galleries and museum shops often have long-established relationships with some of the very best Native artisans, and can provide shoppers with information on art trends, investment considerations, and provenance (documented information on the artist, and background and history of the artwork).

BUYING DIRECTLY FROM NATIVES

One of the most gratifying shopping experiences is purchasing crafts directly from Native artisans, who are found at the major tourist destinations. These craftsmen are either beginners or mid-level artisans, and the prices are usually very reasonable.

- Exercise normal caution. Look for flaws such as uneven edges or curling in rugs, and lopsidedness in pottery.
- Do not purchase expensive articles if you do not know how to determine quality. Avoid making large purchases from unknown vendors.
- Don't be too aggressive while bargaining. A good price is usually 70 to 80 percent of the originally offered price.
- Remember Native etiquette. Speak softly and clearly. Don't point, and if you shake hands, do so gently.
- If you want a photograph of the artist, they may ask for money ($2–$10 is normal).

Navajo weaver working outdoors

Carvings *are primarily represented by* kachina *or* katsina *dolls – beautifully painted, ornate representations of the* kachina *spirits of the Hopi and the Pueblo peoples. Although popular with tourists, they have deep significance for the Hopis, and should be handled and treated with respect. Other tribes occasionally make* kachina *-like dolls for the tourist trade.*

ENTERTAINMENT IN ARIZONA

Arizona's lively blend of cultures and increasing population have made it a thriving center for arts and entertainment. The large cities of Phoenix and Tucson have vibrant artistic communities, and offer opera, ballet, classical music, and major theatrical productions. Sedona is famous for its resident painters and sculptors, and regularly hosts prestigious touring productions, as well as regional theater, dance, and musical events. Also, almost every city and major town has a lively nightlife that includes popular music such as country, jazz, and rock, and dinner theater and standup comedy.

Museum Club sign

Sport is a popular pastime in Arizona, and fans can find major league and college football, baseball, and basketball teams playing across the state.

Bull riding, a popular rodeo event in Arizona

INFORMATION

The best information source on entertainment and events are local newspapers.

Phoenix's *The Arizona Republic* and Tucson's *Daily Star* are useful, and they also have websites with up-to-date information. Several magazines also review events and nightlife. Most hotels offer magazines, such as *Where* and *Key*, that feature dining, attractions, and entertainment. **Jazz in Arizona**'s website details upcoming events. You can book tickets for most events through **Ticketmaster** outlets, or at www.ticketmaster.com, their online booking service.

RODEOS, WILD WEST SHOWS, & HISTORICAL TOURS

Since Buffalo Bill's first Wild West show in the 1880s, Arizona has been a mecca for Western-style entertainment. Traditional cowboy skills, such as roping steers and breaking wild mustangs, are now part of rodeo contests that offer substantial money prizes. Rodeo is the Spanish word for round-up, harking back to the 19th century when herds of cattle crossed the Southwest on their way to California. Today's rodeo circuit is very competitive and dangerous, attracting full-time professionals whose high pay reflects this risky career. Some of the most popular rodeos in Arizona are Tucson's Fiesta de los Vaqueros Rodeo, The Payson Rodeo, The Summer Rodeo Series in Williams, and Frontier Days Rodeo in Prescott.

Arizona offers plenty of opportunities to sample the Wild West atmosphere, either in the many ghost towns or in historic frontier towns such as **Tombstone** *(see p98)*, which stages mock-gunfights at the OK Corral. Western towns that were built as film studios, such as **Old Tucson Studios** *(see p90)*, offer tours of their working movie sets. Similar entertainment can be found at **Rawhide**, north of Scottsdale, which has a museum, an old-fashioned ice cream parlor, and a famous music venue. Goldfield, near Apache Junction, which was once the richest gold mining town in America, offers a train tour of the original gold mine site, a working saloon, and a bordello museum.

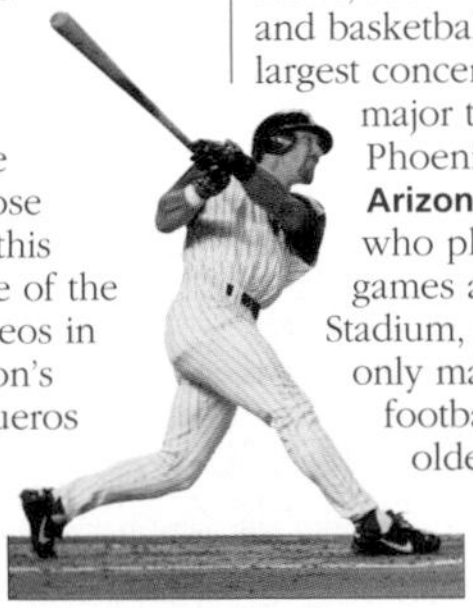
Baseball player

SPORTS

The three most popular spectator sports in Arizona, as in the rest of the United States, are football, baseball, and basketball. The state's largest concentration of major teams is in the Phoenix area. The **Arizona Cardinals**, who play their home games at the Sun Devil Stadium, are the state's only major league football team, and the oldest continually operating NFL football team in the country. The Arizona Diamondbacks baseball team joined the major league in 1998 and is based at the $275-million **Chase Field** in Phoenix.

Professional basketball is represented by the Phoenix Suns, who share the **USAirways Center** with the American Football team, the Arizona Rattlers.

While tickets may be hard to obtain for league games, it is relatively easy to gain entrance to the many college games in any sport throughout the region. Phoenix's warm climate also attracts the Cactus League, a series of training games for seven major league baseball teams in February and March.

CLASSICAL MUSIC, BALLET, & OPERA

Phoenix has an excellent reputation for music. Both the Phoenix Symphony and Arizona Opera perform at the **Phoenix Symphony Hall** building. The city's $14-million refurbishment of the Spanish Baroque-style **Orpheum Theater** has created the state's top venue for big name Broadway shows, and a stunning addition to more than 20 major venues for arts, sports, and entertainment in and around Phoenix. Arizona Theater Company and Actors Theater occupy the **Herberger Theater Center**, offering a regular program of performances. With more than 20 theater companies in Phoenix, there is an impressive array of plays to choose from, as well as touring stage shows and big name entertainers.

In Tucson, the **Arizona Opera** stages its impressive productions at the Tuscon Convention Center Music Hall, which is also home to the award-winning **Tucson Symphony Orchestra**.

Dancing couple at The Museum Club in Flagstaff, Arizona

NIGHTLIFE

Arizona has a vibrant nightlife which caters to most visitors. In almost every town there are restaurants, bars, and nightclubs that offer country music and dancing. Among the most famous country music venues is the Wild West theme-town of Rawhide in Scottsdale, where a large number of well-known bands play. **The Museum Club** in Flagstaff is a legendary Route 66 *(see p29)* roadhouse that has hosted such top country music names as Hank Williams and Willy Nelson, and still offers a lively selection of South-western bands.

The major cities of the state have virtually every type of evening entertainment on offer. For example, trendy dance clubs and jazz bars and cafés are gaining in popularity, and standup comedy and rock music are available in countless venues. In Tucson, **The Rialto Theatre** brings a wide variety of live entertainment – from punk rock to salsa – to the stage of this renovated 1918 playhouse. Clubs and arenas based in Phoenix and Tucson are regular stops for big stars on US tours.

Phoenix Symphony Hall, home to Phoenix Symphony and Arizona Opera

DIRECTORY

INFORMATION

Jazz in Arizona
www.jazzinaz.org

Ticketmaster
Tel *(800) 745-3000.*

RODEOS, WILD WEST SHOWS, & HISTORICAL TOURS

Old Tucson Studios
Tel *(520) 883-0100.*
www.*oldtucson.com*

Rawhide Western Town
Tel *(480) 502-5600.*
www.*rawhide.com*

Tombstone Visitor Center
Tel *(520) 457-3929.*

SPORTS

Arizona Cardinals
Tel *(800) 999-1402.*
www.*azcardinals.com*

Chase Field
Tel *(602) 462-6000.*

USAirways Center
Tel *(602) 379-7833.*
www.*usairwayscenter.com*

CLASSICAL MUSIC, BALLET, & OPERA

Arizona Opera (Tucson)
Tel *(520) 293-4336.*
www.*azopera.com*

Herberger Theater Center
Tel *(602) 252-8497.*
www.*herbergertheater.org*

Orpheum Theater
Tel *(602) 262-7272.*

Phoenix Symphony
Tel *(602) 495-1999.*
www.*phoenixsymphony.org*

Tucson Symphony Box Office
Tel *(520) 882-8585.*
www.*tucsonsymphony.org*

NIGHTLIFE

The Museum Club
Tel *(928) 526-9434.*

The Rialto Theatre
Tel *(520) 740-0071.*
www.*rialtotheatre.com*

SPECIALTY VACATIONS & ACTIVITIES

With hundreds of miles of deep rock canyons, spectacular deserts, and towering, snow-capped mountains, Arizona offers a wide and tempting array of outdoor adventure activities. Much of the state's wilderness is protected by the federal government in national parks, national recreation areas, and lands administered by the National Forest Service and the Bureau of Land Management. An increasing number of visitors are being drawn to the region, and it is now a magnet for climbers, mountain bikers, hikers, and 4WD enthusiasts. The range of organized tours includes whitewater rafting and horseback riding, as well as cultural heritage tours of the many ancient Native American sites. Wildlife enthusiasts, particularly birdwatchers, can spot rare species on the spring and fall migration routes that cross the Southwest. The region is also a center for sports activities, especially for golfers *(see pp154–5)*, who can choose from over 300 courses, some of which are the world's finest.

Powerboating near Parker Dam in Arizona

GENERAL INFORMATION

The main centers for outdoor activities in the region are Phoenix *(see pp76–83)*, Tucson *(see pp88–94)*, Flagstaff *(see pp64–6)*, and Sedona *(see p68)*. These towns have excellent equipment shops and visitor information centers. It is advisable to spend some time planning your trip in advance.

Hikers and campers exploring national park backcountry will need permits from the National Park Service as well as detailed maps, which can be obtained from the **USDA Forest Service**, or the **US Geological Survey (USGS)**. National parks have excellent, well-marked trails, and fascinating ranger-led hikes that focus on the local flora, fauna, and geology. Advice on trails, permits, and weather conditions at most attractions can be obtained at both the state and local tourist offices. Anyone exploring desert or canyon country should be aware of the potential for flash floods, and should check weather reports daily, especially during the summer months of July and August.

HIKING

The single most popular outdoor activity in Arizona is hiking. Day hikes and longer trips attract large numbers of residents and visitors, who feel that this is one of the best way to see the region's stunning scenery.

Hikers on the trail to Pueblo Alto at Chaco Canyon

Popular hiking areas include Mount Lemmon *(see p94)* outside Tucson, Camelback Mountain *(see p81)* and the Superstition Mountains *(see pp84–5)* outside Phoenix, Oak Creek Canyon *(see p69)* near Sedona, and the vast desert expanses of Glen Canyon Recreation Area *(see pp62–3)*.

For easier hiking and driving tours, contact **Walk Softly Tours**, which offers single- and multi-day adventures in the Sonoran Desert and Four Corners areas. Utah-based **Nichols Expeditions** offers five-day hiking tours to the Canyon de Chelly National Monument *(see pp106–9)*, in the midst of the Navajo Reservation.

Arizona Trails is a travel agency that custom-designs hiking adventures in Arizona, matching individuals or groups to experienced guides for one- to three-day desert, canyon, or mountain hikes.

ROCK CLIMBING

Arizona's dry, sunny climate and extensive mountains, canyons, and sheer rock faces make it one of America's most popular climbing destinations.

There are excellent, and often busy, climbing locations near each city, and nearly all the major cities have first-rate climbing shops and schools. **Arizona Climbing and Adventure School**, in Carefree, provides full- and half-day climbs across the state, for groups as well as individuals.

One of the oldest rock climbing resources in Arizona is the **Rocky Mountain Climbing School** in Tucson, which offers professional climbing instruction and guiding for both beginners and intermediate climbers. All guides are certified by the American Mountain Guides Association.

Mountain biking on red rock in Coconino National Forest, Sedona

MOUNTAIN BIKING & FOUR-WHEEL DRIVING

With so much wilderness crisscrossed by trails and jeep tracks, mountain biking and 4WD touring are two of the fastest growing sports in Arizona. Casual riders will find plenty of thrills in Phoenix's Papago Park *(see p82)*. In Tucson, there are numerous trails in the Mount Lemmon area.

Bikeapelli Adventure Tours offers single- and multi-day adventures on rough desert single-tracks and slickrock rides. Sedona is also a hotbed for 4WD adventures, and local legend **Pink Jeep Tours** offers guided 4WD tours, including one of the Grand Canyon. Monument Valley *(see pp102–3)* is a prime location for 4WD tours, which are often led by Navajo guides from **Goulding's Lodge Monument Valley Tours**. Glenn Canyon National Recreation Area's miles of trails and dirt roads make it a hotspot for both mountain bikers and 4WD enthusiasts.

A Pink Jeep in Sedona

WHITEWATER RAFTING & KAYAKING

When people think of whitewater rafting in Arizona, they often dream of the 16-day run through the Grand Canyon *(see pp48–61)*. But, as incredible as this trip is, it requires time, and up to a year of advance planning. When time is short, Arizona offers plenty of other whitewater and flatwater rafting choices. If you want to see the Grand Canyon, several operators, including **Tour West**, offer three- to five-day trips through the lower Grand Canyon, beginning at Diamond Creek on Hualapai reservation and ending at Lake Mead. The Salt River is a raging torrent in the White Mountains, where **Wilderness Aware** offers one- to five-day rafting trips. On the Colorado Plateau, **Wild River Expeditions** offers a gentle one-day float through the canyons of the San Juan River that includes stops to see petroglyphs and Ancestral Puebloan ruins.

OTHER WATERSPORTS

Artificial lakes along the Colorado River – formed because of the damming of the river – offer a variety of watersports, including powerboating and jetskiing. Lake Powell is famous for houseboat cruises, which showcase remote beaches, canyons, and the desert beauty for which the lake is known. **Lake Powell Resorts & Marinas** rents out houseboats and powerboats.

At **Lake Mead** *(see p72)*, shops rent fishing boats and jetskis, and offer waterskiing lessons. All kinds of equipment, from waterskis to tubes, can be taken on rent from **Fun Time Boat Rentals**, which is near Lake Havasu *(see p73)*.

FISHING

Lakes Mead, Powell, and Havasu are also noted as excellent fishing destinations. The lakes are well stocked with game fish during the fishing season, which runs from March to November. River anglers can also fish for salmon and trout. Fishing licenses are required almost everywhere, and catch and release is the rule in many areas. Information about licenses, tournaments, and tours can be obtained from marinas, outdoor equipment stores, local gas stations, and the **Arizona Game and Fish Department**.

HOT AIR BALLOONING

Cool, still mornings, dependable sunshine, and steady breezes have made Arizona one of the top hot air ballooning destinations in America. Around Phoenix, several operators, including **Hot Air Expeditions**, offer Champagne flights over the Sonoran Desert. You can also drift gently over the canyons of Sedona with **Northern Light Balloon Expeditions**.

Whitewater rafting trip on the Colorado River

BIRDWATCHING

With more than 200 species of birds, including many rare breeds, birdwatching is a popular pastime in Arizona, particularly in spring, early summer, and fall. These are the peak migration seasons for many species such as warblers and flycatchers, and for shorebirds.

Cibola National Wildlife Refuge is home to a wide variety of birds, including nesting waders, ducks and a winter population of snow geese, and more than 1,000 sandhill cranes. Several habitats across the region suit desert birds such as the roadrunner and elf owl; Saguaro National Park *(see p90)*, located in the Sonoran Desert, is a notable example. Southern Arizona is also home to America's greatest variety of hummingbirds. The **Southeastern Arizona Bird Observatory**, a non-profit organization, offers educational tours in the region.

LEARNING VACATIONS

Some of Arizona's most interesting learning vacations focus on Native cultures and ancient civilizations. Two organizations, **The Crow Canyon Archeological Center** and **The Four Corners School**, offer vacation courses on geography, flora and fauna, ancient ruins, and Native arts. Archaeology courses often involve working on digs with professional archaeologists. Most programs last between four and ten days, and visitors are housed either in college campuses or in motels. Several of Arizona's top museums offer a variety of learning vacations. The **Smithsonian Institution** also offers popular programs such as the past and present arts of the Hopi and Navajo tribes.

SPA VACATIONS

Arizona's warm winter weather and spectacular outdoors have resulted in the blossoming of high-end spas in Phoenix,

Telemark turns on San Francisco Peaks, near Flagstaff

Tucson, and Sedona *(see p68)*. These spas offer everything from posh pampering to serious diet and fitness programs, and a host of New Age wellness experiences.

Broad-billed hummingbird

Tucson's **Canyon Ranch**, considered one of the world's finest destination spas, offers a stunning array of programs incorporating tennis, hiking, biking, yoga, tai chi, and meditation. Nearby, **Miraval** is famous for its blend of pampering and physical regimen, offering over 100 facial and body treatment options, including acupuncture, Shiatsu, and Trager. The spa's immaculate grounds feature waterfalls, tennis courts, stables, and a Zen garden.

SKIING & WINTER SPORTS

Featuring 2,300 ft (700 m) of vertical drop and a network of superb trails serviced by five chairlifts, the 12,600-ft (3,840-m) **Arizona Snowbowl** *(see p65)*, which lies just north of Flagstaff, is the undisputed champion of downhill ski resorts in Arizona. Another major resort, **Sunrise Park**, in the White Mountains, features ten lifts and 65 runs, and is a favorite with many visitors, particularly snowboarders. Also growing in popularity is the southernmost ski resort in the country, **Mount Lemmon Ski Valley**, which is located just outside Tucson. The Grand Canyon's North Rim *(see p55)* is particularly sought after by cross-country skiing enthusiasts.

HORSEBACK RIDING

Horseback riding is synonymous with Arizona. Even large cities have stables that offer trail rides through the desert. **OK Corral Stables**, at Apache Junction near Phoenix, offers horseback trail camping trips for one to five days. Cooler summer locations, such as Sedona and Pinetop-Lakeside, are also popular. Dude ranches offer a range of experiences, from pampered luxury with daytime trail rides, to real cattle ranches that offer visitors the chance to live and work as a cowboy. The **Arizona Dude Ranch Association** can help plan a dude ranch vacation.

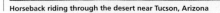

Horseback riding through the desert near Tucson, Arizona

DIRECTORY

INFORMATION

A wealth of information on using and enjoying public lands is available at **www**.recreation.gov

USDA Forest Service
333 Broadway SE, Albuquerque, NM 87102.
Tel *(505) 842-3898.*

USGS
12201 Sunrise Valley Dr, Reston, VA 20192.
Tel *(888) 275-8747.*
www.usgs.gov

HIKING

Arizona Trails
16824 Avenue of the Fountains, Suite 27B, Fountain Hills, AZ 85268.
Tel *(888) 799-4284.*
www.arizonatrails.com

Nichols Expeditions
497 N Main St, Moab, UT 84532.
Tel *(800) 648-8488.*
www.nicholsexpeditions.com

Walk Softly Tours
PO Box 5510, Scottsdale, AZ 85261-5510.
Tel *(480) 473-1148.*
www.walksoftlytours.com

ROCK CLIMBING

Arizona Climbing and Adventure School
PO Box 3094, Carefree, AZ 85377.
Tel *(480) 363-2390.*
www.climbingschool.com

Rocky Mountain Climbing School
8009 E Snakeroot Drive, Tucson, AZ 85710.
Tel *(520) 721-6751.*
www.climbarizona.com

MOUNTAIN BIKING & 4WD

Bikeapelli Adventure Tours
1695 W Hwy 89a, Sedona, AZ 86336.
Tel *(928) 282-1312.*

Goulding's Lodge Monument Valley Tours
Hwy 163, Goulding, UT 84536.
Tel *(435) 727-3231.*
www.gouldings.com

Pink Jeep Tours
PO Box 1447, Sedona, AZ 86339.
Tel *(928) 282-5000, (800) 873-3662.*
www.pinkjeep.com

WHITEWATER RAFTING & KAYAKING

Tour West
PO Box 333, Orem, UT 84059.
Tel *(800) 453-9107.*
www.twriver.com

Wilderness Aware
PO Box 1550WS, Buena Vista, CO 81211.
Tel *(800) 462-7238, (719) 395-2112.*
www.inaraft.com

Wild River Expeditions
PO Box 118/101, Main St, UT 84512-0118.
Tel *(800) 422-7654.*
www.riversandruins.com

OTHER WATERSPORTS

Fun Time Boat Rentals
1685 Industrial Blvd, Lake Havasu City, AZ.
Tel *(928) 680-1003, (800) 680-1003.*
www.funtimeboatrentals.com

Lake Mead Visitor Center
601 Nevada Hwy, Boulder City, NV 89005.
Tel *(702) 293-8990.*

Lake Powell Resorts & Marinas
PO Box 1597, Page, AZ 86040.
Tel *(928) 645-2433, (602) 278-8888, (888) 896-3829.*
www.lakepowell.com

FISHING

Arizona Game & Fish Department
2222 Greenway Rd, Phoenix, AZ 85023.
Tel *(602) 942-3000.*

HOT AIR BALLOONING

Hot Air Expeditions
2243 E Rose Garden Loop, Phoenix, AZ 85024.
Tel *(480) 502-6999, (800) 831-7610.*

Northern Light Balloon Expeditions
PO Box 1695, Sedona, AZ 86339.
Tel *(928) 282-2274, (800) 230-6222.*
www.northernlightballoon.com

BIRDWATCHING

Cibola National Wildlife Refuge
Rte 2, Box 138, Cibola, AZ 85328.
Tel *(928) 857-3253.*

Southeastern Arizona Bird Observatory
PO Box 5521, Bisbee, AZ 85603.
Tel *(520) 432-1388.*
www.sabo.org

LEARNING VACATIONS

The Crow Canyon Archeological Center
23390 County Road K, Cortez, CO 81321.
Tel *(970) 565-8975.*

The Four Corners School
Box 1028, Monticello, UT 84535.
Tel *(800) 525-4456.*
www.fourcornersschool.org

Smithsonian Institution
1000 Jefferson Dr SW, MRC702, Washington DC 20560.
Tel *(877) 338-8687.*
www.smithsonianjourneys.com

SPA VACATIONS

Canyon Ranch
8600 E Rockcliff Rd, Tucson, AZ 85750.
Tel *(520) 749-9655, (800) 742-9000.*
www.canyonranch.com

Miraval
5000 E Via Estancia, Catalina, AZ 85739.
Tel *(800) 232-3969.*
www.miravalresort.com

SKIING & WINTER SPORTS

Arizona Snowbowl
PO Box 40, Flagstaff, AZ 86002.
Tel *(928) 779-1951.*
www.arizonasnowbowl.com

Mount Lemmon Ski Valley
10300 Ski Run Rd, Mt. Lemmon, AZ 85619.
Tel *(520) 576-1321.*

Sunrise Park Ski Resort
PO Box 117, Greer, AZ 85927.
Tel *(928) 735-7669, (800) 772-7669.*
www.sunriseskipark.com

HORSEBACK RIDING

Arizona Dude Ranch Association
PO Box 603, Cortaro, AZ 85652.
www.azdra.com

OK Corral Stables
2665 E Whiteley St, Apache Junction, AZ 85219-8981.
Tel *(480) 982-4040.*
www.okcorrals.com

Golfing in Arizona

Golfer Casey Martin

Boasting over 300 golf courses, many of which are among the world's finest, Arizona is a golfer's paradise. With so many courses, golf enthusiasts have a dazzling array of terrains and levels of challenge to choose from. Green fees can range from nominal to expensive. Private courses are open to club members exclusively, and to those with reciprocal memberships. Semi-private courses are reserved for members, but do accept paying guests at certain times. Public courses are open to all, but golf resorts prefer guests staying with them, though they are opened to the public occasionally. The legendary Boulders Club, near Phoenix, rotates access to its two world-class courses between resort guests, private members, and the public.

A private golf course in the cooler climes of Flagstaff

FLAGSTAFF & NORTHERN ARIZONA

Golf on the Colorado Plateau, at elevations between 5,000 ft (1,524 m) and 7,000 ft (2,134 m), is played throughout the year, although some courses close in winter. In summer, the northern courses usually bustle as they are cooler by 15°F, on an average, than courses in Phoenix. Busy is relative, however, and seldom will the Northern Arizona courses be as crowded as their southern cousins.

In Sedona, the Gary Pranks-designed course at **Sedona Golf Resort** is one of Northern Arizona's must-play venues. Regularly featured in lists of the state's best courses, this par 71 course features lush greens and stunning views of the surrounding red rock canyons.

Surrounded by pine-covered mountains, Prescott is one of the busiest golf regions in Northern Arizona. One of the best deals can be found at **Antelope Hills Golf Course**. For a modest fee of about $55, players can choose from the 50-year-old, 18-hole North Course, with its towering elm trees, classic layout, and challenging doglegs, or the links-style South Course, opened in 1992. In nearby Prescott Valley, the par 72 **Stoneridge Golf Course** is one of Northern Arizona's bright new stars with a visually stunning and physically challenging links-style course that features over 350 ft (107 m) of vertical rise and fall across its 18 holes.

Golfer Charlotta Sorenstam at a golf resort in Phoenix

PHOENIX & CENTRAL ARIZONA

The valley of the sun has perhaps more golf courses per capita than anywhere in the world, 180 and counting, including some of the world's very best. Since this is a spot that must satisfy not only its residents, but also over a million visiting golfers every year, it's no surprise that many of the courses are public or resort courses with generous public access.

Golf is big business here, particularly in Scottsdale, a town virtually synonymous with the concept of luxurious golf resorts such as **The Boulders Club** and **Troon North Golf Club**, which offer some of the best courses in the world. In fact, the Tom Weiskopf-designed course at Troon North is a desert golfer's dream, and is rated No. 1 public golf course in Arizona by *Golf Digest*. Like many Scottsdale courses, the amenities and services at Troon North are

PGA TOUR

Arizona's sunshine and warm winter temperatures make it a favorite of the Professional Golfer's Association (PGA), which holds two important tournaments here early in the year. In late January (or sometimes early February) the FBR Open (formerly the Phoenix Open) attracts huge crowds to the Tournament Players Club of Scottsdale. The club's unusual layout allows for virtually unlimited viewing, and as many as 400,000 people have attended a single tournament. A month later, The PGA Chrysler Classic, with its purse of $3 million, attracts golf fans by the thousands from all over the world to the beautiful Omni Tucson National Golf Resort.

Tiger Woods hits a tee shot during the Phoenix Open

Randolph Park in Tuscon – one of the top ten public golf courses in Arizona

top-notch, but all this comes at a steep price, at up to $295 a round. In Phoenix, there is the **Wildfire Golf Club**, which features two first-class courses, a classic Arnold Palmer Signature course, and the desert-style Faldo Championship Course.

Those wanting to opt for a public course can head east to **Gold Canyon Resort**, which has the Sidewinder and Dinosaur Mountain courses, both top-rated public courses since they opened. Both courses are visually stunning and among the best value in this land of golf and sunshine.

TUCSON & SOUTHERN ARIZONA

Set in the verdant Sonoran Desert, surrounded by stunning landscape and boasting over 350 days of sunshine every year, Tucson is one of America's best golf destinations. The city has fantastic offerings, including **Ventana Canyon Resort**, whose Tom Fazio-designed Mountain Course offers immaculate greens. Listed among North America's best courses, it offers enough challenge to keep even the most experienced golfers focused. Another rewarding course is the classic **Randolf Park**, with its broad water hazards and towering eucalyptus trees. A popular PGA venue in the 1980s, Randolf Park now hosts LPGA events.

South of Tucson, the suburbs of Green Valley have some of the finest courses in Southern Arizona. One of these is **Torres Blancas**, a Lee Trevino-designed course with a monster 484-yard (442-m), par 4 signature 17th hole that gives players something to talk about back at the clubhouse.

DIRECTORY

GENERAL

Arizona Golf Association
7226 N 16th St, St 200, Phoenix, AZ 85020.
Tel (602) 944-3035.

Golf Arizona
Tel (866) 444-0992.
www.golfarizona.com

FLAGSTAFF & NORTHERN ARIZONA

Antelope Hills Golf Course
1 Perkins Dr, Prescott, AZ 86301.
Tel (303) 644-5993.
www.antelopehillsgolfcourse.com

Sedona Golf Resort
35 Ridge Trail Dr, Sedona, AZ 86351.
Tel (877) 733-6630, (928) 284-9355.
www.sedonagolfresort.com

Stoneridge Golf Course
1601 N Bluff Top Rd, Prescott Valley, AZ 86314.
Tel (928) 772-6500.
www.stoneridgegolf.com

PHOENIX & CENTRAL ARIZONA

The Boulders Club
34831 N Tom Darlington, PO Box 2090, Carefree, AZ 85377.
Tel (480) 488-9028.
www.thebouldersclub.com

Gold Canyon Golf Resort
6100 S Kings Ranch Rd, Gold Canyon, AZ 85219.
Tel (480) 982-9449.
www.gcgr.com

Troon North Golf Club
10320 E Dynamite Blvd, Scottsdale, AZ 85255.
Tel (480) 585-7700.
www.troonnorthgolf.com

Wildfire Golf Club
5350 E Marriott Drive, Phoenix, AZ 85054.
Tel (480) 473-0205, (480) 293-5000.
www.wildfiregolf.com

TUCSON & SOUTHERN ARIZONA

Randolph Park Golf Course
600 S Alvernon Way, Pima County, Tucson, AZ 85711.
Tel (520) 791-4161.
www.tucsoncitygolf.com/randolph.html

Torres Blancas Golf Club
3233 S Abrego Dr, Pima County, Green Valley, AZ 85614.
Tel (520) 625-5200.
www.torresblancasgolf.com

Ventana Canyon Golf Resort
6200 N Clubhouse Lane, Tucson, AZ 85750.
Tel (520) 577-1400. www.ventanacanyonclub.com

SURVIVAL GUIDE

PRACTICAL INFORMATION

A vast region of fascinating and spectacular natural beauty, Arizona is dotted with dramatic rock formations, canyons, ancient archeological sites, and wild desert scenery that offers visitors a choice of pleasures, including a wide variety of outdoor activities.

Arizona State Parks' sign

Arizona's cities are famous for their combination of a laid-back Southwestern culture, and sophisticated urban pursuits such as excellent museums and great dining. In addition, unique attractions located on Native reservations provide a wonderful opportunity to observe American Indian cultures. Accommodations are excellent *(see pp122–31)*, and visitor information centers are plentiful, even in the small towns.

The following pages contain useful information on planning a trip to this region. Personal Security *(see pp160–61)* recommends a number of precautions to visitors, while Travel *(see pp162–5)* provides information on travel by both public transportation and car.

WHEN TO GO

Arizona is a year-round destination, and its climate is dictated by elevation. The higher elevation areas have cold, snowy winters, making them a popular destination for skiing and other winter sports activities. In contrast, lower elevations in Southern Arizona are noted for the warm and sunny winter weather, with temperatures averaging a comfortable 70°F (21°C) in Phoenix. Be aware, however, that the average temperature in the summer months of July and August touches 100°F (37°C) in Phoenix, making it one of the hottest cities outside the Middle East. Spring and fall are ideal seasons to visit Arizona – there are fewer visitors, and the milder temperatures make outdoor activities a popular option. However, some services may be closed at these times: the North Rim of the Grand Canyon *(see p55)* is open only between May and October. Whatever the time of year, this is a region known for having a great deal of sun, with the northern areas averaging over 200 days of sunshine each year, and the southern parts famous for having more than 300 sunny days in a year.

TOURIST INFORMATION

Visitor information centers in Arizona offer everything from local maps to hotel and B&B bookings. Special tours, such as guided history walks, ranger-led archaeological tours, and wildlife expeditions, can also be arranged through these offices. In addition, the national and state parks have their own visitor centers that provide hiking maps, safety advice, and special licenses for hiking and camping out in the wilderness.

Arizona has a department of tourism, as do all the major towns and cities in the state. Contact the **Arizona Office of Tourism** when planning your trip and they will be pleased to send an information pack. Smaller urban centers and sights of special interest have offices that provide maps and guides. Information can also be obtained from the network of chambers of commerce in the region. Websites of the departments of tourism, as well as those of individual sights, also offer information and online booking services for accommodations.

Ranger on a guided tour at Keet Seel, Navajo National Monument

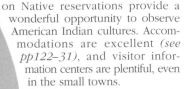

Many tourist attractions, such as Canyon de Chelly *(see pp106–9)*, are located on Native reservations and are managed by tribal councils. For advice on etiquette, opening times, and admission fees, contact the local **Bureau of Indian Affairs** or the **Navajo Tourism Department**.

TIME ZONES

The state is located in the Mountain Standard Time zone, but it does not follow Daylight Saving Time. From late spring to early fall, all of the neighboring states in the Mountain Standard Time zone (New Mexico, Colorado, and Utah) set their clocks forward by one hour, but not Arizona.

To confuse matters even more, it is important to be aware that the Navajo Nation (across Arizona and part of New Mexico) does use Daylight Saving Time, but the Hopi Indian Reservation (in the middle of the Navajo Reservation) does not.

SENIOR TRAVELERS

Although the age when you are considered a senior is 65, a multitude of discounts are available to people over 50. Reduced rates can apply to meals, accommodations, public transportation, and entrance fees, and are often

◁ Highway to mesa, butte, and spire formations at Monument Valley National Monument

better than student discounts. The **National Park Service** offers Golden Age Passports that reduce the cost of park tours and services. **Elderhostel** arranges educational tours, which include inexpensive accommodations, lectures, and meals. The **American Association of Retired Persons (AARP)** offers good travel discounts.

TRAVELERS WITH DISABILITIES

Arizona has excellent facilities to cater to the physically disabled traveler. All public places and buildings are legally required to be wheelchair-accessible, and to have suitably designed restrooms. However, call and check on the accessibility in smaller inns and B&Bs, and in small, local restaurants. Public transportation also comes under this law, and road crossings in city centers have dropped curbs to enable easier access. Service animals, such as guide dogs for the blind, are the only animals allowed on public transportation.

Many national parks and archaeological sights have paved walkways for wheelchairs. The National Park Service grants free entry, for one year, to those who are disabled or blind. The **Disabled Travelers** website and the **Society for Accessible Travel & Hospitality** are two organizations that offer advice on traveling to the disabled, from how to rent specially adapted cars to qualifying for parking permits.

Wheelchair access sign

STUDENT TRAVELERS

The largest provider of student travel products and services is **STA Travel**. It offers discounted accommodations, rail passes, phone cards, email options, travel packages, and cut-rate student airfares. The best deals are available at offices near colleges and universities. **Student Universe** offers similar services via the Internet. If you are planning to stay in youth hostels, you will need to join **Hostelling International/American Youth Hostels (HI/AYH)**.

Water fountains in the courtyard of the Heard Museum in Phoenix

DIRECTORY

STATE & LOCAL OFFICES

Arizona Office of Tourism
1110 W Washington St, Phoenix, AZ 85007.
Tel (866) 298-3795.
www.arizonaguide.com

Bureau of Indian Affairs
PO Box 10, Phoenix.
Tel (602) 379-6600.

Flagstaff Visitor Center
One E Route 66, Flagstaff, AZ 86001.
Tel (800) 842-7293.
www.flagstaffarizona.org

Greater Phoenix Convention & Visitors Bureau
400 E Van Buren St, Suite 600, Phoenix, AZ 85004.
Tel (877) 225-5749.
www.visitphoenix.com

Metropolitan Tucson Visitors Bureau
100 S Church Ave, Tucson, AZ 85701.
Tel (800) 638-8350.
www.visittucson.org

Navajo Tourism Department
PO Box 663, Window Rock, AZ 86515.
Tel (928) 871-6436.

SENIOR TRAVELERS

American Asso. of Retired Persons
201 E Washington St, Suite 1795, Phoenix AZ 85004.
Tel (866) 389-5649.
www.aarp.org

Elderhostel
11 Avenue de Laffayette, Boston, MA 02111.
Tel (877) 426-8056.
www.elderhostel.org

National Park Service
(see also under individual sights)
Intermountain Area, PO Box 25287, Denver, CO 80225.
www.nps.gov

DISABLED TRAVELERS

Disabled Travelers
PO Box 492, Yucca, AZ 86438.
www.disabledtravelers.com

Society for Accessible Travel & Hospitality (SATH)
347 Fifth Ave, Suite 610, New York, NY 10016.
Tel (212) 447-7284.
www.sath.org

STUDENT TRAVELERS

Hostelling International/ American Youth Hostel (HI/AYH)
8401 Colesville Rd, Suite 600, Silver Spring, MD 20910.
Tel (301) 495-1240.
www.hiusa.org

STA Travel
5900 Wilshire Blvd, Suite 900, Los Angeles, CA 90036.
Tel (800) 781-4040, (800) 836-4115.
www.statravel.com

Student Universe
230 Third Ave, Watertown, MA 02472.
Tel (800) 272-9676.
www.studentuniverse.com

Personal Security & Health

Fire Department badge, Sedona

Arizona is a relatively safe place as long as some general precautions are observed. Arizona's urban centers have lower crime rates in contrast to other US cities, but it is still wise to be cautious and to find out which parts are unsafe at night. When traveling across remote areas, take a reliable local map, and follow the advice of local rangers and visitor centers. These sources also offer invaluable information on survival in the wilderness and on safety procedures that should be followed during outdoor activities *(see pp58–61 & 150–55)*. It is also advisable to check the local media such as newspapers, television, and radio for current weather and safety conditions.

PERSONAL SAFETY

Most tourist areas in Arizona are friendly and non-threatening. However, to avoid being a victim of crime, it is wise to observe a few basic rules. Never carry large amounts of cash, wear obviously expensive jewelry, or keep your wallet in your back pocket. Wear handbags and cameras over one shoulder with the strap across your body. Keep your identification separate from your cash and traveler's checks. Most hotels have safety deposit boxes or safes in which you should store any valuables.

If you are driving, be sure to lock any valuables in the trunk where they are out-of-sight, and to park only in well-lit parking lots. Also, it is wise to have a roadside assistance service plan, such as AAA *(see p165)*, which sends licensed service representatives in case assistance is needed. Similarly, at night it is better to stay where there are other people and be aware of which areas could be unsafe. It is a good idea to carry a cell phone so that you can call 911 in an emergency. In tourist destinations, lock the car when stepping out. Parking areas in national parks, particularly overlooks and trailheads, are extremely popular targets for thieves.

Police officer on horseback patrol in Nogales

MEDICAL TREATMENT

For emergencies that require assistance from the medical, police, or fire services call 911. **Traveler's Aid Society**, a national organization, extends help to needy travelers. City hospitals with emergency rooms can be found in the directory, but they are often overcrowded. Private hospitals offer more personalized treatment and are listed in the Yellow Pages. Walk-in clinics offer basic medical services, and are usually less expensive and more efficient than hospitals for non-emergencies. You may be required to provide evidence of your ability to pay before a doctor will agree to treat you, hence the importance of adequate medical insurance. Hotels will usually call a doctor or recommend a local dentist.

TRAVEL INSURANCE

Arizona has excellent medical services, but as in the rest of the US they are very expensive. Visitors are strongly advised to make sure they have comprehensive medical and dental coverage for the duration of their stay. Visitors planning to take part in outdoor activities in remote areas or stay on Native reservations should consider including medical air evacuation insurance as well.

TRAVEL SAFETY

There are plenty of remote areas and lightly traveled roads in Arizona. Before you go, check that your car has a spare tire, and the tools required to change it, and that you know how to replace a flat tire. Carry a cell phone, blanket, and emergency food and water in case of a breakdown in a remote area.

Lone truck on rough Arizona desert road

Park ranger at the Petrified Forest National Park, Arizona

OUTDOOR SAFETY

The weather in the Southwest can present a number of dangerous situations, especially in Southern Arizona, where sudden summer storms may cause flash floods. Weather information can be obtained from ranger stations, and through reports on radio and television. If you are planning a drive or hike in remote territory, always tell someone where you are going and when you expect to return.

The dry summer heat is often underestimated, and hikers are advised to carry at least a gallon (4 liters) of drinking water per person for each day of walking. Dry conditions also pose the risk of forest fires at higher elevations, and it is advisable to check with forest service rangers regarding fire danger before lighting any flame.

The sun is surprisingly strong at higher elevations, and an effective sunscreen and sunhat should always be worn. Temperatures can change rapidly in Arizona. It may be 80°F (26°C) during the day, and then drop to 30°F (-1°C) at night. Be prepared and dress accordingly.

Dangerous creatures are found in the wilderness *(see p19)*, but these animals generally avoid humans and it is unlikely you will be bitten if you avoid their habitats.

Do not turn over rocks or reach up to touch rock ledges. Shake out clothes and shoes that have been on the ground before putting them on. Venomous stings and bites may hurt but are rarely fatal to adults with prompt medical attention. Always carry a first aid and snakebite kit if you are going into snake country.

TRAVELING ON THE RESERVATIONS

Visitors are welcome on reservations, and will generally find Natives to be friendly and helpful. However, take the same care as when traveling in any remote rural area of the US. Services such as restaurants, motels, gas stations, and ATMs are only located in towns and at major crossroads. Call 911 in case of an emergency. If a serious medical situation develops, you will be provided first-line treatment and then shifted to a hospital off the reservation. Most reservations also have their own highly trained police forces, which enforce the laws and assist lost tourists. It is illegal to bring alcohol onto reservations – even a bottle visible in a locked car will land you in trouble. Always ask before photographing anything, and be prepared that a fee may be requested. Do not wander off marked trails as this is forbidden. Dress respectfully – for example, the Hopi request that people do not wear shorts.

Navajo security personnel

Speak softly when talking to Natives as loud voices are considered rude. Speak clearly and remember that English is a second language for many Native Americans.

DIRECTORY

EMERGENCY SERVICES

All emergencies
Tel *911* and alert police, fire, or medical services.

Police Non-Emergency Line
Phoenix
Tel *(602) 262-6151.*

Traveler's Aid Society
Sky Harbor Airport Chapel, Terminal 4, Phoenix.
Tel *(602) 244-1346.*

American Express
Stolen credit & charge cards
Tel *(800) 992-3404.*

Diner's Club
Lost & stolen credit cards
Tel *(800) 234-6377.*

MasterCard
Lost & stolen credit cards
Tel *(800) 307 7309.*

Visa
Lost & stolen credit cards
Tel *(800) 336-8472.*

Police department sign on the Navajo Reservation

TRAVEL INFORMATION

Phoenix, followed by Tucson, is the main gateway for visitors arriving in Arizona by air. There are other major airports in neighboring states that also serve as entry points, including the cities of Las Vegas in Nevada, Salt Lake City in Utah, and Albuquerque in New Mexico. Visitors also arrive by long-distance bus or, less frequently, by Amtrak train. However, the automobile remains the preferred mode of transport. Arizona has an excellent, well-maintained network of highways, service stations, and comfortable, air-conditioned cars for rent.

American Airlines

Public transportation options are increasing in major urban centers of the state – a light rail service has been implemented, and local bus systems have expanded their hours of operation. The downtown shuttle is used by visitors during weekday working hours.

An airplane flying over the Phoenix skyline at sunset

VISAS

British citizens, members of many EU countries, and citizens of Australia and New Zealand do not need a visa provided they have a return ticket and their stay in the US does not exceed 90 days. Regulations require visitors to register with the Electronic System for Travel Authorisation (ESTA) before departure. It is valid for two years. It is advisable to apply well in advance.

Other citizens must apply for a nonimmigrant visa from a US consulate, while Canadians need only a passport. Before you travel, it is advisable to check the most up-to-date information, available at www.uscis.gov.

ARRIVING BY AIR

Mesa Airlines logo

Phoenix's Sky Harbor International has three terminals and receives the bulk of domestic and international arrivals. Sky Harbor and Tucson International Airport are centers for major US airlines that offer both international and domestic routes; these include **American Airlines, Continental Airlines, Delta Airlines**, **Frontier Airlines**, **Southwest Airlines**, and **United Airlines**.

From Phoenix, **USAirways** flies to the cities of Tucson, Flagstaff, Sedona, and Yuma, while **Mesa Airlines** flies to a variety of Southwestern destinations.

There are very few non-stop flights into Arizona from outside the United States. Most international visitors have to connect via one of the country's major airports, such as Los Angeles, San Francisco, Chicago, Atlanta, or Dallas. Travelers from Pacific countries generally change at Honolulu, Hawai'i. Those foreign carriers that do have direct flights to Phoenix include **British Airways**, **Air Canada**, and **AeroMexico**.

AIR FARES

There is an array of fare types and prices available. The cheaper tickets are usually booked early, especially between June and September, as well as around the Christmas and Thanksgiving holidays.

Direct bookings can be done through an agent, travel website or through an airline. Agents are a good source of information on bargains and ticket restrictions. Fly-drive deals, where the cost of the ticket includes car rental, may also be a lower-priced option.

Although there are several websites offering bargains on

AIRPORT	*TEL* INFORMATION	DISTANCE TO CITY CENTER	TRAVEL TIME BY ROAD
Phoenix	(602) 273-3300	4 miles (6.4 km)	15 minutes
Tucson	(520) 573-8000	8 miles (12.8 km)	30 minutes
Flagstaff	(928) 556-1234	7 miles (11.3 km)	10 minutes

A Grand Canyon Railway train on its way to Grand Canyon Village

last minute bookings, travel websites offer the convenience of price comparisons. Prices can change daily, so check at various times before buying tickets that impose penalties for changes. However, the travel websites may not always have the best prices on tickets or packages. Part of your comparison shopping should include visiting the websites, and calling up individual airlines, hotels, and rental car outfits.

TRAVELING BY TRAIN & BUS

Train and bus travel in Arizona can be a slow but enjoyable means of exploring the region.

Long-distance **Greyhound** buses are the least expensive way to travel, and they also offer the widest choice of destinations. There are 27 daily routes throughout Arizona, as well as eight daily trips direct to Tucson, from Phoenix's Sky Harbor airport. Greyhound and a number of other companies also offer package tours. Destinations include national parks, such as Grand Canyon, and casinos, as well as urban and historical tours on luxury, air-conditioned buses. **Amtrak** offers two train routes – Southwest Chief runs daily between Chicago and Los Angeles, through the Navajo and Hopi reservations, Winslow, Gallop, and Flagstaff, while the Sunset Limited travels three times a week between Orlando and Los Angeles, passing through Tucson and Yuma. Both offer National Park Service cultural and natural heritage programs.

Greyhound bus crossing South-western desert landscape

For rail enthusiasts, the **Grand Canyon Railway** offers both diesel and steam rail trips from Williams *(see p29)* to the Grand Canyon. The two-hour trip offers packages with meals and overnight accommodations. Western entertainment – including a posse of bad guys staging an attack on the train is also included.

PUBLIC TRANSPORTATION IN CITIES

With the exception of Flagstaff, which can be explored on foot, the major cities in Arizona, such as Phoenix and Tucson, are large areas and are plagued by traffic problems. Visitors could use public transportation, such as local buses, to tour these. Booking a tour can often be the best way of seeing major city sights and some remote scenery.

Phoenix and Scottsdale *(see pp76–80)* are covered by the **Valley Metro** bus and light rail system, as well as by **Ollie the Trolley**, a bus service that runs between Scottsdale's resorts and its shopping districts. Downtown Phoenix also has the convenient **Downtown Dash**, which travels between the State Capitol, Arizona Center, and the Civic Plaza. Tucson *(see pp88–91)* has the **Sun Tran** bus system.

DIRECTORY

TRAVEL SITES & AIRLINE CARRIERS

www.lastminute.com

www.expedia.com

www.orbitz.com

AeroMexico
Tel (800) 237-6639.

Air Canada
Tel (888) 247-2262.

American Airlines
Tel (800) 433-7300.

British Airways
Tel (800) 247-9297.

Continental Airlines
Tel (800) 525-0280.

Delta Airlines
Tel (800) 221-1212.

Frontier Airlines
Tel (800) 432-1359.

Mesa Airlines
Tel (888) 435-9462.

Southwest Airlines
Tel (800) 435-9792.

United Airlines
Tel (800) 241-6522.

USAirways
Tel (800) 428-4322.

RAIL & BUS COMPANIES

Amtrak
Tel (800) 872-7245.

Grand Canyon Railway
Tel (800) 843-8724.
Tel (928) 773-1976.

Greyhound
Tel (800) 231-2222.

CITY PUBLIC TRANSIT

Downtown Dash
Phoenix. *Tel (602) 253-5000.*

Ollie the Trolley
Scottsdale. *Tel (480) 970-8130.*

Sun Tran
Tucson. *Tel (520) 792-9222.*

Valley Metro
Phoenix. *Tel (602) 253-5000.*

Traveling By Car & Four-Wheel Drive

Sign for RV parking

When the movie characters Thelma and Louise, in the film of the same name, won a kind of freedom on the open roads of the Southwest, they promoted the pleasures of driving in this visually spectacular and dramatic region. However, for both residents and visitors, driving is a necessary part of life in Arizona, and a car is often the only means of reaching remote country areas. Tours of picturesque regions, such as the North Rim of the Grand Canyon *(see p55)*, Canyon de Chelly National Monument *(see pp106–9)*, or the Organ Pipe Cactus National Monument *(see p96)*, are best made by car. The entire state is served by a network of well-maintained roads, from multilane highways to winding, scenic routes that lead to even the remotest areas.

RENTING A CAR

Most of the major car rental businesses, such as **Alamo**, **Avis**, and **Hertz**, and some budget dealers, such as **Budget, Dollar Rent-A-Car**, and **Thrifty Auto**, have outlets at airports, and in towns and cities across Arizona. However, for those planning to fly into Phoenix, the least expensive option may be to arrange a fly-drive deal *(see p162)*.

There is a central computerized booking system for most of the car companies – use the toll-free number and the Internet to find the best rates. Bargains can also be found by booking in advance and for travel during the off-season.

Hertz car-rental logo

RENTING SUVS & 4WDS

Visitors planning to travel the back roads of Arizona to explore places like Chaco Canyon *(see pp112–3)* or Monument Valley *(see pp102–3)* may want to rent a sports utility vehicle (SUV) or a four-wheel drive (4WD) vehicle; such vehicles provide greater road clearance. Roads that require high clearance in Arizona are usually marked as such. In wet conditions, it is safest to travel by a 4WD on these roads, and it is also advisable to use 4WD vehicles on dirt roads. Most of the major car rental companies offer 4WD SUVs, but you must ask for guaranteed delivery, specify the 4WD you want, and make sure you understand the usage restrictions, if any. Also, some car rental agreements do not allow travel on unpaved roads.

For serious off-road 4WD use, **Farabee** in Sedona rents modified jeeps for four to eight hours of use on designated trails.

RENTING RVS

One of the most interesting and cost-effective ways of enjoying Arizona's vast and fascinating outdoors is in a recreational vehicle (RV). An RV gives you more freedom to explore on your own schedule, the ease of unpacking only once, and the convenience of cooking in your own kitchen.

Campgrounds are plentiful, and you can choose between the grounds of the National Park Service, Forest Service, Bureau of Land Management and private companies *(see pp150–53 & p159)*. The **Recreation Vehicle Rental Association (RVRA)** offers tips on selecting a rental RV, campground information, as well as rental agreement information. Make sure that the rental company provides roadside assistance if required, and that it explains the operations and usage of all the features of the RV. Also, plan to spend your first night near the dealer in case you require additional information after driving and sleeping in the RV.

Sports utility vehicle moving through Canyon de Chelly

Recreational vehicle in Arizonan backcountry

BACKCOUNTRY DRIVING

For any travel in the remote parts of Arizona, such as the desert regions and Native reservations, it is very important to check your route to see if a 4WD vehicle is required. Although many backcountry areas have graded dirt and gravel roads, which can be used by conventional cars, a 4WD is essential in some wild and remote areas. Monument Valley, for example, has a self-guided driving tour on dirt roads. Contact motoring organizations and tourist centers for information to assess your backcountry trip properly.

Unimproved road sign

There are certain basic safety points that should be observed on any trip of this kind. Plan your route and carry up-to-date maps. When traveling between remote destinations, inform the police or National Park Service wardens of your departure and expected arrival times. Check weather and road conditions before you start, and be aware of seasonal dangers such as flash floods. Carry plenty of food and water, and a cell phone as an added precaution. If you run out of gas or break down, call for help and stay with your vehicle since it offers protection from the elements.

Native flora and fauna must not be removed or damaged. Also, visitors should not drive off-road unless they are in a specially designated area, and especially not on Native reservation land. If driving an RV, you must stop overnight in designated campgrounds.

ROADSIDE SERVICES

Although Arizona has many remote destinations, service stations are usually located in towns and at the intersections of major highways. Most have small stores that offer drinks, snacks, and basic automotive parts. Seldom are they more than 60 miles (96 km) apart. Not all stations provide mechanical assistance, so visitors may want to join a roadside assistance organization, such as the **American Automobile Association (AAA)**, that will come to their aid at a call. In the Phoenix area, Freeway Safety Patrol vehicles assist stranded motorists by diagnosing minor vehicle problems, helping with repairs, and calling a tow truck.

DIRECTORY

CAR RENTAL COMPANIES

Alamo
Tel *(800) 354-2322.*
www.alamo.com

Avis
Tel *(800) 331-1212.*
www.avis.com

Budget
Tel *(800) 527-0700.*
www.budget.com

Dollar Rent-A-Car
Tel *(800) 800-4000.*
www.dollar.com

Hertz
Tel *(800) 654-3131.*
www.hertz.com

Thrifty Auto Rental
Tel *(800) 847-4389.*
www.thrifty.com

OFF-ROAD 4WDS

Farabee Jeep Rentals
3009 W Hwy 89A,
Sedona, AZ 86336.
Tel *(928) 282-8700.*

USEFUL ORGANIZATIONS

American Automobile Association
742 E Glendale Ave,
Phoenix, AZ 85027.
Tel *(602) 285-6241.*
www.aaaaz.com

Recreational Vehicle Rental Association
3930 University Dr,
Fairfax, VA 22030.
Tel *(703) 591-7130.*
www.rvra.org

Gas service station on the legendary Route 66

General Index

Page numbers in **bold** type refer to main entries.

Acknowledgments

Main Contributor
Paul Franklin is a travel writer and photographer specializing in the United States and Canada. He is the author of several guide books and magazine articles, and is based in Livingston, Texas.

Contributors
Nancy Mikula, Donna Dailey, Michelle de Larrabeiti, Philip Lee.

Factcheckers
Paul Franklin and Nancy Mikula.

Proofreader
Sonia Malik.

Indexer
Chumki Sen.

DK London
Publisher
Douglas Amrine.

Publishing Managers
Fay Franklin, Jane Ewart.

Additional Picture Research
Rachel Barber, Ellen Root.

Revisions Editors
Anna Freiberger, Catherine Palmi.

Revisions Designers
Julie Bond, Conrad Van Dyk.

Editorial & Design Assistance
Brigitte Arora, Claire Baranowski, Sonal Bhatt, Uma Bhattacharya, Tessa Bindloss, Nicola Erdpresser, Mariana Evmolpidou, Vinod Harish, Mohammad Hassan, Laura Jones, Jasneet Kaur, Juliet Kenny, Vincent Kurien, Sands Publishing Solutions, Azeem Siddiqui, Brett Steel, Ros Walford.

Additional Photography
Paul Franklin, Steve Gorton, Dave King, Andrew McKinney, Neil Mersh, Ian O'Leary, Tim Ridley, Clive Streeter.

Cartography
Uma Bhattacharya, Alok Pathak, Ben Bowles, Rob Clynes, Sam Johnston, James Macdonald (Colourmap Scanning Ltd).

Senior DTP Designer
Jason Little.

Senior Cartographic Editor
Casper Morris.

DK Picture Library
Gemma Woodward, Hayley Smith, Romaine Werblow.

Production Controller
Louise Daly.

Dorling Kindersley would like to thank the following people whose contributions and assistance have made the preparation of this book possible.

Special Assistance
Many thanks for the invaluable help of the following individuals: Juliet Martin, Heard Museum; Stacy Reading and Brett Brooks, Phoenix CVB; Barbara MacDonald and Hope Patterson, Tucson CVB; Leslie Connell and Ana Masterson, Flagstaff CVB; Michelle Mountain, Museum of Northern Arizona; Tom Pittinger, Grand Canyon National Park; Russ Bodner, Chaco Culture National Historic Park; and all the national park staff in the region.

Photography Permissions
Dorling Kindersley would like to thank all the cathedrals, churches, museums, hotels, restaurants, shops, galleries, national and state parks, and other sights for their assistance and kind permission to photograph at their establishments.

Placement Key – t=top; tl=top left; tlc=top left center; tc=top center; trc=top right center; tr=top right; cla=center left above; ca=center above; cra=center right above; cl=center left; c=center; cr=center right; clb=center left below; cb=center below; crb=center right below; bl=bottom left; b=bottom; bc=bottom center; bcl=bottom center left; br=bottom right; d=detail.

Works of art and images have been produced with the permission of the following copyright holders: Frank Lloyd Wright Foundation 23ca, 81b; University of Arizona Fine Arts Oasis Barbara Grygutis *Front Row Center* 88tl.

The publishers would like to thank the following individuals, companies, and picture libraries for their kind permission to reproduce their photographs:

AFP: Spaceimaging.com 11t; ALAMY: 72t, 161c; ALAMY IMAGES: Stefan Binkert 62tr; Andreas Keuchel 91bl; Rollie Rodriguez 8tc; ARIZONA GAME & FISH DEPARTMENT: Pat O'Brien 14tc; ARIZONA OFFICE OF TOURISM: Chris Coe 28tr; ARIZONA STATE LIBRARY: Archive+Public Records, Archive Division, Phoenix no.99–0281 34; ARIZONA STATE PARKS: K. L. Day 99t; ASSOCIATED PRESS: Louisa Gauerke 29cl, Roy Dabner 148b; AURA/NOAO/NATIONAL SCIENCE FOUNDATION: 94b.

BRANSON REYNOLDS: 25b; BRIDGEMAN ART LIBRARY: Christie's London Walter Ufer (1876–1936) *The*

Southwest 6–7; Frederic Remington (1861–1909) *Aiding a Comrade* c.1890 26–7, *The Conversation, or Dubious Company* 26b.

CORBIS: 41t, 41clb, 41b; Art on File 23clb, 23br; Bettman *Cowboy on a Horse* Frederic Remington (1861–1909) 20cl, 26cb, 26tr, 38cb, 39bl, 43c, 109b, 162tc; Duomo/Jason Wise 154t; New Sport/Gark Newkirk 154b; James L. Amos 110t; Tom Bean 2–3, 14b, 19br, 26tr, 26b, 30cra, 33b, 37cr, 49b, 60b, 68bc, 142br, 151t, 151c, 152t; Patrick Bennett 68br; Geoffrey Clements 147t; Richard A. Cooke 20b; Richard Cummins 15t, 68t, 68c, 73b; Owen Franken 165t; Marc Garanger 161b; Raymond Gehman 84cla, 85cb; Lowell Georgia 84bl, 84br; Mark E. Gibson 95b; Darrel Gulin 19tr, 19bc; Richard Hamilton 160b; Jan Butchofsky-Houser 27t, 164t; Dave G. Houser 85clb, 144b; George H. H. Huey 86–7, 96c; Liz Hymans 37t; Dewitt Jones 36tr; Catherine Karnow 24ca, 68clb, 68cb, 164b; Layne Kennedy 58c, 98b; Douglas Kirkland 120–21; Danny Lehman 59t, 142c; James Marshall 22tr; Joe McDonald 91t; David Muench 1c, 19cr, 36–7, 51c, 73t, 85t, 114–5; Marc Muench 58b; Pat O'Hara 52bl; Gabe Palmer 25c; Greg Probst 84cl; Carl & Ann Purcell 60t; Roger Ressmeyer 94c; Tony Roberts 154cl, 154cr, 155t; Joel W. Rogers 61t, 162c; Bob Rowan 3c, 24tl; Pete Saloutos 147crb; Phil Schermeister 30bl; Richard Hamilton Smith 143b; Scott T. Smith 19clb; Kennan Ward 18tr; Ron Watts 48cl; Nik Wheeler 122c; CORBIS SYGMA: Stone Les 160c.

DAVE G. HOUSER: 31b; © Mrs. Anna Marie Houser/The Allan Houser Foundation 21t; DIANA DICKER: 36b; DIGITAL CLARITY: Hayden Houser 83t, 83b.

GETTY IMAGES: Car Culture 8br; Collection Mix: Subjects/Car Culture 133tr; National Geographic/ Martin Gray 9br; Stone/John Elk 9tl; GRAND CANYON CAVERNS: 28br; GRAND CANYON RAILWAY: 163tl; GRAND CANYON WEST: 61TR; GREYHOUND LINES, INC.: 163b; GOULDINGS LODGE: 103b.

HEARD MUSEUM: Fred Harvey Collection/Daniel Namingha *Red-Tailed Hawk* 20–21, 78tr, 79t; HOPI LEARNING CENTER: 20tr, 146cl; HOUSERSTOCK: Ellen Barone 32.
IMPACT PHOTOS: Jacquie Spector 28bl; INDEXSTOCK IMAGERY: Mark Gibson 144t; James Lemass 149b.

JOHN RUNNING: 24crb, 25t.

KOBAL COLLECTION, LONDON: Paramount Pictures 27b.

LEONARDO MEDIA LTD.: 123cb.

MASTERFILE: G.D.Gifford 148c; MESA AIR GROUP: 162cb; MUSEUM OF NEW MEXICO: Fray Orci *Portrait of Don Juan Bautista de Anza* 1774 neg. no. 50828 39br(d).

NHPA: 18br; John Shaw 18clb; courtesy of the NATIONAL PARK SERVICE, CHACO CULTURE NATIONAL HISTORIC PARK: 36cb, 37b, 112tl; NEW MEXICO TOURISM: 30tc.

PAUL FRANKLIN: 15c, 50br, 55tr, 59b, 116 all, 117t, 117b, 143t; PETER NEWARK PICTURES: 26cla, 27tl, 35c, 39t, 40t, 40br; PHOTOLIBRARY: Roland Mayr 8cl; PHOTOSHOT: Newscom 49cr; PRIVATE COLLECTION: 7c, 39cb, 157c.

RAMAN SRINIVASAN: 97t.

SHARLOT HALL MUSEUM: 31t; STONE: Tom Bean 33tc; Paul Chesley 100; Steve Lewis 29cr.

UNIVERSITY OF ARCHEOLOGY & ANTHROPOLOGY: 146bl; UNIVERSITY OF ARIZONA: 88tl.

YUMA CONVENTION AND VISITORS BUREAU: ©Robert Herko 1999 95t.

Front endpaper: all special photography except STONE: Paul Chesley cr.

Jacket
Front – ALAMY IMAGES: Rollie Rodriguez main image; CORBIS: Dewitt Jones clb. Back – ALAMY IMAGES: David Ball bl; Robert Harding Picture Library Ltd/Tony Gervis tl; Chris Selby bl; DK IMAGES: Demetrio Carrasco cla, clb. Spine – ALAMY IMAGES: Rollie Rodriguez t; DK IMAGES: Tim Ridley b.

Road Map of Arizona & the Four Corners

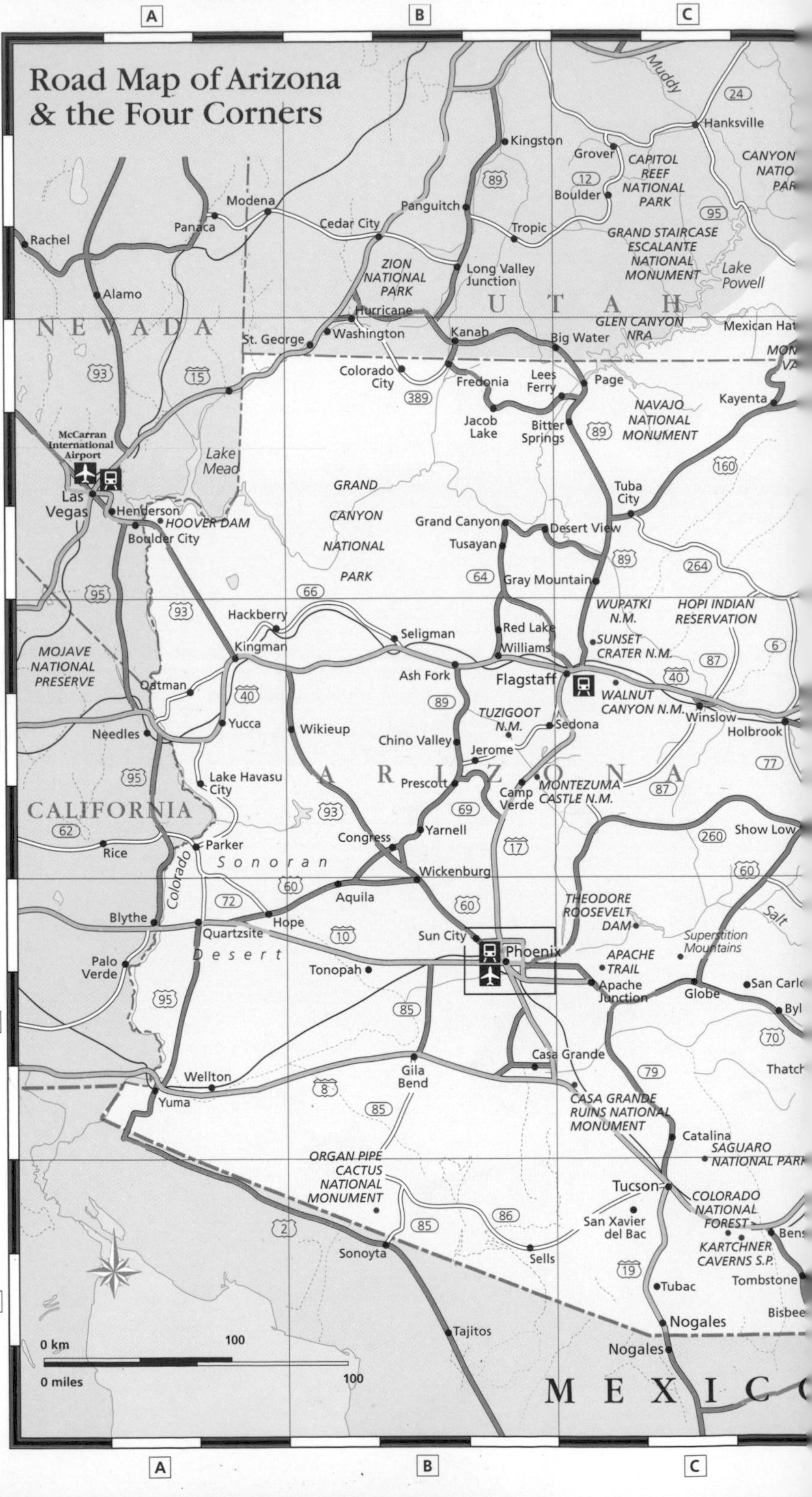